POPULAR POLITICS
AND BRITISH
ANTI-SLAVERY

The mobilisation of public opinion

against the slave trade

1787–1807

J. R. OLDFIELD
University of Southampton

D1352569

FRANK CASS
LONDON PORTLAND, OR

First published in 1995 by Manchester University Press, Manchester
This edition published in 1998 in Great Britain by
FRANK CASS PUBLISHERS
Newbury House, 900 Eastern Avenue
London, IG2 7HH

and in the United States of America by
FRANK CASS PUBLISHERS
c/o ISBS, 5804 N.E. Hassalo Street
Portland, Oregon 97213-3644

Copyright © 1998 Frank Cass Publishers

Website: http://www.frankcass.com

British Library Cataloguing in Publication Data
Oldfield, J.R.
Popular politics and British anti-slavery: the mobilisation
of public opinion against the slave trade, 1787–1807. –
2nd ed. – (Studies in slave and post-slave societies and
cultures; v. 6)
1. Slavery—Great Britain—Public opinion 2. Antislavery
movements—Great Britain—Public opinion
I. Title
326'.0941

ISBN 0–7146–4462–5 (paper)
ISSN 1462–1770

Library of Congress Cataloging-in-Publication Data
Oldfield, J.R. (John R.)
Popular politics and British anti-slavery: the mobilisation of
public opinion against the slave trade, 1787–1807/J.R. Oldfield.
p.   cm. — (Studies in slave and post-slave societies and
cultures, ISSN 1462–1770)
Includes bibliographical references and index.
ISBN 0–7146–4462–5
1. Antislavery movements—Great Britain. 2. Slave-trade—
Great Britain—Public opinion. 3. Public opinion—Great Britain.
I. Title. II. Series.
HT1162.O57   1998
326'.8'094209033—dc21   98–29907
CIP

Printed in Great Britain by
Biddles Ltd, Guildford and King's Lynn

CONTENTS

LIST OF ILLUSTRATIONS

FOREWORD

The Atlantic slave trade was a critical element in the transformation of the Americas and in the dislocation of wide areas of
African life. In its early Iberian days it seemed a marginal issue.
But the establishment of the sugar industry, first in Brazil, then in
the British West Indies, and the development of the tobacco
plantations of the Chesapeake, quickly established the economic
importance of African labour. A critical formula emerged, of
American lands, European investment and technology and African
labour. There followed that transformation of the Atlantic world
into a familiar mould; vast numbers of enslaved Africans toiling
for the material betterment of white settlers and their European
backers, with a consequential improvement in the material
advancement of western Europe. It is hard to recall, today, that
until the 1820s it was the African, not the European, who was the
typical migrant to key areas of the Americas. But, of course the
Africans were not migrants in the conventional sense. They were
victims of a rapacious trading and colonising system which
reached from Europe, to Africa and thence to the Americas.

Early proponents of overseas settlement and trade had long
argued that major economic benefits would accrue to the Mother
Country. And by the 1680s few could doubt that they were correct.
Yet much of the material well-being which came the way of the
colonising British came from slave labour. Moreover, the slave
contribution to British life could be seen in everyday British domestic settings; in the vast amounts of sugar consumed with tea and
coffee, and used as an ingredient in an array of popular dishes, and
in the smoking habits of men across the length and breadth of
Britain. There were also the human reminders, notably that handful of blacks who settled in Britain (normally against their will) and
who often found work as domestics to propertied employers.

Despite these local reminders of the slave impact on British life,
the slaves were, in general, out of sight and out of mind; labouring
helots on the far side of the Atlantic whose conditions scarcely
ruffled the conscience of the people who benefited most from their
efforts – British consumers. It is true of course that the British did

v

not invent or devise the Atlantic slave trade or the plantation system. But it was the British who shipped more Africans than any other nation in the course of the eighteenth century and whose shippers and merchants honed and finely tuned the Atlantic system as no others before. It was the British whose domestic life was so thoroughly permeated by the consequences of slave labour, from the simple fact of domestic sugar consumption, to the economic benefits which flowed to London, Bristol, Liverpool (and the hinterlands which serviced those and other slaving ports). The Atlantic slave system was too prospering a form of trade and commerce to criticise or diminish. Yet, by the 1780s at a time when the system was as prosperous as ever a small band of critics met to consider how best to civilise slavery, and ultimately to bring it to its knees.

Historians continue to puzzle about the process of abolition. Why, if the slave system remained buoyant and profitable, did the British turn against it? Why turn against the slave trade in the last two decades of the eighteenth century, and not before? There have of course been a number of explanations, beginning with the justifications of the abolitionists themselves. They led by Thomas Clarkson and by the descendants of Wilberforce were in a unique position to provide insiders' answers. Indeed the historiography of British abolition has been haunted by the abolitionists or by the more prominent abolitionists. In recent years, however, scholars have shifted their attention, away from the 'high politics' of formal, parliamentary abolition, to the more popular aspects of the abolition campaign. To view the campaign against the slave trade (and later against slavery) as a parliamentary affair is to see only one aspect of a highly complex process. Though parliamentary history (tactics, party politics, personal biographies) remains important (Abolition and Emancipation were, after all, Acts of Parliament), recent scholars have sought to explore the *roots* of abolition.

The importance of J.R. Oldfield's book, now appearing in paperback for the first time, is that he advances the broadly based study of popular abolition further than any previous scholar. Building on the work of earlier scholars, notably Seymour Drescher, Oldfield's research serves to clinch a simple but critical issue, namely that in the attack on the slave trade, popular revulsion was crucial. What follows is the teasing out of that basic

Foreword

point; that in generating hostility to the continuation of the British involvement in the Atlantic slave trade, the abolition movement after 1787 laid special stress on rallying popular feeling.

It is of course a great curiosity. The nation which had perfected Atlantic slaving, which benefited most from its material and commercial rewards, very quickly turned its back against it. Nor was this merely a question of formal propertied politics. The importance of Oldfield's carefully researched argument is to illustrate and prove the emergence and extent of popular abolition. It was, in many respects, the first modern successful campaign of popular politics. Others were to follow with varying success (the Corresponding Societies, Chartism, Free Trade), but abolition now stands out as the pioneer. In explaining the details of popular abolition its political and intellectual roots, its geographical location, its intersection with the world of popular print and graphic illustration, Oldfield places the campaign at the centre of late-eighteenth century social and political life. As such, the broader campaign to end the Atlantic slave is more easily understood. This study is an important contribution to out awareness not simply of abolition, but of the changing nature of popular politics in the last years of the eighteenth century.

James Walvin
University of York
May 1998

ACKNOWLEDGEMENTS

THE research for this book would not have been possible without the help of archivists and librarians on both sides of the Atlantic. In particular, I would like to thank the staffs of the following libraries, galleries, and record offices: Birmingham Public Library; the Bodleian Library; Bristol Record Office; the British Library; the British Museum; Devon Record Office; the Friends House Library; the Moorland-Spingarn Research Center, Howard University, Washington, D.C.; Keele University Library; Liverpool Record Office; Manchester City Art Gallery; the Menil Foundation, Houston, Texas; Northamptonshire Record Office; St John's College, Cambridge; Sheffield City Library; Shropshire Record Office; Tyne and Wear Archives Service; the Wedgwood Museum; West Devon Record Office; the Westcountry Studies Library; and the Wordsworth Library, Grasmere.

While working on this project, I was also fortunate enough to spend a long summer at the Huntington Library in San Marino, California. I am indebted to the then Director of Research, Martin Ridge, for giving me this opportunity, and to Virginia Renner and Mary Wright for making my stay so pleasurable. A grant from the Committee for Advanced Studies at Southampton University made possible a shorter trip to Washington, D.C., while the Faculty of Arts Research Sub-Committee very generously funded my repeated forays into the West Country. I am extremely grateful for their assistance.

Various colleagues and friends have helped along the way, among them John Brewer, Cathy Cherbosque, Aileen Dawson, Virginia Hewitt, Nicholas Kingwell, Tony Kushner, Tom Lange, Lynn Miller, Jane Newman, Martin Phillips, Jack Pole, Richard Wall, James Walvin, and Rob Weir. I also owe a particular debt to the work of Hugh Honour, Clare Midgley, and, of course, Seymour Drescher. While I do not always agree with Professor Drescher's interpretation and understanding of the early abolitionist movement, his research has nevertheless helped me to

Acknowledgements

clarify my own ideas, not least with regard to the respective roles of London and the provinces. Some of these ideas were first worked out in an article in *The Historical Journal* (1992), which forms the basis of Chapter Two. Portions of Chapters One and Five have previously appeared in *The Huntington Library Quarterly* (1993) and *Slavery and Abolition* (1989), and are reproduced here with the kind permission of the editors and Frank Cass & Co. Ltd.

In Manchester University Press I could not have wished for a more attentive or efficient publisher. I would like to say a special word of thanks to Jane Thorniley-Walker, who commissioned the book, and to her assistant, Michelle O'Connell, and the press's excellent production staff. My final acknowledgement is to my wife, Veronica, whose loving support has been a constant source of inspiration. Thank you a thousand times over.

J. R. O.

For Veronica

INTRODUCTION

DESPITE a constant stream of books and articles, abolition, slavery, and the slave trade still pose some of the most challenging problems of historical interpretation. In the space of some twenty-six years, between 1807 and 1833, Britain not only outlawed the slave trade, but abolished the institution of slavery throughout her colonial possessions. How this came about has absorbed the attention of a generation of historians, among them David Brion Davis, Seymour Drescher, and James Walvin.[1] And thanks to their efforts we now have a much better understanding of the 'ecology' of British anti-slavery, its origins, its dynamics, and the reasons for its vast popular appeal. This book is not an attempt to rehearse those arguments, or, indeed, to write a history of British anti-slavery during its initial, formative period (1787–1807).[2] Rather, it is concerned with a part of that history, namely, the petition campaigns of 1788 and 1792. In the first of these campaigns over 100 petitions condemning the slave trade were presented to Parliament. Four years later 519 petitions were mobilised against it, involving perhaps as many as 400,000 people. What follows explains how this remarkable expression of support for black people was organised and orchestrated, and how it contributed to the growth of popular politics in Britain.

When I started work on this project I had a number of questions in mind. How were the petition campaigns of 1788 and 1792 organised? How was it possible to mobilise public opinion on such a wide scale and, seemingly, at such short notice? These questions led me, first, to the minutes of the Committee for the Abolition of the Slave Trade, or London Committee. Here a very clear picture quickly began to emerge. The Committee's opinion-building activities—its publication programme, its use of advertising and subscription lists, and its large number of correspondents—hinted at ingenuity and sophistication. The members of the Committee, it seemed, were not 'Saints' but practical men who understood about the market and about consumer choice.

Josiah Wedgwood, elected a member of the Committee in August 1787, is a case in point. What Wedgwood brought to the Committee was an innovative genius that was perfectly attuned to the demands and rigours of eighteenth-century business.

It is a central contention of this book that the role and significance of the London Committee has been grossly misunderstood by historians. So far from being a low-level lobby, in its original guise the Committee was the prototype of the modern (nineteenth-century) reform organisation. Its self-appointed task was to create a constituency for anti-slavery through books, pamphlets, prints, and artefacts; indeed, the same sort of paraphernalia that had characterised the Wilkite agitation of the 1760s. The Committee also had its own network of local and regional contacts in the shape of 'agents' and 'country committees' scattered across the length and breadth of the country. And, finally, there was Thomas Clarkson, a sort of 'travelling agent' who provided a vital link between London and the provinces, organising committees, distributing tracts, and offering advice and encouragement to hundreds of local activists.

It follows that we must take a fresh look at the role of the provinces in the early abolitionist movement, not least when it comes to petitioning. Of course, local initiatives were always welcomed. Manchester, for instance, was an important centre of popular abolitionism, thanks largely to the efforts of men like Thomas Walker and Thomas Cooper. But the recent emphasis on Manchester, and the lead it took in the petition campaign of 1788, runs the risk of attaching too much importance to the provinces, and the industrial north in particular. Walker and his friends, it needs to be stressed, did not act alone in 1788. Like other parts of the country, they were in regular contact with abolitionists in London, and, as far as one can judge, ready to follow their lead. The impetus, in other words, came from London, and it is to London that we must turn if we are to understand how the movement was given political shape and significance.

Manchester, moreover, raises a problem of a different kind. That there was a link between abolition and industrialisation seems indisputable. New modes of production undoubtedly changed perceptions about the organisation of labour and, with it, notions about property. Drescher may also be right in speculating that the rapid growth of towns like Manchester encouraged a sense of identity with the 'uprooted' and a concern with loss of kin, home, and community.[3] But Manchester was only part of the picture. What was it, for instance, that united towns like Exeter, Maidstone, Norwich, and Shrewsbury in their condemnation of the trade? And what about small towns and villages like Tregony in Cornwall, Chesham in Buckinghamshire, or Wooler in Northumberland, all of which petitioned Parliament in 1792? To understand their concerns we need to get closer to the mental outlook of those men (and women) who shaped the movement at the grassroots level, namely, the middling sort: merchants, professionals, manufacturers, and shopkeepers.

Thus part of the purpose of the present study is to try and locate abolition within the context of broader socio-economic trends, the contours of which are still emerging. Chapter One describes some of these trends and in doing so draws on literary sources (children's literature and eighteenth-century drama, for instance) to reconstruct the world view of the provincial middle classes. And in Chapters Four and Five I have tried to look in greater detail at the dynamics of popular abolitionism, its relevance and its meaning. An important theme here, and throughout the book, is the role of social emulation in the early abolitionist movement. As men like Wedgwood demonstrated, abolition could be made fashionable and given its own status meaning. Wedgwood's special contribution to British anti-slavery and the link between abolition, visual culture, and popular politics are discussed at length in Chapter Six.

In drawing attention to the social and cultural context of British anti-slavery, I have been strongly influenced by recent work on eighteenth-century towns, the history of childhood, women, leisure, the press, and the book trade. In particular, I have made extensive use of the growing literature on consumption and the world of goods. I am fully aware that some critics have questioned the usefulness of terms and concepts like 'consumer revolution'.[4] But there seems little doubt that during the eighteenth century 'more men and women than ever before in human history enjoyed the experience of acquiring material possessions'.[5] More important still, the 'birth of a consumer society' brought with it new techniques (advertising, catalogues, inertia selling) that were to have a profound impact on the reform sphere. The significance of these techniques for the early abolitionist movement is explored in Chapter Two.

Of course, to some extent the commercialisation of abolition had been anticipated by John Wilkes and his followers. Recent work on the Wilkite agitation has brought into focus the emergence of a new kind of politics during the eighteenth century: popular, broad-based, entertaining, and sociable. Wilkite propaganda, John Brewer argues, created a movement not confined to the constituency of Westminster, but extending to 'the even wider ambit of the whole kingdom'.[6] As a result, by the late 1780s 'a market in politics and a market in protest existed for the abolitionists to exploit'.[7] Indeed, as we shall see, a strong link emerges at the local level between Wilkes and abolition, and, just as important, between abolition and conciliation with the American colonies.

At the same time, however, there was an implicit danger in being too closely identified with radical causes, as witness the following letter from 'Rachel Mend'en' in the *London Chronicle*:

> While Crispin [her husband] was in trade he kept tolerably clear of the reforming passion, but even then I could observe it stealing on him by degrees; and I remember, when there was so much stir about Mr Wilkes, he got from London a picture, in which that great patriot was represented turning his back to a purse of gold, and his face to the cap of liberty . . . But the maddest part of his conduct I am yet to relate. Some time ago he began to be very clamorous about the slave trade and the condition of the negroes in the West Indies; and under pretext of obtaining information he took into the house two of the vagrant blacks that were unemployed in our country . . . One of the men has been taught to talk fluently about liberty, and nature and so forth, and Crispin is convinced that he will be a Member of Parliament; nay, he said the other day, that if there must be such a thing as a King of this country, he saw no reason why Quashi should not sit on the throne at the next revolution.[8]

This was in 1788. Similar alarms and protests accompanied the petition campaign of 1792, linking abolition with the democratic tendencies released by the French Revolution. Ultimately, radicalism was to prove the Achilles heel of the early abolitionist movement. The rising tide of revolutionary violence in France and, with it, the growth of political reaction at home forced abolition underground after 1793, leading in some cases (Manchester, for instance) to splits and recriminations.

With hindsight, we can see that the petition campaigns of 1788 and 1792 took place during a period of anxiety for many Britons, wedged between the American war and the mounting conflict with Revolutionary and Napoleonic France. Fleetingly, abolition succeeded in bringing together different elements from within the middle classes: dissenters, Evangelicals, radicals, patriots, men, women, and children. In doing so, it created strength, unity, and, above all, a growing sense of purpose. What follows is an attempt to describe and explain this 'moment' in British history. It is, if you will, a piece of 'thick description',[9] intended to offer fresh insights into the increasingly powerful role of the middle classes in influencing Parliamentary politics from outside the confines of Westminster.

Notes

1. David Brion Davis, *The Problem of Slavery in Western Culture*, Ithaca, New York, and London, 1966; *The Problem of Slavery in the Age of Revolution, 1770–1823*, Ithaca, New York, and London, 1975; *Slavery and Human Progress*, New York, 1984: Seymour Drescher, *Econocide: British Slavery in the Age of Abolition*, Pittsburgh, 1977; *Capitalism and Antislavery: British Mobilization in Comparative Perspective*, New York, 1987: James Walvin, *The Abolition of the Atlantic Slave Trade: Origins and Effects in Europe, Africa and the Americas*, Madison, Wisconsin, 1981; *England, Slaves and Freedom*, London, 1987. See also David Eltis, *Economic Growth and the Ending of the Transatlantic Slave Trade*, Cambridge, 1987; Barbara Solow and Stanley Engerman, eds., *British Capitalism and Caribbean Slavery: The Legacy of Eric Williams*, Cambridge, 1987.

2. The best general history of the early abolitionist movement is still Roger Anstey's *The Atlantic Slave Trade and British Abolition, 1760–1810*, London, 1975.

3. Drescher, *Capitalism and Antislavery*, pp. 73–4.

4. See, for instance, E. P. Thompson, *Customs in Common*, London, 1991, pp. 18–19.

5. Introduction to Neil McKendrick, John Brewer and J. H. Plumb, *The Birth of a Consumer Society: The Commercialization of Eighteenth-Century England*, London, 1982, p. 1.

6. John Brewer, *Party Ideology and Popular Politics at the Accession of George III*, Cambridge, 1976, pp. 190–1, 198.
7. *The American Experience: The Collected Essays of J. H. Plumb*, Athens, Georgia, 1989, p. 151.
8. *London Chronicle*, 27–9 March 1788 (p. 311).
9. Clifford Geertz, 'Thick Description: Toward an Interpretative Theory of Culture', in *The Interpretation of Cultures*, New York, 1973, pp. 3–30.

Chapter One

THE EIGHTEENTH-CENTURY
BACKGROUND

BETWEEN 1788 and 1792 the slave trade became a matter of absorbing interest to thousands of Britons. The response surprised even abolitionists. Writing at the height of the petition campaign of 1788, Joseph Woods felt moved to liken the humanity of the British people to 'Tinder which has immediately caught fire from the spark of Information which has been struck upon it'.[1] To understand this enthusiasm for abolition, and how it was exploited and developed, it is necessary first to know something about eighteenth-century society. Only then do the petition campaigns of 1788 and 1792 begin to make sense. The group most directly involved with the early abolitionist movement was the provincial middle classes; these were the men and women who rushed forward to sign petitions, organise committees, subscribe funds, and distribute books and pamphlets. They engineered the breakthrough. And it is their eighteenth-century world which forms the subject of what follows.[2]

'Urban renaissance' and 'consumer revolution' are just two of the terms that have been used to describe a series of changes which transformed England between 1660 and 1800.[3] Historians may still disagree as to why, how and precisely when these changes began, but the signs of progress and improvement are obvious enough. One important indicator is population growth. The population of England and Wales approximately doubled during the eighteenth century, and much of this increase took place in towns. Even historic regional centres like Norwich, Chester, and York experienced modest growth. But the real expansion came in the 'new' manufacturing towns of the north and north-east. Manchester, for instance, grew from 18,000 in 1750 to 89,000 in 1801. Birmingham, meanwhile, grew from 24,000 to 74,000 and Leeds from 16,000 to 53,000. Indeed, the population of the four largest manufacturing towns in England almost quadrupled in the second half of the eighteenth century, a rate of increase that overturned the traditional English urban hierarchy.[4]

Striking as they are, these figures only hint at a second important trend, namely, the emergence of a rapidly expanding and increasingly leisured middle class. It is scarcely possible to estimate the size of this group; as Borsay points out: 'the make-up of the middling stratum could vary from place to place'.[5] Nevertheless, the underlying trend is unmistakable. More people meant more goods and services. The explosion in the professions is just one indication of the changing structure of English society.[6] So, too, is the increasing number of 'carters, carriers, and innkeepers: booksellers, printers, entertainers, and clerks: drapers, grocers, druggists, stationers, ironmongers, shopkeepers of every sort'.[7] Doubtless, the list could be extended—the classification, in any case, is an imprecise one—but what lifted these men (and women) 'out of the mechanick part of mankind was the fact that their activities not only fed and clothed them but also enabled them to accumulate on a regular basis and so improve themselves'.[8]

The growth of the middle class, their ease and their comfort, became at once a source of comment and reflection. If some reacted anxiously, others could only wonder at the standard of living enjoyed by many in the middling ranks. Even 'inferior tradesmen' now lived in comparative luxury:

> their tables are served as well as those of rich merchants were an hundred years ago: their houses good and ornamented; what formerly was a downfall gable end, covered with thatch, is now brick and tile, and a sashed front, with white pales before it; and the furniture strangely improved from the last age; in dress, see the sons and daughters tricked out in all the little ornaments which make a country church gay, grogram changed for silk, and thousands of ribbons where peckthread once sufficed. See the amusements of these people; they resort to their theatres, and are busy in visits, and tea-drinkings and cards; as much ceremony is found in the assembly of a country grocer's wife, as that of a countess.[9]

Nor did the writer exaggerate. Lorna Weatherill's pioneering work on late seventeenth- and early eighteenth-century inventories reveals that many 'higher status tradesmen' possessed new and imported goods (china, pictures, earthenware). Even those of

8

lower status were more likely to own household items than yeomen farmers, for instance, while some tradesmen displayed 'distinctly consumerist tastes and a need to assert their position in society through the ownership of goods'.[10]

There is no doubting the growing range of goods available to eighteenth-century consumers or the fact that more social groups were in a position to purchase and enjoy them. The key to this bustling consumer society was fashion. New marketing devices, especially fashion magazines, stimulated the public's thirst for the latest styles and colours and began increasingly to mould their tastes and preferences.[11] In the process, material objects acquired a new kind of status meaning, a meaning that was inseparable from their novelty value. To quote Grant McCracken:

> with the growth of fashion grew an entirely new habit of mind and behavior. Increasingly, aesthetic and stylistic considerations took precedence over utilitarian ones. That an object had not exhausted its usefulness was no longer sufficient grounds for its preservation. Whether it could satisfy the more important condition of fashionableness was now the deciding factor.[12]

No one understood this better than the potter, Josiah Wedgwood, who quite consciously exploited the world of fashion in order to make his wares more exclusive and hence desirable. Entrepreneurs like Wedgwood transformed the world of eighteenth-century business, devising techniques and strategies that were not only intended to satisfy demand but to create it.[13]

Leisure, too, became increasingly commercialised between 1660 and 1800. Even small towns had their balls and assemblies, while lectures, concerts, exhibitions, and horse-race meetings (indeed, sport of all kinds) grew in popularity. Finally, improvements in travel (better vehicle design and more roads and canals) stimulated trade and touring.[14] At times the pace of change was almost breathtaking. 'Before the turnpike road, the Taunton stage to London did not finish its journey, in less than 4 days', mused Joshua Toulmin in 1791. Now it took only two:

> [The stage] sets out from Taunton and from London, every Mon., Wed. and Fri. a.m., at 4, and arrives at each place in the evening of the following day: and, in the summer months, by going all night, arrives in London at noon. . . . A stage runs

[daily] through this town, from Exeter to Bristol; and another from Exeter to Bath: meeting others running from Bristol and Bath to Exeter. On Sunday and Thursday evenings a coach, now, arrives at Taunton from Barnstaple, and leaves it, for that place, on Monday and Friday mornings. And last summer, a new coach was set up to go twice a week between Taunton and Sidmouth.[15]

Faster still, the mail coach from London to Exeter, introduced in 1785, did the journey in twenty-four hours, a remarkable feat which spoke volumes about middle-class expectations.[16]

If the provincial middle classes were more mobile they were also better informed. By 1800 between sixty and seventy per cent of adult males in England and Wales could read; the corresponding figure for women was probably somewhere in the region of forty per cent.[17] Literacy, as we know, was closely linked with social and economic position. The growth of the retail sector, of trade and business, rested on the ability to read. David Cressy estimates that in the period 1754–84 illiteracy was only 5 per cent among shopkeepers. Among building workers, by contrast, it was fifty-one per cent and among labourers and servants fifty-nine per cent.[18] Literacy was also closely linked with urbanisation and the demands of urban living: it was 'part of the agenda for modernity, the city and the Enlightenment, as well as for religious leaders and social reformers'.[19]

High literacy rates, together with rapid population growth, created a seemingly insatiable demand for all kinds of printed matter. Pride of place must go to the provincial press. By 1760 there were thirty-five country newspapers in England alone; two decades later this number had risen to fifty.[20] Competition was fierce. Several provincial towns had more than one newspaper, while for a time Newcastle and Manchester could boast as many as three.[21] Circulation figures also increased over the course of the century. Cranfield estimates that before 1740 few country newspapers had a circulation of more than two or three hundred copies a week. But numbers steadily increased thereafter. Certainly, by the 1780s and 1790s it was not unusual for a provincial newspaper to be selling 3,000 copies a week, and in some cases the circulation may have been higher still.[22]

Newspapers brought the provinces into closer contact with London and with the outside world. They were a vital source of news and information about the court, politics, the changing fortunes of trade, fashion, gossip, and scandal. At the same time, however, newspapers brought London into closer contact with the provinces. The point can be made by looking at the career of George Packwood of Gracechurch Street, who sold razor straps. Between 1794 and 1796 Packwood launched a carefully orchestrated assault on consumer choice, placing over sixty advertisements in twenty-six different newspapers, including the *Caledonian Mercury*, the *Cork Gazette and General Advertiser*, and the *Dublin Evening Post*.[23] Packwood's campaign, though exceptional, hinted at the increasing importance of newspaper advertising during the eighteenth century. Patent medicines, perfumes, face-creams, soaps, hats, gloves, and corsets are just some of the other goods that appear prominently in local newspapers. Even Wedgwood, who is sometimes thought to have been above such things, was not averse to using the press as part of his marketing programme.[24]

Newspapers were also behind another development that began to have a significant impact after 1750, namely, the growth of the provincial book trade. Many newspaper printers were themselves booksellers; many, in addition, acted as agents for London publishers keen to exploit the huge potential market for books. The agency system, really a network of local distributors, stimulated growth at all levels of the bookselling business.[25] Whereas at the beginning of the century most readers in the provinces had to send to London for their books, by 1800 there were an increasing number of local businesses competing for their custom. Indeed, one of the features of the expansion of the second half of the eighteenth century was the growth of booksellers (and printers) in small towns like Fareham, Peterborough, St Ives, and Alcester. Romsey, for instance, boasted two booksellers in 1789, the Isle of Wight three, possibly more.[26] The major centres continued to prosper, offering greater variety and choice, but for many readers it was the developments closer to home that were the surest indication of change and progress.

The growth of the provincial book trade also brought with it new innovations like the subscription or circulating library.[27] The earliest of these libraries probably contained around 3,000 volumes, but holdings undoubtedly increased over the course of the century. By 1798 Thomas Baker claimed to have over 7,000 volumes in his library in Southampton and Joseph Watts's library in Gosport was larger still. The books themselves were selected for their maximum possible appeal, which, in practice, meant a high proportion of novels, romances, and plays, the standard fare of most circulating libraries. Proprietors stocked what was generally described as a 'selection of the most useful and entertaining French and English Books in every department of Polite Literature', and nearly all of them guaranteed to procure new publications 'regularly every week'.[28] Such promptness was evidently considered essential to the success of a flourishing circulating library. Subscribers expected to be kept abreast of the latest tastes and fashions and to be able to read new titles almost as soon as they were published in London.

The circulating library was in essence a leisure facility where people went to socialise as much as to buy or borrow books. Thomas Baker boasted that his library near the West Quay was 'the morning rendezvous of ladies and gentlemen, who come to read the London Papers, which are taken in every day, and to form riding and sailing parties'.[29] Most proprietors kept newspapers for the benefit of their customers and some even provided a reading room specifically for this purpose. At Moses Dimmock's library and coffee shop in Winchester, subscribers could read the *London Gazette* (published twice a week), the *Sun*, *Star*, and *Courier* (weeklies), the *Times*, *Morning Post*, and *Gazetteer* (dailies), as well as three provincial newspapers, the racing calendar, and a selection of monthly publications. Entertainment of this kind was not cheap: by 1800 charges ranged anything from 10s. 6d. to a guinea per annum, 5s. to 7s. per quarter, and 5s. for the season.[30] But for a growing number of people (women as well as men) the circulating library offered access to a broad range of printed material: to fiction and non-fiction, to plays and political pamphlets, to prints, cartoons, and newspapers.

Another indication of growing middle-class independence was the establishment of literary and philosophical societies. Perhaps the best known of these was the Birmingham Lunar Society, of which Josiah Wedgwood, Matthew Boulton, and Joseph Priestley were all members. But there were similar societies in Bath, Newcastle, and Manchester.[31] Science and scientific inquiry were only part of the impetus here; in Newcastle, for instance, 'practical questions' were studiously avoided. Rather, what many members wanted (and evidently got) was 'broad access' to Enlightenment culture: to literary pursuits, music, history, and the visual arts. Potent symbols of modernity, of civility, and sociability, lit-and-phils 'offered a leg-up from rusticity, associated with barbarity and riot, towards metropolitan—indeed, cosmopolitan—urbanity'.[32] The same thing was true of book clubs and debating societies, of coffee houses and private schools and academies. Everywhere, it seems, the urban bourgeoisie felt the need to impose their will on their surroundings, to create harmony, decency, and good order.

In short, the eighteenth century witnessed a narrowing of the gap between London and the provinces. More mobile, better informed, provincial elites imported (and assimilated) metropolitan ideas and fashions with astonishing speed. Expectations changed perceptibly. James Linden, printer of the *Hampshire Chronicle*, boasted in 1774 that he could get new books from London 'at three days notice'.[33] Of course, not all of these developments took place overnight. But from mid-century onwards the opening up of the provinces to merchandise, to fashion, and to news and information accelerated at an increasing pace. And as it did so the potential for popular protest, for new kinds of political expression, changed with it. This, after all, was the meaning of the Wilkite agitation of the 1760s. Wilkes and his supporters created a market in politics which they exploited through their use of propaganda: pamphlets, prints, circular letters, medallions, and badges.[34] Abolitionists built on these successes, using many of the same strategies to create a movement that hinted at an even greater depth of popular feeling.

There is no doubting the increasing presence of the capital in provincial life. At the same time, however, the provinces were also beginning to develop their own regional identities. The growth of town guides, of directories, of town and county histories all hint at the emergence of civic pride as a factor in eighteenth-century politics.[35] So, too, does the massive expenditure on town halls, urban walks, theatres, assembly rooms, pavements, and lighting. Yet many of these same towns, particularly the 'new' manufacturing towns, lacked a voice in national affairs. Manchester is the classic example. The second largest town in England by 1800, it nevertheless had no representatives in Parliament; and the same was true of Birmingham and Sheffield. Viewed in this light, the growing appeal of political radicalism, of calls for greater representation, in the decades after 1760 is not surprising. Neither is it surprising that many (notably radicals) should have made the connection between political reform and abolition of the slave trade. Both were part of an attack on a system that increasingly began to appear outmoded and in urgent need of repair.

The growth in wealth and numbers of the middling ranks; the growth of a consumer society, leisure, and public facilities—all this was undoubtedly taking place during the eighteenth century. Yet at the same time there was a darker, more anxiety-ridden side to the 'making' of the middle class. One reason for this was a largely informal credit system and the concomitant threat of bankruptcy. As John Brewer has shown, tradesmen tried to deal with the difficulties created by a volatile economy as best they could.[36] But still the threat of bankruptcy was a real one. Figures fluctuated, sometimes wildly so, but the American Revolution seems to have precipitated a particularly severe crisis. In 1777 and again in 1778 the number of bankrupts reached record levels and a fresh panic in 1788 saw 587 businesses fail in only ten months.[37] Of course, these figures reflected in part an increase in population and trade. Nevertheless, to quote Brewer: 'there is hardly a single account of a Georgian tradesman or merchant, and not very many that flowed from aristocratic and genteel pens, that does not make reference to the frightful prospect of indebtedness'.[38]

We do not need to look too closely at the reasons for the number of business failures during the eighteenth century, but part of the problem, especially in the retail sector, was increased competition. The more businesses there were—and the amount of duplication is surprising, even in medium-sized provincial towns—the greater was the pressure to expand and diversify. Expansion, however, brought with it the threat of financial ruin. William Dawkins, a bookseller in Gosport, is a case in point. In the early part of 1773 Dawkins decided to enlarge his circulating library, and, in what was a new departure for him, set up a printing press; nine months later he was declared bankrupt.[39] Many other booksellers suffered the same fate, but so, too, did grocers, linen drapers, druggists, publicans, printers, and cabinet-makers. The list is endless.

Dawkins clearly expanded his business in a vain attempt to keep his head above water. Nevertheless, there was a natural tendency to associate bankruptcy with extravagance of one sort or another. 'One thing is certain', noted the *London Chronicle* in 1788,

> that while gaming and every species of luxury so much prevail among men of business we are not to be surprised if bankruptcies continue more frequent than when men were contented with a more simple mode of living, and did not grasp at riches beyond the fair returns of trade.[40]

Behind such comments was a growing unease over the consumerist tendencies of the middle classes and, in particular, the example set by the aristocracy, their social superiors. Even those who applauded the general diffusion of wealth in eighteenth-century Britain and, significantly, its humanising effects, were forced to concede that among the very wealthy 'it is no longer expense, but profusion and manners are not elegant, but fashionably capricious'.[41] Worse still, merchants, manufacturers, farmers in some counties, 'even the common people, professional men's children, such as Doctors and Lawyers sons and daughters'; all imitated 'the detestable manners and vices of the embroidered rabble'.[42]

Of course, not everyone was in awe of the dictates of fashion. In her fascinating study of Elizabeth Shackleton of Alkincoats (1726–81), Amanda Vickery shows how at least one eighteenth-century consumer was able to impose her will on the market. Shackleton, Vickery tells us, 'was not a slavish imitator of elite modes, nor a passive victim of the velocity of fashion'. On the contrary, she was rational, sensible, discerning: 'some designs were accepted *tout court*, and some adapted for use in Lancashire, and others rejected out of hand'.[43] But how typical was Shackleton? And how easy was it to make decisions of this kind? Shackleton, it needs to be said, was thirty-eight years of age when she married her second husband, John Shackleton, a local woollen merchant, and clearly knew her own mind. Others, one suspects, lacked her singleness of purpose or, indeed, her self-confidence. It was easier, and certainly more tempting, to flow with the tide, whatever the consequences.

For this very reason the excesses of the 'fashionable Great', and their spectacular failures, were held up repeatedly before the aspiring middle classes. The term itself became synonymous with extravagance and ruin. The 'fashionable Great', explained the author of *The Auction: A Town Eclogue* (1788),

> are those Persons of rank and spirit, who sacrifice to the follies of the present moment all the comforts of future life; who will expend an immense sum in Furniture, Equipage, etc. to possess an unimportant splendour for three or four winters, when, amid the smiles of those who partook of it, and who in the midst of it foretold its conclusion, they must consign it all to the disposal of an Auctioneer, who, perhaps, to save the indignity of a sale at their own Houses, will, as a particular mark of respect to them, purchase it at a fourth part of the original value.

Far better, the writer implied, to emulate those persons of rank and fortune who, 'contented with a wise maintenance of their dignity, pleased with domestic society, and honoured by acts of well-applied bounty and hospitality, have not the spirit to practise these vices, nor the taste to engage in those follies, which end in ruin'.[44]

These different pressures, the threat of bankruptcy and the contemporary discourse on fashion and luxury, helped to define an emerging middle-class consciousness.[45] We can see this process at work in the children's literature of the period. In recent years children's literature, like the history of childhood, has attracted growing attention from scholars on both sides of the Atlantic. As a result, we probably know more than we ever did about the number of children's books published during the eighteenth century, the range of titles available, and the authors and publishers involved.[46] More problematic, it seems to me, is how we should tackle these books as historical sources. One approach, adopted here, is to treat them as 'a kind of linguistic behavior addressed to children by adults'.[47] Children's books, according to this view, convey messages and meanings not about children themselves, but about the beliefs thought necessary to sustain a given way of life. They are, in other words, part of the process whereby standards and modes of behaviour are transmitted from one generation to another.

Eighteenth-century children's literature, written by and for the urban middle classes, filled an obvious need. Pioneers like John Newbery understood this only too well. 'My design', he explained in *The Lilliputian Magazine* (1783), 'is, by way of *history* and *fable*, to sow in [the minds of young children] the seeds of polite literature, and to teach them the great grammar of the universe; I mean, the knowledge of men and things'.[48] 'The great grammar of the universe'. Urban life provided eighteenth-century consumers with a bewildering variety of choice. The problem was knowing which choices were the right ones. Recently, J. Paul Hunter has argued that the rise of the novel was linked with problems of socialisation.[49] Children's books can be viewed in a similar light. Put simply, they sought to help middle-class children interpret the world they saw around them. More than that, they sought to persuade them 'to acknowledge, and finally to act on, particular definitions of self and society'.[50]

To this end, writers of children's books set up a deliberate tension between two quite different belief systems. Witness the following exchange from *The Young Ladies Magazine* (1780):

Miss Sophia. Do you not know, Miss, that five thousand pounds is but two hundred by the year? What is that for a woman of quality?

Miss Rural. She may find lodgings, food, and raiment. What need of more?

Lady Sincere. She must have a coach, money to pay servants' wages, to bestow in charities, and to gratify fancy and whims.

Miss Rural. What need of a coach, when I am able to walk? Can't I do with one maid? And, if I have not money to give away in charities, may not I be in some condition or other to do for the poor? And as to whims and fancies, if I have none, there is none to gratify; if I have, I must make it my business to get rid of such guests.

Lady Sincere. How is it possible to live without some whim or fancy? I think without some whim or other I should be tired of my life.[51]

Eighteenth-century children's literature is full of characters like 'Lady Sincere'—vain, proud, obstinate, and empty-headed. But there is never any doubt who is right in these situations, and the outcome is usually the same; 'Lady Sincere' is made to see the error of her ways and harmony is restored.

Young girls seem to have been a particular target of this sort of moralising. John Gregory put the case succinctly in his 'legacy' to his daughters in 1774. What they should aspire to, he maintained, was 'a retiring delicacy', 'dignity without pride, affability without manner'.[52] 'Shun affectation in all its odious forms', echoed Thomas Percival. 'Assume no borrowed airs, and be content to please, to shine, or to be useful in the way nature points out, and which reason approves'.[53] But young boys, too, were constantly reminded of the folly of extravagance. 'Why all this anxiety, this longing after riches?' asks Billy Hiron, a character in Newbery's *Lilliputian Magazine*. 'You can eat no more, sleep no more, than you do now. Believe me, friends, a woollen coat is as warm as a silken one, and there is as much comfort in a cap as in a crown'.[54] The author of *The Amusing Instructor* (1769) agreed. It was absurd, he argued, to value oneself on rank or riches, for the simple reason that 'in reality' these things possessed no 'intrinsic worth'.[55]

Yet no one went so far as to suggest that wealth or possessions did not matter at all. It was simply a matter of proportion. 'I mean not, that fortune and beauty should be despised', explained the Rev. J. Cooper in *The Blossoms of Morality* (1789). 'I mean only that they should be used properly, and that the possessor of them should not imagine, that they will supply the place of education, industry, benevolence, charity and virtue'.[56] What gave added resonance to this sort of advice was its appeal to nature. The place of the natural world in eighteenth-century children's literature is sometimes overlooked, but it deserves closer attention. The stories themselves are often set in the country and frequently they contain quite detailed information about birds, flora, and wildlife. This was by no means accidental. There was an important discourse going on here; one that set artificial city values against a romanticised view of simple, rural values. Needless to say, nature ('Miss Rural') more often than not emerged triumphant.

Appropriately, young children were encouraged to respect and value God's creation. Pulling the wings off harmless insects, baiting or torturing dogs and cats with sticks and stones, and robbing birds' nests, all met with the condemnation of writers of children's books. Even fishing did not escape their censure. As Mary Pilkington put it:

Fishing is not only a *cruel*, but a *treacherous* amusement, for the unsuspecting little animal is allured under the pretence of a favourite regale. Suppose we were invited to a feast, and in the most luxurious dishes a deadly poison was concealed?[57]

Such sentiments were already commonplace by 1800 and few middle-class children would have been unaware of the consequences of disregarding them. 'The encouragement given to boys to destroy the labours of these poor little innocent creatures [birds], and deprive them of their tender nestlings, is often productive of much evil in future life', proclaimed John Marshall's *Juvenile Correspondence* (1783). 'Can you wonder to see men cruel, oppressive, unjust, when we suffer children to be so?'[58]

Changing attitudes towards the natural world went hand in hand with a more enlightened attitude towards the poor and the dispossessed. 'It is our duty to help everyone we may meet with in distress', wrote William Darton in *Little Truths* (1787). 'We should not, like the Priest and the Levite mentioned in the parable, pass by the man, who, in travelling from Jerusalem to Jericho, fell among thieves, was robbed, and grievously wounded; but, like the good Samaritan, render every service in our power'.[59] Almsgiving and acts of charity were accordingly encouraged and applauded; miserliness and prejudice roundly condemned. 'Fill the poor with food, and you shall never want treasure', was one characteristic comment.[60] Nevertheless, the pressing claims of men and women who were 'too idle to work and too impudent to solicit' prompted some writers to counsel caution. 'Though I wish to inspire you with the spirit of charity', Mary Pilkington warned young readers, 'yet I would not have you indulge it in opposition to your reason, and in defiance of common sense'.[61]

If we accept that children's literature can help us to reconstruct a group's world view, then it is quite clear that many middle-class Britons, the 'authors' of this linguistic behaviour, now endorsed a different set of values: decency, moderation, compassion, and good order. Not all of them, of course. Some were content to make their way as best they could, while others like Thomas Turner veered anxiously between extremes of behaviour, at one moment coming home drunk after a night of carousing, at another full of remorse.[62] But the vast market for children's literature, the growth of private schools and academies, libraries, and literary and philosophical societies—all of these things suggest that the middling sort were beginning to assert their independence and find a distinctive voice. (Political clubs, fraternities, and manufacturing organisations like the General Chamber of the Manufacturers of Great Britain were all part of the same phenomenon.[63]) And as they did so they became increasingly frustrated with their exclusion from political influence, at both a local and a national level. They became frustrated with ministerial incompetence and, as they saw it, the decline of national affairs. And, finally, they became frustrated with the follies of the 'fashionable Great', with luxury, extravagance, and corruption.

What united these men (and women) was a shared set of assumptions, a common outlook that for want of a better term can be described as 'enlightened'. This applied to towns like Taunton and Exeter in the south-west of England, undergoing profound dislocation as they shifted to a broader-based service economy, as much as to 'new' manufacturing centres like Manchester and Birmingham. In each case we can see the emergence of a vocal middle class eager to advance its own ideas and interests and keenly aware of its own unique virtues. As a correspondent in the *Gentleman's Magazine* put it in 1791, commenting on the debate on the slave trade: 'they [the Commons] have made us more contemptible, both in our own sight, and in the eyes of Europe, than we should have been respectable. It has only confirmed what I have long suspected, that the manners of the Great are in general so corrupt, that it is not from them we are to expect reformation, but from the middling ranks of the community'.[64]

The growth of compassion, of civility and sociability, also affected attitudes towards blacks and the related questions of race and slavery. By 1750 there were perhaps as many as 20,000 blacks in Britain. This community, of course, had its origins in the Atlantic slave trade. There are no reliable estimates for the number of slaves who found their way into Britain during the seventeenth and eighteenth centuries, but it was certainly large.[65] Fuelled by the aristocratic taste for the rare and exotic, black servants, particularly young boys, were soon familiar sights in larger country houses. By degrees the fashion spread to wealthy merchants and the urban gentry. We can trace this process of social emulation in the paintings of the period, from Peter Mignard's elegant portrait of the Duchess of Portsmouth (1682) to George Morland's genre paintings of the 1780s.[66] The blacks portrayed in these paintings are, for the most part, objects of display, intended to tell the viewer something about the 'owner's' wealth, status, and respectability. They are props, fashionable possessions, as important in their way as a piece of china or the cut of a dress.

As the black population grew so did it become more visible and more mobile. By 1800 blacks were scattered all over Britain, although the largest concentration of numbers was still to be found in London and ports like Bristol and Liverpool. Visiting Lewes in Sussex in 1783, Sylas Neville noted that one of the maids at the 'White Hart' was 'a thin pretty black girl'.[67] Meanwhile at Weston Longville, near Norwich, Parson Woodforde recorded the following incident in his diary on 21 July 1787:

> This Evening as we were going to Supper, a covered Cart drove into my Yard with 3 Men with it, and one of them, the principal, was a black with a French Horn, blowing it up the Yard to the kitchen Door, to know if we would [like to see] a little Woman only 33 Inches high and 31 Years of Age. As we did not give our Dissent, she was taken out of the Cart and brought into our Kitchen, where we saw her and heard her sing two Songs. I don't think she was any taller than represented, but rather deformed, seemed in good Spirits, sang exceedingly high with very little Judgement and was very talkative. She was called by the black Polly Coleshill of Glocester (sic). The Black told me that he had formerly lived with the Earl of Albemarle.[68]

A similar scene is visualised in William Henry Pyne's *Outside the Tavern* (n.d.), which depicts the arrival of 'Mr Ranter's (Theatrical) Company' outside a village inn. The troupe hangs out of a covered cart, among them a black who looks directly at the viewer, his arms outstretched, seemingly oblivious to the confusion going on around him.[69]

As these few examples suggest, many blacks upon leaving domestic service were forced to make a living as best they could, as entertainers or showmen. Others fell into poverty, theft, and crime. One of Isaac Cruikshank's satirical prints, *Foot Pad's—Or Much Ado About Nothing* (1795), portrays a poor black woman and her accomplice, a one-legged beggar, in the act of holding up and robbing a well dressed man-about-town.[70] Cruikshank hinted at an important reality. By the 1790s there were an increasing number of black poor, many of them 'seamen who had been disbanded after the peace of 1783'.[71] Nevertheless, it is easy to exaggerate the size and scale of this 'black problem', easier still to ignore the number of blacks who enjoyed a measure of financial security, or, like Ignatius Sancho and Olaudah Equiano, earned the respect and admiration of prominent whites.[72] There was, it seems, no typical black experience during the eighteenth century. As James Walvin puts it:

> They could be found grouped together in the wretched slums of the capital; they could be found in stately homes in remote rural communities, living the respected but rugged life of the servant class. Some behaved like black English gentlemen, and had been educated to that end. Others stalked the major ports of the country or settled in the smallest of rural villages where they had found themselves in the train of a retiring planter or official.[73]

This much is in no doubt. Less clear is the way in which the black community in Britain, and blacks generally, were perceived. Certainly, there was distrust and a good deal of hostility. 'Black is a colour which nature abhors', noted the *English Review* in 1788. 'The eye startles and shrinks from it when it is first presented; nothing inanimate wears this horrid gloom; and, in the living world, a black skin is peculiar to animals of the most odious and loathsome kind'.[74] Yet at the same time there is plenty of evidence to suggest that a more enlightened attitude towards blacks was emerging during the second half of the eighteenth century. Again, we can see this in the children's literature of the period. John Newbery's *Tom Telescope* (1761), for instance, took issue with a man who doted on his household pets yet as a slave merchant thought nothing of 'separating the husband from the wife, the parents from the children, and all . . . from their native country, to be sold in foreign markets, like so many horses'.[75] As far as we know, this is one of the first references to the slave trade in children's literature, and its appearance in a book ostensibly about the Newtonian system of philosophy is highly suggestive. Slavery was not only cruel and oppressive, *Tom Telescope* seemed to be saying, it was also irrational and contrary to natural law.

No less striking in this regard is Thomas Percival's *A Father's Instructions to his Children* (1776). Percival's book, a collection of tales, fables, and reflections, deals only incidentally with the subject of the slave trade, but what it does have to say is highly revealing. Volume one contains a powerful and evocative description of a fine Arabian horse trapped by hunters and sold to the British envoy at Constantinople—a narrative that has obvious parallels with the abolitionist rhetoric of the 1780s and 1790s.[76] In the second volume, published in 1777, Percival turns his attention to the horrors of the slave trade itself, the human plunder carried out on the west coast of Africa, and the cruelties endured during the Middle Passage. He ends with an appeal not to reason or, indeed, to his readers' finer feelings, but to their patriotism and their sense of honour:

—I am shocked to inform you, that this infernal commerce is carried on by the humane, the polished, the christian inhabitants of Europe, whose ancestors have bled in the cause of liberty, and whose breasts still glow with the same generous flame![77]

The same ideas and assumptions can be found in contemporary drama, a source which has been strangely neglected by historians. Not content with questioning the morality of slavery itself, eighteenth-century playwrights experimented increasingly with themes and characters that portrayed blacks not as inferior objects, but as human beings. If the results were sometimes comical and frequently prone to caricature, the plays nevertheless helped to create a climate in which abolition, both inside and outside Parliament, acquired an urgent moral force.

The literature on blacks and the theatre is, by any standard, remarkably thin. In the only relevant study of early British drama, that by Elliot Tokson, negative images abound. 'The black characters who parade across the English stage', he concludes, 'lie, cheat, kill, worship the sun and moon, and act in passionate disorder'.[78] Significantly, Tokson's survey ends in 1688 with the publication of Aphra Behn's *Oroonoko*, which broke new ground in its portrayal of a black—in this case an African prince who, snatched from the west coast of Africa by an unscrupulous slave merchant, is willing to contemplate death rather than submit to the ignominy of colonial slavery.[79] Such was the success of Behn's novel that it was dramatised by Thomas Southerne in 1695 and the play went on to become one of the most frequently performed works in the eighteenth-century theatre.[80] Southerne's *Oroonoko*, however, deviated from the original in a number of important respects. Not only did he add a comic sub-plot involving a grasping widow in pursuit of a wife for her witless son, but he insisted on making Oroonoko's wife, Imoinda, white, an added complication that helped to seal the couple's fate.[81] For in this version of the story Oroonoko destroys himself as well as Imoinda, following an abortive slave rebellion inspired by Aboan, one of his followers.

Despite the early success of Southerne's *Oroonoko*, by 1750 the play was clearly losing its appeal, and this undoubtedly had something to do with the fact that no fewer than three revised versions appeared between 1759 and 1760. There is a tendency to dismiss these adaptations as being of very little consequence, involving, as each of them did, the removal of all the comic scenes, but closer analysis reveals a more deliberate purpose. This is most obvious in John Hawkesworth's version of the play, which was first performed at Drury Lane on 1 December 1759.[82] Many of Hawkesworth's alterations were concerned with small inconsistencies in plot and character, but more significant for our purposes was the drastically revised first act. Hawkesworth's *Oroonoko* opened with a new scene clearly intended to expose the inhumanity and hypocrisy of the West Indian planter class. Several 'Christian' planters are discovered discussing the finer details of slave management. 'Pox on 'em, a parcel of lazy, obstinate, untractable Pagans', says one as the group awaits another cargo of slaves (among them Oroonoko) to come ashore. He goes on: 'Half of 'em are so sulky when they first come, that they won't eat their Victuals when it's set before 'em, and a Christian may beat 'em till he drops down before he can make 'em eat, if they han't a mind to it'. 'Aye, in truth', replies another,

> a Christian Colony has a hard time of it, that is forced to deal in this cursed Heathen Commodity: Here every time a Ship comes in, my money goes for a great raw-boned negroe Fellow, that has the Impudence to think he is my Fellow-Creature, with as much Right to Liberty as I have, and so grows sullen and refuses to work; or for a young Wench, who will howl Night and Day after a Brat or a Lover forsooth, which nothing can drive out of her Head but a Cat-o'-nine-tails; and if Recourse is had to that

Remedy, 'tis ten to one but she takes the next Opportunity to pick my Pocket by hanging herself.[83]

Hawkesworth's images were carefully chosen. The play upon the words 'Christian' and 'Heathen' was heavily ironic, as was the contrast drawn between the 'poor industrious Planter', on the one hand, and his 'lazy, obstinate' charges, on the other. Almost at once, then, in the first scene, Hawkesworth had set about altering the whole moral emphasis of Southerne's original play.

Later in the same act Hawkesworth added another new scene, which was intended to account for the precipitate attempt of Aboan to recover his liberty and, with Oroonoko's co-operation, to form and carry out a slave rebellion. The scene hinges on the cowed, submissive air of three of Aboan's fellow field workers. 'You are a Stranger, ign'rant of your Duty', says one,

> Or else this Idleness had been chastis'd
> With many a smarting Blow.
> 3. Aye, good Aboan
> Come, come with us, for if the Overseer
> Ev'n now surprise us—
> 2. Hush, I hear his Voice—
> 1. No, no 'tis not he—
> Aboan. Wou'd he scourge us then?
> 3. Wou'd he? Experience
> soon will tell you that.
>
> (1. 3; pp. 9–10)

The first act of Hawkesworth's *Oroonoko*, therefore, served to reorient the action that followed. Whereas Southerne had been concerned with the tragedy of a noble prince enslaved and, as a consequence, had said very little about slavery itself, Hawkesworth recast Oroonoko in the role of a victim of a system that was impossibly cruel and inhumane.

Francis Gentleman's adaptation of *Oroonoko*, published in 1760, was, in many respects, unremarkable. But, like Hawkesworth, Gentleman was at pains to give the play a clear moral stance on the slave issue. Blandford, for instance, who is the only member of the planter elite sympathetic to the plight of his charges, greets the slave dealer, Captain Driver, in the following manner:

But see, here comes the sordid Buccaneer,
With a malicious joy upon his brow,
To boast the merit of his savage trade:
A wretch as ruthless as the prowling wolf,
Without one human feeling in his breast;
Yet vaunts, that, as a Christian, he has right
To make the most of infidels—he's here.[84]

Gentleman pursues this theme further in an exchange between two slaves, one of whom, Massingano, is bent on Oroonoko's destruction. 'Here I shall not need thy honest aid', Massingano tells his companion,

I must become a Christian in my scheme,
Invert my nature, bend my stubborn heart,
And work, by stratagem, to gain my end.
Thy fraudless bosom knows not arts like these;
But here, 'tis common, to betray with smiles,
And pierce the heart, that meets thee as friend.

(Act 1; p. 25)

Oroonoko, too, strikes out at the Christian's alleged superiority:

You cast the name of savage with contempt,
But know, proud boasters, those unletter'd shores,
Claim brighter virtues far than art e'er taught;
Learning and fraud are equally unknown.

(Act 1; p. 19)

It would not do to leave *Oroonoko* without saying something about the third, anonymous, version of the play, also published in 1760.[85] Of all three adaptations this was the one that addressed slavery most directly, a fact which may help to explain why it was never performed. The author first introduces the subject in the form of a dialogue between Imoinda and a new character, Maria, who is engaged to Blandford. 'I have heard', says Imoinda,

. . . the Isle which gave thee birth,
Is mark'd for hospitable Deeds, humane
Benevolence, extended Charities—
With ev'ry social Virtue—Is't possible?
A Nation thus distinguish'd, by the Ties,
Of soft Humanity, shou'd give its Sanction,

To its *dependent* States, to exercise,
This more than savage Right, of thus disposing,
Like th' marketable Brute,
Their Fellow-Creatures Blood?

'Too just the Charge', comes the reply,

    —too closely urg'd—for one,
Unknowing in the hidden Paths of States,
T'answer, with that Energy of reas'ning,
Thou, so forcibly, hast given it—Yet—
I am well persuaded—Justice, Equity,
With Wisdom blended, of the sage Rulers,
Of my parent Country, cou'd furnish forth,
Fit Argument; and with Humanity,
Conjoin'd, to authorise an Act, I must with thee,
Confess, has much alarm'd, and shock'd my feeling Soul.

           (1.1.; pp. 5–6)

Later Maria returns to the morality of slavery in yet another conversation, this time with Blandford, which is remarkable also for its allusion to pro-slavery arguments. Pressed by Maria, Blandford admits that it is unfortunate that a more humane expedient cannot be found for the cultivation of the West Indian islands. 'And yet', he goes on,

There are those, who say, this Practice carries Mercy,
Rather than Marks of an unfeeling Stamp—
Since in th' Wars, they wage, each with the other—
Were not this Channel of commercial Intercourse
Kept open, th' Pris'ners taken, would exchange
This Slavery, for cruel, and tormenting Deaths.

           (4.1; p. 42)

The question therefore remains unresolved and, as a result, the play tends to lose direction and, ultimately, moral purpose. More significant for our concerns, however, is the fact that the author should have felt it necessary to address such issues at all. These adaptations of *Oroonoko* warrant close scrutiny because they hint at a subtle but important intellectual shift. By 1760, clearly, it was no longer enough to interpret Aphra Behn's novel in the way that Southerne had done. The reality of a greatly increased black population in Britain, not to mention changing attitudes towards man and the natural world, called for new responses and new strategies.[86] What, indeed, we can discern in the rewritings of Southerne's play is a willingness to take issue with the morality of slavery and, just as important, a ready acceptance of the black's humanity. In short, authors like Hawkesworth and Gentleman (and how many others?) now read *Oroonoko* in a startlingly different way. And, of course, their adaptations of the play invited theatregoers to do likewise.

Despite these attempts to make *Oroonoko* more realistic, the central character remained a dramatic invention. Oroonoko was an exotic—a tragic, noble figure who happened to be black. Increasingly, however, such images came to lack authenticity and immediacy. One of the playwrights who experimented with more realistic, or at least more recognisable, black figures was Isaac Bickerstaffe.[87] For a period during the eighteenth century Bickerstaffe enjoyed considerable popular success, not least because of his comic operas, a genre that he can lay some claim to have created. His choice of material is of interest in part because he was almost certainly homosexual:[88] although many of his plays and comic operas were, admittedly, loose adaptations of foreign texts, his work reveals a deep sympathy with outsiders, often women or blacks, and a fascination with the overturning of established conventions. In *The Sultan* (1775), for instance, an ungovernable female slave, Roxalana, wins the heart of her master and persuades him to throw open the gates of his seraglio. An earlier piece, *The Captive* (1769), plots the downfall of an avaricious cadi whose daughter is determined to become a Catholic and go to Spain.[89]

It is perhaps understandable, given these concerns, that Bickerstaffe should have turned his attention to the subject of colonial slavery, as he did in *Love in the City* (1767). The play was ostensibly a satire on the pretensions of London's middle class, but the heroine was Priscilla Tomboy, a West Indian orphan forced to take up lodgings in the capital with her aging guardian and his two children, Penelope and Young Cockney. Priscilla is a frightening yet compelling creation. In the first scene we learn that she has been expelled from her 'Hackney boarding-school' for beating the governess, behaviour which, significantly, is put down to her upbringing 'in the plantations'.[90] Needless to say,

Priscilla's treatment of her black servant, Quasheba, is uncompromising:

> *Pris.* . . . Quasheba, get out, I want to talk with Miss Penny alone—or stay, come back, I will speak before her—But if ever I hear, hussy, that you mention a word of what I am going to say to any one else in the house, I will have you horse-whipp'd till there is not a bit of flesh left on your bones.
>
> *Pen.* Oh, poor creature!
>
> *Pris.* Psha,—what is she but a Neger? If she was at home at our plantations, she would find the difference; we make no account of them there at all; if I had a fancy for one of their skins I should not think much of taking it.
>
> *Pen.* I suppose then you imagine they have no feeling?
>
> *Pris.* Oh! we never consider that there—
>
> (1.2; p. 5)

Priscilla's progress through the play is unremitting. Determined not to marry her guardian's son, as planned, she sets her heart on a young captain and pursues her quarry with characteristic ruthlessness. Bickerstaffe's obvious intention was to provoke and unsettle his audience. Priscilla's disregard for Quasheba, for instance, is set in sharp contrast to her guardian's attention to his servant, Margery:

> Come, Friend Margery, let us see how you have settled things— have you dusted well, and swept . . . But what have you done in the other chamber, Friend Margery—
>
> (3.9; p. 62)

No less striking is the character of Penelope, who is aptly portrayed as the embodiment of all domestic virtues. Penelope represents everything that Priscilla is not, and her disquiet at Priscilla's treatment of Quasheba is intended to draw attention to the boorishness, and hence the unfemininity, of Priscilla's behaviour. Priscilla's bantering exchanges with Young Cockney are designed to have the same effect. Young Cockney may be vain and a social climber—certainly this is the view of his uncle—but he is instantly recognisable as a model of urban gentility. So while we are invited to laugh at Priscilla's antics we are left in no doubt that she represents the antithesis of middle-class sensibilities. She is, in other words, a subversive character, and it is this knowledge that creates the dramatic tension at the heart of the play.

Bickerstaffe sought to confront white racial attitudes again in *The Padlock* (1768). Loosely based on a short story by Cervantes, *The Padlock* concerns a middle-aged merchant, Don Diego, who takes in Leonora, a neighbour's daughter, for three months in the hope of making her his wife. Convinced that the most rigorous confinement has bent the young girl to his will, Don Diego sets out to arrange matters with her parents, leaving Leonora in the care of his two servants, Ursula and Mungo. As a precaution, however, he locks up his house (hence the title of the play), taking the key with him. But in his absence the household rebels. Don Diego returns to find Mungo intoxicated and Leonora in the arms of a young student, Leander. Confused and distraught, Don Diego at last sees the error of his ways. Not only does he give up Leonora to Leander, but in a final act of contrition he orders the grills to be removed from the windows of his house.

The Padlock was for Bickerstaffe familiar territory, involving as it did the themes of liberty and captivity, submission and rebellion, jealousy and trust, and it was an instant success.[91] But the key to its popularity was not the plot or the moral drawn but Mungo, Don Diego's black servant.[92] Here was a very different kind of black character; lazy, gullible (it is Mungo who is first taken in by Leander), and untrustworthy, it is true, but at the same time quick-witted, worldly, and, above all, human:

> *Don Diego.* Can you be honest?
>
> *Mungo.* Me no savee, Massa, you never ax me before.
>
> *Don Diego.* Can you tell truth?
>
> *Mungo.* What you give me, Massa?
>
> *Don Diego.* There's a pistreen for you; now tell me, do you know of any ill going on in my house?
>
> *Mungo.* Ah, Massa, a damn deal.
>
> *Don Diego.* How! that I'm stranger to?
>
> *Mungo.* No, Massa, you lick me every day with you rattan: I'm sure, Massa, that's mischief enough for poor Neger man.[93]

When in act two Mungo finally loses his temper and rebels, Bickerstaffe uses humour again to soften the edges of a potentially threatening situation:

Don Diego. Horrid creature! what makes you here at this time
of night; is it with a design to surprise the innocents in their
beds, and murder them sleeping?

Mungo. Hush, hush—make no noise—hic-hic.

Don Diego. The slave is intoxicated.

Mungo. Make no noise, I say; deres young Gentleman wid
young Lady; he plays on guitar, and likes him better dan
she likes you. Fal, lal, lal.

Don Diego. Monster, I'll make an example of you!

Mungo. What you call me names for, you old dog?

Don Diego. Does the villain dare to lift his hand against me!

Mungo. Will you fight?

Don Diego. He's mad.

(2.6; p. 26)

Mungo, of course, is a comic figure, but behind such exchanges
there was a more serious intent, namely, to provide a critique of
the master–slave relationship. Mungo appealed to the consciences
of white audiences, gently prodding them in a manner that was
both light and entertaining.

This is not to deny the persistence of racist attitudes during the
eighteenth century or the fact that characters like Mungo were
demeaning or crudely drawn. Unwittingly, perhaps, Bickerstaffe
fostered an image of blacks as servants or menials with certain
identifiable traits, not least of which was a distinctive way of
speaking. (Representations of African or West Indian dialect
were extremely rare on the British stage before 1768; Oroonoko,
for instance, spoke in the manner of an educated Englishman, and
this was as true of the various adaptations of the play produced
between 1759 and 1760 as it was of Southerne's original.) Be that
as it may, such characters did succeed in evoking more positive
images of blacks than those common a century before. Plays like
The Padlock therefore deserve close attention. Highly successful
entertainments, they helped to build 'a bridge of sympathy and
understanding' between the races which, in turn, made abolition
seem possible as well as desirable.[94]

In a parallel trend there were rising doubts in some quarters
about 'holding private property in the person of man'. For radicals
like Granville Sharp the issue went beyond the domain of morals
or religious sensibilities. 'The perpetual service of a slave cannot,

with propriety, be compared to the temporary service of an apprentice', Sharp argued,

> because the latter is due only in consequence of a voluntary contract, wherein both parties have a mutual advantage; but in the former case, there is no contract, neither can a contract be even IMPLIED, because the free consent of both parties cannot possibly be IMPLIED likewise; and, without this, every kind of contract (in the very nature and Idea of such an obligation) is absolutely null and void.[95]

Sharp, of course, was making a case against the legality of chattel slavery in England, but the logic of his argument was inescapable. Slavery, wherever it existed, was a form of 'vassalage'; it denied men their natural rights (and, not least, their right to enter freely into a contract) and robbed them of their humanity.

Doubts about slavery as a species of property also found an echo in changing attitudes towards labour. Throughout the second half of the eighteenth century the old compulsions gave way to a 'growing belief amongst industrialists that men and women could be entitled to work hard by rewards as well as penalties'.[96] Compassion was only part of the issue here. Industrialisation simply offered a more effective means of organising labour. Entrepreneurs like Wedgwood and Matthew Boulton understood this only too well. Wedgwood's factory at Etruria was disciplined, highly productive, and, by the standards of the time, friendly and humane: it was modern. The gap between capitalist and pre-capitalist modes of production widened perceptibly during the eighteenth century and as it did so slavery began to seem curiously outmoded. None of this is to suggest that the spread of abolitionist ideas *had* to rest on industrialisation and the growth of wage labour. But that there was a link of some sort, perhaps 'a transformation of consciousness', seems indisputable.[97]

These different trends—a rapidly expanding middle class, consumerism, better communications, the growth of compassion and sensitivity—made organised anti-slavery, in the shape of the early abolitionist movement, possible. But why did it take until the 1780s for that movement to emerge?

In part, the answer to this question has to do with middle-class formation. As E. P. Thompson and others point out, the middling sort were understandably slow to assert their independence in the face of the 'ever-present controls of clientage, of patronage and "interest"'.[98] The Wilkite agitation of the 1760s was a turning-point for many. But of far greater moment, in retrospect, was the American Revolution. At an ideological level the revolution unleashed a heated debate about political representation, both at home and abroad. There is no need to rehearse those arguments here.[99] But I do want to say something about the rhetoric of radicalism during the 1780s. Almost without exception, radicals likened their own plight to that of slaves. 'To be free', wrote Capel Lofft in 1780, 'is to be in a condition of giving assent to the laws of the state, either in *person*, or by a representative . . . To be enslaved is to have no will of our own in the choice of law-makers; but to be governed by rulers whom other men have set over us'.[100] Disfranchisement, echoed John Cartwright, 'is the very definition of slavery'.[101] In this way, slavery began to take on a more immediate significance, related to the political condition of thousands of native-born Britons.

The revolution, in other words, gave slavery political meaning. But it also had a more far-reaching effect. Defeat in the American war brought with it a searching and sometimes painful re-evaluation of Britain's standing as a once victorious Protestant nation. As Linda Colley reminds us, one of the results of the loss of the American colonies was a move to tighten the reins of empire elsewhere, in Canada and Ireland. Another, however, was 'a rise in enthusiasm for Parliamentary reform . . . for religious liberalisation, for the reform of goals and lunatic asylums; for virtually anything, in fact, that might prevent a similar national humiliation in the future'.[102] Here, in other words, was the catalyst that abolitionists had been looking for. The American war came to an end in 1783. Four years later Sharp and his friends organised the Society for the Abolition of the Slave Trade. Can this have been coincidence?

Notes

1.   Joseph Woods to William Matthews, 28 January 1788, Matthews MSS, A1/5, Friends House Library, London.

2. For grass-roots support for abolition see Chapter Five. I am quite aware that other groups played their part, but the main impetus came from the middling ranks.

3. For the whole concept of an 'urban renaissance' see Peter Borsay, *The English Urban Renaissance: Culture and Society in the Provincial Town, 1660–1770*, Oxford, 1989; Angus McInnes, 'The Emergence of a Leisure Town: Shrewsbury, 1660–1760', *Past and Present*, CXX, 1988, pp. 53–87; Peter Borsay, 'The Emergence of a Leisure Town: or an Urban Renaissance?' and Angus McInnes, ' A Reply', *Past and Present*, CXXVI, 1990, pp. 189–202. For the 'consumer revolution' of the eighteenth century see Neil McKendrick, 'The Consumer Revolution of Eighteenth-Century England', in McKendrick, Brewer and Plumb, *The Birth of A Consumer Society: The Commercialization of Eighteenth-Century England*, pp. 9–33; Grant McCracken, *Culture and Consumption: New Approaches to the Symbolic Character of Consumer Goods*, Bloomington and Indianapolis, 1988; John Brewer and Roy Porter, eds., *Consumption and the World of Goods*, London and New York, 1993.

4. E. Anthony Wrigley, 'Urban Growth and Agricultural Change: England and the Continent in the Early Modern Period', in Peter Borsay, ed., *The Eighteenth-Century Town: A Reader in English Urban History, 1688–1820*, London, 1990, pp. 42–50.

5. Introduction to Peter Borsay, ed., *The Eighteenth-Century Town*, p. 12.

6. For the professions see Wilfrid Prest, ed., *Lawyers in Early Modern Europe and America*, London, 1981; Roy Porter, *Doctor of Society: Thomas Beddoes and the Sick Trade in Late Enlightenment England*, New York, 1982; Geoffrey S. Holmes, *Augustan England: Profession, State, and Society, 1680–1730*, London, 1983.

7. John Brewer, 'English Radicalism in the Age of George III', in J. G. A. Pocock, ed., *Three British Revolutions*, Princeton, 1980, p. 333. See also P. J. Corfield, *The Impact of the English Town, 1700–1800*, Oxford, 1982, pp. 130–3.

8. Peter Earle, *The Making of the English Middle Class: Business, Society and Family Life in London, 1660–1730*, London, 1989, pp. 4–5. For classification of the middle class see Keith Wrightson, 'The Social Order of Early Modern England: Three Approaches', in L. Bonfield, R. M. Smith and K. Wrightson, eds., *The World We Have Gained*, Oxford, 1986, pp. 177–202; P. Corfield, 'Class by Name and Number in Eighteenth-Century Britain', *History*, LXXII, 1987, pp. 38–61; Lawrence Stone, *The Past and the Present Revisited*, London, 1987, pp. 222–40; John Seed, 'From "Middling Sort" to Middle Class in Late Eighteenth- and Early Nineteenth-Century Britain', in M. L. Bush, ed., *Social Orders and Social Classes in Europe Since 1500*, London, 1992, pp. 114–35.

9. *Letters Concerning the Present State of England. Particularly Respecting the Politics, Arts, Manners, and Literature of the Times*, London, 1772, p. 228.

10. Lorna Weatherill, 'The Meaning of Consumer Behavior in Late Seventeenth- and early Eighteenth-Century England', in Brewer and Porter, eds., *Consumption and the World of Goods*, pp. 210–11.

11. See Neil McKendrick, 'The Commercialization of Fashion', in McKendrick, Brewer and Plumb, *The Birth of a Consumer Society*, pp. 34–99.

12. McCracken, *Culture and Consumption*, p. 19.

13. For Wedgwood's marketing techniques see Neil McKendrick, 'Josiah Wedgwood and the Commercialization of the Potteries', in McKendrick, Brewer and Plumb, *The Birth of a Consumer Society*, pp. 100–45.

14. Borsay, *The English Urban Renaissance*, pp. 117–96. For travel see J. Money, 'Birmingham and the West Midlands, 1760–1793: Politics and Regional Identity in the English Provinces in the Later Eighteenth Century', in Borsay, ed., *The Eighteenth-Century Town*, pp. 296–7; Linda Colley, *Britons: Forging the Nation, 1707–1837*, London and New Haven, 1993, pp. 39–40, 172–3.

15. Joshua Toulmin, *The History of the Town of Taunton, in the County of Somerset*, Taunton, 1791, pp. 185–6.

16. W. G. Hoskins, *Two Thousand Years in Exeter*, Exeter, 1960, pp. 91–2.

17. For literacy see Lawrence Stone, 'Literacy and Education in England, 1640–1900', *Past and Present*, XLII, 1969, esp. pp. 104–9; J. Paul Hunter, *Before Novels: The Cultural Context of Eighteenth-Century English Fiction*, New York and London, 1990, pp. 66–73; David Cressy, 'Literacy in Context: Meaning and Measurement in Early Modern England', in Brewer and Porter, eds., *Consumption and the World of Goods*, pp. 305–19.

18. Cressy, 'Literacy in Context', p. 317.

19. Hunter, *Before Novels*, p. 84.

20. G. A. Cranfield, *The Development of the Provincial Newspaper, 1700–1760*, Oxford, 1962, p. 22; John Brewer, *Party Ideology and Popular Politics at the Accession of George III*, pp. 142–3.

21. Cranfield, *The Development of the Provincial Newspaper*, p. 173. The *Manchester Mercury*, the *Gazette* and the *Herald* were all being published in Manchester during the 1790s.

22. Cranfield, *The Development of the Provincial Newspaper*, p. 175. Christine Ferdinand estimates that between the 1760s and 1780 the circulation of the *Salisbury Journal* increased from 2,500 to 4,000 copies a week. See C. Y. Ferdinand, 'Selling it to the Provinces: News and Commerce round Eighteenth-Century Salisbury', in Brewer and Porter, eds., *Consumption and the World of Goods*, p. 398.

23. Neil McKendrick, 'George Packwood and the Commercialization of Shaving: The Art of Eighteenth-Century Advertising or "the Way to Get Money and be Happy"', in McKendrick, Brewer and Plumb, *The Birth of a Consumer Society*, pp. 152, 163–4.

24. McKendrick, 'Josiah Wedgwood and the Commercialization of the Potteries', pp. 123–6.

25. For the agency system and the book trade in general see John Feather, *The Provincial Book Trade in Eighteenth-Century England*, Cambridge, 1985.

26. Borsay, *The English Urban Renaissance*, pp. 131–2; J. R. Oldfield, 'Printers, Booksellers and Libraries in Hampshire, 1750–1800', *Hampshire Papers*, No. 3, Winchester, 1993, p. 8.

27. For circulating libraries see Paul Kaufman, *Libraries and their Users*,

London, 1969, pp. 6–25, 50–3; Borsay, *The English Urban Renaissance*, pp. 133–5; J. Fergus, 'Eighteenth-Century Readers in Provincial England: The Customers of Samuel Clay's Circulating Library and Bookshop in Warwick, 1770–72', *Papers of the Bibliographical Society of America*, LXXVIII, 1984, pp. 179–91; Oldfield, 'Printers, Booksellers and Libraries in Hampshire', pp. 16–20.

28. Oldfield, 'Printers, Booksellers and Libraries in Hampshire', p. 17.

29. Ibid., p. 17.

30. Ibid., p. 20.

31. Roy Porter, 'Science, Provincial Culture and Public Opinion in Enlightenment England', in Borsay, ed., *The Eighteenth-Century Town*, pp. 243–67. For the Birmingham Lunar Society see R. E. Schofield, *The Lunar Society of Birmingham*, Oxford, 1963.

32. Porter, 'Science, Provincial Culture and Public Opinion in Enlightenment England', p. 253.

33. Oldfield, 'Printers, Booksellers and Libraries in Hampshire', p. 8.

34. For Wilkes see Brewer, *Party Ideology and Popular Politics at the Accession of George III*, esp. pp. 163–200; John Brewer, 'Commercialization and Politics', in McKendrick, Brewer and Plumb, *The Birth of a Consumer Society*, pp. 231–62; Colley, *Britons*, pp. 105–17.

35. There seems to have been a vogue for town and county histories during the late eighteenth century. See, for example, John Brand, *The History and Antiquities of the Town and County of Newcastle upon Tyne*, Newcastle-upon-Tyne, 1789; *The History and Antiquities of the Town and County of Nottingham; containing the whole of Thoroton's Account of that Place. By John Thorsby*, Nottingham, 1795; Richard Warner, *The History of the Isle of Wight, Military, Ecclesiastical, Civil, Natural*, Southampton, 1795; R. H. Cumyns, *The Ancient and Modern History of Portsmouth*, Gosport, 1799.

36. Brewer, 'Commercialization and Politics', pp. 214–30.

37. *London Chronicle*, 1–3 May, 6–8 May, 10–13 May, 13–15 May, 15–17 May, 20–2 May, 21–3 August, 30 October–1 November 1788.

38. Brewer, 'Commercialization and Politics', p. 210.

39. Oldfield, 'Printers, Booksellers and Libraries in Hampshire', p. 12.

40. *London Chronicle*, 30 October–1 November 1788.

41. *Letters Concerning the Present State of England*, pp. 231–2.

42. *Female Government! Or, Letters from a Gentleman to his Friend on the Education of the Fair Sex*, London, 1779, p. 15.

43. Amanda Vickery, 'Women and the World of Goods: A Lancashire Consumer and Her Possessions, 1751–81', in Brewer and Porter, eds., *Consumption and the World of Goods*, p. 291.

44. *The Auction: A Town Eclogue*, London, 1788, p. 4.

45. Of course, there were other factors, too, not least of which were Enlightenment culture and the rise of religious Nonconformity. But there is little doubt that as a secular trend the spread of civility, of moderation, and good order was linked with problems of socialisation and the difficulties created by a volatile economy. For the debate on luxury see John Sekora, *Luxury: The Concept in Western Thought, Eden to Smollet*, Baltimore, Maryland,

1977; T. H. Breen, 'The Meaning of Things: Interpreting the Consumer Economy in the Eighteenth Century', in Brewer and Porter, eds., *Consumption and the World of Goods*, esp. pp. 254–7.

46. For children's literature see Percy Muir, *English Children's Books, 1600–1900*, London, 1954; F. J. Harvey Darton, *Children's Books in England: Five Centuries of Social Life*, new ed., London, 1982; J. H. Plumb, 'The New World of Children in Eighteenth-Century England', in McKendrick, Brewer and Plumb, *The Birth of a Consumer Society*, pp. 300–6; Bette P. Goldstone, *Lessons to be Learned: A Study of Eighteenth-Century English Didactic Children's Literature*, New York, 1984.

47. R. Gordon Kelly, 'Literature and the Historian', *American Quarterly*, XXVI, 1974, p. 154.

48. *The Lilliputian Magazine: or, the Young Gentleman and Lady's Golden Library. Being an Attempt to mend the World, to render the Society of Man more amiable, and to establish the Plainness, Simplicity, Virtue and Wisdom of the Golden Age, much celebrated by the Poets and Historians*, London, 1783, p. 2. Earlier editions of *The Lilliputian Magazine* appeared in 1752, 1765, 1768, 1772, and 1777. Note the wording of the subtitle.

49. Hunter, *Before Novels*, esp. chaps. 5 and 6.

50. Kelly, 'Literature and the Historian', p. 154.

51. *The Young Ladies Magazine, or, Dialogues between a Discreet Governess and Several Young Ladies of the first Rank under her Education. By Mrs Le Prince de Beaumont*, London, 1780, p. 35.

52. John Gregory, *A Father's Legacy to his Daughters*, London, 1774, pp. 26, 45–6.

53. Thomas Percival, *A Father's Instructions to His Children: Consisting of Tales, Fables and Reflections; Designed to Promote the Love of Virtue, a Taste for Knowledge, and an Early Acquaintance with the Works of Nature*, London, 1776, I, p. 78.

54. *The Lilliputian Magazine*, p. 33.

55. *The Amusing Instructor: or, Tales and Fables in Verse, for the Improvement of Youth*, London, 1769, p.21.

56. *The Blossoms of Morality. Intended for the Amusement and Instruction of Young Ladies and Gentlemen. By the Author of the Looking-Glass for the Mind*, London, 1789, p. 93.

57. Mary Pilkington, *The Calendar; or, Monthly Recreations; Chiefly consisting of Dialogues between an Aunt and her Nieces, designed to inspire the juvenile Mind with a Love of Virtue, and a Study of Nature*, London, 1807, pp. 201–2.

58. *Juvenile Correspondence; or, Letters suited to Children, from Four to above Ten Years of Age*, London, 1783, p. 99.

59. William Darton, *Little Truths better than great Fables; Containing Information for the Instruction of Children*, London, 1787, pp. 110–11.

60. *Wisdom in Miniature; or, the Young Gentleman and Ladies Pleasing Instructor: Being a Collection of Sentences, Divine, Moral, and Historical: Selected from the Writings of many ingenious and learned Authors, both ancient and modern*, Coventry, 1791, p. 84.

61. Mary Pilkington, *Obedience Rewarded, and Prejudice Conquered; or, the History of Mortimer Lascells. Written for the Instruction and Amusement of Young People*, London, 1797, pp. 22–3.

62. David Vaisey, ed., *The Diary of Thomas Turner, 1754–1765*, Oxford, 1984, pp. 24, 26–7, 76, 138, 141–3, 155–7, 172, 193.

63. See Brewer, 'Commercialization and Politics', pp. 217–30; Money, 'Birmingham and the West Midlands', pp. 297–301.

64. *Gentleman's Magazine*, LI, 1791, p. 538.

65. See Folarin Shyllon, *Black People in Britain, 1555–1833*, Oxford, 1977, pp. 10–16, 39–44; Peter Fryer, *Staying Power: The History of Black People in Britain*, London, 1984, pp. 14–32.

66. For George Morland see Chapter Six.

67. Basil Cozens-Hardy, ed., *The Diary of Sylas Neville, 1767–1788*, Oxford, 1950, p. 118. Characteristically, Neville asked the young girl for a kiss.

68. David Vaisey, ed., *James Woodforde: The Diary of a Country Parson, 1758–1802*, Oxford, 1984, p. 306.

69. Sale catalogue, Phillips, London, sale on 2 November 1987, London, 1987, p. 18 (No. 18).

70. Robert R. Wark, ed., *Isaac Cruikshank's Drawings for Drolls*, San Marino, California, 1968, catalogue No. 46.

71. Quoted in Shyllon, *Black People in Britain*, p. 120.

72. For Ignatius Sancho and Olaudah Equiano see Fryer, *Staying Power*, pp. 93–9, 102–12.

73. James Walvin, *Black and White: The Negro and English Society, 1555–1945*, London, 1973, p. 72.

74. *English Review*, XI, 1788, p. 277. Interestingly, these comments were made in a review of Hannah More's *Slavery: A Poem* (1788).

75. *The Newtonian System of Philosophy Adapted to the Capacities of Young Gentlemen and Ladies, and familiarised and made entertaining by Objects with which they are intimately acquainted: Being the Substance of Six Lectures read to the Lilliputian Society by Tom Telescope, A.M.*, London, 1761, pp. 121–2.

76. Percival, *A Father's Instructions to His Children*, I, pp. 157–68.

77. Ibid., II, pp. 23–8.

78. Elliot H. Tokson, *The Popular Image of the Black Man in English Drama, 1550–1688*, Boston, Massachusetts, 1982, p. 16.

79. *Oroonoko; or, the Royal Slave*, introduction by Lore Metzger, New York, 1973; David Brion Davis, *The Problem of Slavery in Western Culture*, pp. 470–7; Laura Brown, 'The Romance of Empire: Oroonoko and the Trade in Slaves', in Felicity Nussbaum and Laura Brown, eds., *The New Eighteenth Century: Theory, Politics, English Literature*, London and New York, 1987, pp. 41–61.

80. Robert Jordan and Harold Love, eds., *The Works of Thomas Southerne*, 2 vols., Oxford, 1988, II, p. 91.

81. The obvious model here was Shakespeare's *Othello*, but the device seems to have been chiefly designed to account for white male interest in Imoinda.

82. George Winchester Stone, Jr., *The London Stage, 1660–1800: A Calendar of*

Plays, Entertainments and Afterpieces Together with Casts, Box-Receipts and Contemporary Comment, Part 4: 1747–1776, 3 vols., Carbondale, Illinois, 1962, II, p. 759.

83. *Oroonoko, A Tragedy, As it is now Acted at the Theatre-Royal in Drury Lane by His Majesty's Servants. By Thomas Southern [sic]. With Alterations*, London, 1759, 1.1 (pp. 1–2); further references are given in the text.

84. *Oroonoko; or, The Royal Slave. A Tragedy. Altered from Southerne, By Francis Gentleman. As it was Performed at the Theatre in Edinburgh, with universal Applause*, Glasgow, 1760, 1.1 (p. 12); further references are given in the text.

85. *Oroonoko. A Tragedy. Altered from the Original Play of that Name, Written by the late Thomas Southern [sic], Esq; To Which the Editor had added near Six Hundred Lines, in Place of the Comic Scenes, Together With an Addition of Two New Characters. Intended for one of the Theatres*, London, 1760.

86. Keith Thomas, *Man and the Natural World: Changing Attitudes in England, 1500–1800*, London, 1983, esp. part 4.

87. For Bickerstaffe see Peter A. Tasch, *The Dramatic Cobbler: The Life and Works of Isaac Bickerstaffe*, Lewisburg, Pennsylvania, 1971.

88. Ibid., pp. 24–6, 220 and chap. 12.

89. *The Sultan; or, A Peep into the Seraglio. A Farce* (London, 1774); *The Captive. A Comic Opera* (London, 1769).

90. *Love in the City: A Comic Opera. As it is Performed at the Theatre Royal in Covent-Garden. The Words Written, and the Music Compiled by the Author of Love in a Village*, London, 1767, 1.1 (p. 2); further references are given in the text.

91. Between 1768 and 1776 *The Padlock* was performed 142 times at Drury Lane and seventy times at Covent Garden. See Peter A. Tasch, ed., *The Plays of Isaac Bickerstaffe*, New York and London, 1981, I, p. xx. The play quickly became part of provincial repetoires and was still being performed regularly in London as late as 1790–91. See Charles Beecher Hogan, *The London Stage, 1660–1800: A Calendar of Plays, Entertainments and Afterpieces Together with Casts, Box-Receipts and Contemporary Comment, Part 5: 1776–1800*, 3 vols, Carbondale, Illinois, 1968, II, pp. 1279, 1285, 1289, 1321, 1356, 1373.

92. Part of the success of Mungo undoubtedly had something to do with Bickerstaffe's collaborator, Charles Dibdin, who played the part in the original production. By all accounts, Dibdin's Mungo was a great triumph. For a highly subjective view of his contribution see *The Professional Life of Mr Dibdin, written by himself*, London, 1803, pp. 70–1.

93. *The Padlock: A Comic Opera: As it is Perform'd by His Majesty's Servants, at the Theatre Royal in Drury-Lane*, 2nd ed., London, 1768, 1.6 (p. 10); further references are given in the text.

94. Davis, *The Problem of Slavery in Western Culture*, p. 474.

95. Granville Sharp, *A Representation of the Injustice and Dangerous Tendency of Tolerating Slavery; or of admitting the least Claim of Private Property in the Person of Man, in England*, London, 1769, pp. 163–4.

96. *The American Experience: The Collected Essays of J. H. Plumb*, p. 157. See also David Brion Davis, *The Problem of Slavery in the Age of Revolution, 1770–1823*, pp. 453–68, 489–501.

97. David Brion Davis, 'The Perils of Doing History by Ahistorical Abstraction', in Thomas Bender, ed., *The Antislavery Debate: Capitalism and Abolitionism as a Problem in Historical Interpretation*, Berkeley, California, 1992, p. 294.

98. E. P. Thompson, *Customs in Common*, pp. 31–3, 89.

99. But see Brewer, *Party Ideology and Popular Politics at the Accession of George III*, pp. 201–16; Bernard Bailyn, *The Ideological Origins of the American Revolution*, Cambridge, Massachusetts, 1967; H. T. Dickinson, *Liberty and Property: Political Ideology in Eighteenth-Century Britain*, New York, 1977, esp. pp. 214–20.

100. Capel Lofft, *A Summary of a Treatise by Major Cartwright, entitled The People's Banner against undue Influence: or, the Commons' House of Parliament according to the Constitution*, London, 1780 (not paginated). Sharp had made the same point in his *A Representation of the Injustice and Dangerous Tendency of Tolerating Slavery*, p. 99.

101. John Cartwright, *Letter to the Deputies of the Associated and Petitioning Counties, Cities, and Towns; on the means necessary to a Reformation of Parliament*, London, 1781, p. 4. The same rhetoric persisted into the 1790s. See, for example, *Liberty and Equality; treated of in a Short History, addressed from a Poor Man to his Equals*, 2nd ed., London, 1792, p. 15.

102. Colley, *Britons*, pp. 143–5, 353.

Chapter Two

THE VIEW FROM LONDON

Organised anti-slavery, at least on a nationwide scale, began in
1787 with the Society for the Abolition of the Slave Trade. Of
course, there had been initiatives before that date. The Quakers,
for instance, petitioned Parliament against the trade as early as
1783. That same year the London Meeting for Sufferings also
appointed a special committee to distribute books and pamphlets. And in a quite unrelated move (or so it would seem) the
inhabitants of Bridgwater in Somerset petitioned Parliament in
1785.[1] But by and large these were unco-ordinated efforts, involving a relatively small number of people. It was the Society for the
Abolition of the Slave Trade, or, to be more precise, the Society's
guiding London Committee, which set the movement on its
'modern' course, evolving a structure and organisation which
made it possible to mobilise thousands of Britons across the
length and breadth of the country.

Over the years the London Committee has been ignored or
forgotten by historians of British anti-slavery. The Wilberforces,
for instance, attached far greater significance to the opinion-
building activities of their father, William Wilberforce.[2] Latterly,
the Committee has fallen foul of a broader attempt to arrive at a
better understanding of the general social and cultural context of
anti-slavery and, in particular, the linkage between economic
change, protest, and reform. One of the effects of this search for
the 'ecology' of British anti-slavery has been to divert attention
from London and the influence of an abolitionist elite (the
'Saints') to the provinces and the dynamics of popular abolitionism. As a result, the London Committee has been marginalised or
simply dismissed by some recent historians of the movement.[3] And
yet it is clear that the Committee played an indispensable part in
the mobilisation of public opinion against the slave trade.

The London Committee was formally organised on 22 May
1787. The precise details are unclear, but the stimulus undoubtedly came from William Wilberforce, who by that date had already

declared his intention to introduce the subject of the slave trade in the House of Commons.[4] The nucleus of the group was provided by Samuel Hoare, George Harrison, William Dillwyn, John Lloyd, and Joseph Woods, who had all been connected with the Quaker committee established in 1783.[5] In all, nine of the twelve founding members were Quakers, the exceptions being Philip Sansom, Granville Sharp, and Thomas Clarkson. Moreover, Woods, author of *Thoughts on the Slavery of the Negroes* (1784), was related to Hoare by marriage.[6] The other significant feature of the original Committee was its middle-class origins in commerce and business. Two members were bankers, four were merchants or had some experience of trade, while two, John Barton and James Phillips, were manufacturers.[7] By and large, these were practical men, cautious about money, but as it turned out peculiarly suited to the task of mobilising public opinion against the slave trade.

Politically, many members of the Committee were radicals. Sharp, for instance, vigorously supported the movement for Parliamentary reform and wrote extensively on the subject. Clarkson and James Phillips also closely identified themselves with radical causes, Clarkson's visit to Paris in 1789 arousing in him a deep sympathy with the ideals of the French Revolution.[8] In the Committee's affairs these three men formed an influential group that favoured immediate abolition of the slave trade and looked upon abolition as but a step towards the emancipation that would inevitably follow. Others took a more moderate line. John Barton confessed in March 1788 that he saw 'very plainly that many mischiefs would attend the *immediate* abolition of the Slave Trade, wh[ich] need not be feared if that abolition took place *gradually*; and am further convinced that if it takes place at all, the latter and not the former, will be the mode adopted'. Barton's words were to prove prophetic, but for many members of the Committee gradual abolition was a compromise measure and an acceptance of defeat. 'Nothing short of an entire and immediate abolition will satisfy them', Barton admitted, a realisation that undoubtedly had something to do with his decision to resign from the Committee later that year.[9]

Many of those subsequently invited to join the Committee also had radical sympathies. Josiah Wedgwood, elected in August 1787, privately supported extension of the franchise and through the Birmingham Lunar Society was personally acquainted with Joseph

Priestley and Thomas Day; Andrew Kippis, elected in April 1788, was among those who met at the 'Crown and Anchor' in the Strand in July 1791 to celebrate the anniversary of the French Revolution; Benjamin Meggot Forster, elected in March 1792, was involved in a number of other humanitarian causes, among them the prevention of cruelty to animals and the reform of legislation affecting child-theft.[10] Not all of these men took an active part in the running of the Committee's affairs, however. The day-to-day business seems to have remained in the hands of an inner circle that included James and Richard Phillips, George Harrison, William Dillwyn, John Lloyd, Joseph Woods, and Samuel Hoare. Many of the thirty-six members elected between August 1787 and December 1792 made only rare appearances at meetings—this was particularly true of those who were members of Parliament—while others, like Richard Sharp, quickly lost interest altogether. As a result, meetings of eight or nine members were not uncommon, while through the whole period the highest recorded attendance was just seventeen.[11]

In the words of the original minute, the London Committee was conceived as a vehicle 'for procuring such Information and Evidence, and for distributing Clarkson's Essay [on the Inhumanity of the Slave Trade] and such other Publications, as may tend to the Abolition of the Slave Trade'.[12] Accordingly, one of its first actions was to draw up a distribution list, a task which occupied the Committee through most of July. The result was a working list of 132 names, over half of which were provided by James Phillips, whose contacts in thirty-four English counties included Josiah Wedgwood and the Manchester radical, Thomas Walker.[13] Many of those subsequently approached by the Committee clearly felt either unable or unwilling to help. But others were quick to respond and by the end of the year the Committee had in place a network of correspondents in over thirty towns, including Manchester, Bristol, Sheffield, and Leeds, who were prepared to use their influence in circulating tracts and mobilising public opinion against the slave trade.[14]

Phillips's business interests helped to create a channel through which the Committee proceeded to distribute thousands of pamphlets, reports, and circular letters, most of them printed at Phillips's own works in George Yard.[15] The Committee effectively ran its own publishing house, buying up copyrights, as in the case of Carl Wadström's *Observations on the Slave Trade*, which cost the Committee £30 in July 1788, commissioning new titles or simply reprinting old ones. Some idea of the size and scale of this activity emerges from the Committee's accounts. In 1787–88 over fifty per cent of its total expenditure, £1,106, was expended on printing. The following year, 1788–89, this figure fell to thirty per cent (£618), but when Phillips brought in his stock list of the Committee's publications in November 1788 there were already fifteen different titles listed, among them John Newton's *Thoughts upon the African Slave Trade* (1788), Alexander Falconbridge's *Account of the Slave Trade on the Coast of Africa* (1788), and James Ramsay's *Objections to the Abolition of the Slave Trade, with Answers* (1788). Furthermore, new publications would continue to appear at regular intervals throughout 1790 and 1791.[16]

The publishing strategy of the London Committee warrants closer attention, since it reveals how effectively business and marketing skills were transferred to the reform sphere. Early efforts were concentrated on producing cheap promotional literature that could be distributed in large quantities through the Committee's country agents. Thomas Clarkson's *Summary View of the Slave Trade* (1788) and the Dean of Middleham's *Letter to the Treasurer of the Society instituted for the Purpose of effecting the Abolition of the Slave Trade* (1788) both fell into this category. Over 15,000 copies of each of these titles were printed for the Committee in the fifteen months up to August 1788 alone, and the final figure, particularly in the case of the *Letter*, was probably closer to 20,000.[17] Running to just sixteen pages and small enough at 110 mm × 150 mm to pass easily from hand to hand, these publications, really short pamphlets, were intended to introduce readers to the subject of the slave trade and arouse their sympathy and interest. More substantial books and pamphlets were available through the Committee or direct from James Phillips. But the hard work of opening up the market was done by Clarkson's *Summary* and the Dean of Middleham's *Letter*.

The Committee also expended a great deal of time and energy on its subscription lists. Between June 1787 and August 1788 no fewer than four different lists were distributed through the country agents, each one of them longer and more detailed than the last.[18] Subscription lists were important, not simply because of the sums of money involved, but because of the information they supplied about the subscribers themselves, their status, place of residence, and so on. In a bustling consumer society such details assumed particular significance. Subscribing to any type of project, cultural or otherwise, was a form of self-advertisement; it was helpful, therefore, to be able to recognise names one knew and respected, especially in one's own region or locality.[19] 'I have been solicited for Lists of later Date than those of Septr', wrote one of the Committee's correspondents from Suffolk at the end of 1787. 'When the Committee print any a few will be very acceptable in this Neighbourhood'.[20] That social emulation was a factor in the mobilisation of public opinion against the slave trade should not surprise us. Clarkson recognised its influence and so did Wedgwood. Numbers were important, too. The subscription list of August 1788 ran to nearly 2,000 names, a level of support that gave the early abolitionist movement credibility as well as respectability.

Cheap disposable literature, subscription lists: these were the tactics of men who understood about the market and about consumer choice. The Committee revealed a similarly enlightened attitude towards advertising and the press. Besides notices of its own activities, reports and subscriptions, the Committee also published information calculated to win over potential converts. Particular prominence was given to the progress of the abolitionist movement in what until recently had been the American colonies. In October 1787, for instance, the Committee arranged for the London papers to carry the memorial of the Pennsylvania Society for the Abolition of Slavery to the Convention of Delegates sitting in Philadelphia. This was followed in July 1788 by details of the Acts against the slave trade passed by Rhode Island and Massachusetts.[21] Undoubtedly, both of these items were chosen because they gave abolition an international dimension; they also threw down a challenge to Britons who cherished their freedom and liked to think of themselves as a free and enlightened people. Such methods were highly sophisticated, revealing a keen awareness of the influence of the press and how it could be used to mould public opinion.

By these various means the Committee hoped to create enough momentum to launch a petition campaign. The circular letter of June 1787 made this quite clear. 'We are not without hopes of this trade becoming a subject of Parliamentary Investigation early in the next session', it concluded,

> And if that should be the case, it is to be wished that the general sense of the nation (which we are persuaded is in favour of liberty, justice, and humanity) may be expressed by Petitions to Parliament, and by applications to their Representatives, in order to procure their assistance. In the distribution of the [enclosed] Tracts, we therefore recommend this purpose may be kept in view.[22]

There was never any doubt about the Committee's commitment to petitioning; what was less clear in the summer of 1787 was the mood of the country on the subject. By the autumn a picture of sorts was beginning to emerge. En route to Liverpool in September, Thomas Clarkson reported that there was reason to believe that *'when this Committee gives Information of the proper Time for such application'* Bridgwater, Monmouth, Bristol, Gloucester, Worcester, Shrewsbury, and Chester would all petition.[23] At Manchester he was surprised but reassured to learn that the 'spirit which was then beginning to show itself . . . on the subject of the Slave-trade . . . would unquestionably manifest itself further by breaking out into petitions to Parliament for its abolition'.[24] The Committee's growing list of correspondents told a similar story.

Encouraging as these signs were, however, the London Committee knew that it would have to wait on William Wilberforce before it could make any concerted move. At last, soon after Christmas, Wilberforce gave notice that early in the next session he would ask leave to bring in a Bill for the abolition of the slave trade.[25] Taking this as their cue, the members of the Committee moved quickly to rouse local correspondents into action. At the same time, they worked hard to ensure that the petition campaign was as broadly based as possible. On 1 January 1788 a delegation was appointed to wait on the City aldermen 'to confer with them on the proper measures to obtain a petition from the Corporation of London'. Three weeks later two new members, Robert Hunter and Joseph Smith, were delegated to do all they could to procure a petition from Glasgow, while Samuel Hoare was requested to write to 'the Rev. Mr Wyvill at Constable Barton Yorkshire to request his Exertions to obtain a Petition from that County'. The same meeting also directed a small sub-committee to send 'a circular letter with the Report to the Mayor of every Corporate Town that has not yet Petitioned'.[26]

It is important to be clear about the role that the London Committee played in orchestrating the petition campaign of 1788, not least because of the attention that in recent years has been paid to the industrial north, and Manchester in particular.[27] First to take the decision to petition, late in December 1787, Manchester deserves a special place in the history of the early abolitionist movement. Not only this, but in Thomas Walker and Thomas Cooper the town had enthusiasts whose enterprising use of the provincial press ensured that it was placed on the national map as a vital centre of popular abolitionism, a position seemingly confirmed by the 10,639 people who signed its petition.[28] Such fervour has prompted some historians to see Manchester and not London as the key to the petition campaign of 1788. 'It was the booming industrializing North and, above all, Manchester, which made mass-petitioning the principal political weapon of abolitionism', writes Seymour Drescher in *Capitalism and Antislavery.* 'Manchester converted a London committee which was little more than a low-key lobby, like the Protestant dissenters' delegates working against the Test Acts, or the Quakers' representatives handing out pamphlets to MPs at the doors of Parliament, into the prototype of the modern social reform movement'. Manchester, he suggests elsewhere, 'pushed Britain across the psychological threshold into the abolitionist era'.[29]

Central to this thesis is the contention that Manchester took the decision to petition without consulting the London Committee and seemingly against its express wishes.[30] Close examination of the few surviving records suggests otherwise. To judge from local newspapers, rumours that Manchester would petition Parliament were in the air from as early as October, and Walker and his colleagues certainly discussed the question with Clarkson when he visited the town later that same month, by which date Manchester abolitionists were already in contact with the London Committee.[31] In his *History* Clarkson hints that he counselled caution for the moment and Manchester abolitionists evidently took heed. When rumours persisted that a petition was in prospect, Thomas Cooper intervened to assure readers of the *Manchester Mercury* that 'it will certainly be more prudent to confine the Applications for the present, under general Expressions, and to notorious Facts, than to adopt any Specific Plan in a Case, where every separate Person may possibly have his own'. A petition, he was at pains to point out,

> is in itself imprudent under all the Circumstances, and Foreign to the Intention of those who have principally interested themselves in the Business here . . . Subscriptions then have been solicited to procure relief in general, and not any specific Mode of Relief, and the Friends to the Cause will be glad to see Relief afforded to the utmost extent that the present Circumstances will admit.[32]

This was early in December. That same month Walker and Cooper corresponded with the London Committee on no fewer than three occasions, the immediate cause being a proposed meeting of Manchester abolitionists that was scheduled for 20 December and later postponed to 27 December.[33] Sadly, no record of this correspondence survives, but the speed with which Hoare replied to Cooper's letter of 11 December suggests that he tried to persuade Walker and his colleagues—successfully, as it turned out—to postpone their meeting until Wilberforce had made his intentions clear.[34] Certainly, there is nothing to suggest that the London Committee was caught unawares by the proceedings of the meeting held on 27 December, at which a Manchester committee was organised, or by the decision taken at a second meeting on 29 December to petition Parliament. On the contrary, the Committee seems to have welcomed the Manchester initiative. John Barton, for one, noted 'the good effects which are likely to arise from the exertions of the Manchester committee', adding that its 'public advertisements' were sure to be 'of great use'. 'To see so many respectable people so much in earnest', he went on, 'serves to excite the public attention; and the more generally their example is followed by other large towns, the more probable it is that our efforts will be successful'.[35]

None of this is to deny the importance of Manchester in the petition campaign of 1788. But it seems abundantly clear that from the outset the London Committee was in control of the campaign and able to dictate its timing and pace. This much is evident from the fact that most localities sent copies of their petitions to London and at their public meetings proposed votes of thanks to the efforts of the metropolitan group.[36] Important as Manchester was, it could never compete with London in terms of resources, access to Parliament or regional contacts. The London Committee, moreover, was never merely content to lobby MPs at the doors of Parliament. Initially, at least, its efforts were directed towards the country, and petitions, as we have seen, were always central to its political thinking. What compromised the Committee somewhat was its relationship with Wilberforce. Mindful of the niceties that such a relationship involved, the Committee eschewed anything that might be considered 'forced' or 'unnecessary', preferring to co-ordinate a seemingly spontaneous outburst of public feeling by means of personal appeals to magistrates and corporations and the mobilisation of a large network of local correspondents.[37] Such tactics, however, should not be confused with inaction or lack of initiative.

In the same context, it is instructive to compare Manchester with the experience of Maidstone in Kent, a thriving market town that also had strong links with the papermaking industry.[38] Writing to Samuel Hoare on 29 December 1787, James Ramsay explained that Will Bishop, the Mayor of Maidstone, was 'desirous of giving the assistance of his Office for procuring a petition for the abolition of the Slave Trade from the Corporation to Parliament. He only wishes to have a form, that it may meet your wishes, and know when you would that they should come forward'. By way of reply, the Committee sent Bishop 'a rough draft of a Petition' to be used as he saw fit; Clarkson, meanwhile, forwarded to Ramsay a copy of the Manchester resolutions, adding, 'they are very sensible and well drawn up'.[39] Here, in other words, the Committee took a hand in the petitioning process itself, a level of involvement which, if anything, would become more pronounced during the campaign of 1792.

The petition campaign of 1788 fully rewarded the efforts of the London Committee. Between 1 February and 9 May over 100 petitions dealing with the slave trade were presented to the House of Commons, more than half the total number of petitions received in the session.[40] The response surprised even the Committee, but at the same time it revealed the limits as well as the strengths of popular feeling on abolition. While a significant number of petitioners insisted on broadening their appeal to include the abolition of slavery itself, a confusion of aims that the Committee worked hard to stamp out, others called merely for regulation of the slave trade, or an immediate Parliamentary inquiry.[41] Just as telling was the geographical distribution of the petitions. Significantly, almost a third of them came from the industrial area north of the river Severn.[42] East Anglia and the south-west of England petitioned strongly, but Cornwall, which rose up in 1792, was relatively quiet, as indeed was Scotland. More worrying still was the lack of response from the Home Counties. With the exception of Maidstone there were no petitions from the densely populated counties of Kent, Sussex or Surrey and there was only token support from Essex and Hertfordshire.[43]

It was against the background of the petition campaign that on 11 February a committee of the Privy Council was appointed to consider the state of the slave trade.[44] Five days later, following a communication from Wilberforce, Clarkson, Hoare, James and Richard Phillips, Joseph Smith, and William Dillwyn were appointed to collect and arrange suitable evidence.[45] Encouraged by the Privy Council's interest, the Committee looked forward with confidence to Wilberforce's motion in the House of Commons. But as the weeks passed by, and Wilberforce's health finally broke down, the Committee began to grow more anxious. Then, in May, William Pitt announced his intention to bring forward a resolution relative to the slave trade. Accordingly, on 6 May Clarkson and Granville Sharp, among others, were deputed to wait on leading MPs 'to request their support of Mr Pitt's Motion'.[46] Over the years, this would become a familiar pattern. Important as lobbying was, however, it was the gathering of evidence that henceforth would take up an increasing amount of the Committee's time and resources. As first the House of Commons and then the Lords opened their own independent inquiries into the slave trade, the burden on Clarkson, in particular, grew almost insupportable.

The success of Pitt's motion, resulting as it did in a decision to take up the question of the slave trade in the next Parliament, gave fresh impetus to the abolitionist movement. Eager to capitalise on the turn of events at Westminster, the Committee arranged for the immediate distribution of 10,000 copies of the debate on Pitt's motion. Then in June it set about printing the key speeches in the debate on Sir William Dolben's Slave Limitation (or Middle

Passage) Bill, which had passed both Houses late in the same session.[47] In the meantime, the Committee was exploring other ways of pressing home its advantage. One of these, brought to its attention by abolitionists in Plymouth, was the plan and sections of a slave ship, in this case the *Brooks* of Liverpool. First published in the spring of 1789, copies were sent 'to the Members of both Houses of Parliament & to such other persons as may be thought expedient by the Committee of Distribution', the intention being to lobby MPs before Wilberforce's motion came on in the House of Commons on 11 May.[48] But so far from being willing to act on the report of the Privy Council, or even to discuss Wilberforce's proposals for an early abolition of the trade, the Commons resolved to hear evidence at its own bar, a compromise measure which left abolitionists playing a dangerous waiting game.

Another aspect of the opinion-building activities of the London Committee that deserves closer attention is its attempts to create an international movement or coalition against the slave trade. One of the charges most commonly levelled against supporters of abolition was that it was impolitic; put simply, abolition of the slave trade would allow Britain's competitors to seize her share of the trade and profit accordingly.[49] Foreign support and intervention were therefore considered vital to the success of the movement at home. This was why American co-operation was so important. The progress made by many of the states in abolishing the trade, certainly up to 1788, helped to create a special bond that gave added impetus to the British movement. The real challenge for abolitionists, however, was how to influence the course of events in Europe. France, Britain's greatest commercial rival, figured largely in these calculations—many would-be supporters of abolition thought it impossible to proceed without French co-operation—but so, too, did Spain and Portugal.[50]

Personal links between British and American abolitionists had been established during the colonial period. Granville Sharp, for instance, had been introduced to Benjamin Franklin through Anthony Benezet and corresponded with Benjamin Rush of Philadelphia, while for years Quakers on both sides of the Atlantic had been united in their efforts to alleviate the sufferings of blacks.[51] If anything, the revolution strengthened these ties, at the same time setting them on a more formal basis. One of the first acts of the Pennsylvania Abolition Society, for instance, following its reorganisation in 1787, was to open a correspondence with Thomas Clarkson. Eager to repay the compliment, in July 1787 the London Committee instructed four of its members, Dillwyn, Woods, Harrison, and Sansom, to prepare a letter to the societies at Philadelphia and New York 'to inform them of the measures this committee are taking for the abolition of the Slave Trade'.[52]

These overtures opened a new chapter in Anglo-American co-operation. The Pennsylvania Society, in particular, replied enthusiastically to the Committee's letter. 'We had a meeting of the Committee yesterday evening', John Barton wrote excitedly to William Roscoe on 12 December 1787,

> From a similar Society established at Philadelphia (Dr B. Franklin pres.) we rec'd a large pacqt containing numerous testimonials of the good conduct of several negroes set free and the advantages experienced by their masters in employing them as hired servts instead of slaves. It also contained specimens of the writing (& two of drawing) of several young negroes, the name & age of the writers annexed to each specimen & severally attested to be genuine. The writing in many was excellent.[53]

More communications were to follow throughout 1788, bringing with them details of the action taken against the slave trade by Pennsylvania, Rhode Island, Massachusetts, Maryland, and Connecticut. Then early in 1789 another large packet arrived from Philadelphia, this time containing 'a certificate of a wonderful talent for arithmetic calculation, in an African slave at Virginia & also a certificate of the great medical abilities of a black man in the Spanish settlement of New Orleans'.[54]

As we have seen, the Committee took great pains to publicise some of the information supplied by its American correspondents, judging that the progress of the movement in the United States would set an example for Britons to follow. By 1788 no fewer than six states had legislated for the immediate abolition of the slave trade and two more, South Carolina and Delaware, had suspended it temporarily. Other states, like Massachusetts and Pennsylvania, had also gone further and made some provision for the gradual or immediate abolition of slavery itself. This was state action, however. At the federal level there was no getting away from the fact that the Philadelphia Convention of 1787 had agreed to leave the slave trade intact until 1808. How this proposal had come to be adopted, first at Philadelphia and later by the ratifying conventions, bewildered many British abolitionists, but nevertheless it was a part of the constitution, as was the clause recognising slaves as three-fifths of a person for the purposes of representation.[55]

Abolitionists sought to circumvent the constitution by appealing direct to Congress. On 10 February 1790 the Pennsylvania Society presented a memorial against slavery to both Houses, which was followed the next day by a petition from the Friends' yearly meetings of Pennsylvania, New York, Maryland, and Virginia, this time against the slave trade. The ensuing debate determined the broad lines of congressional action for the next eighteen years. On 23 March the House of Representatives affirmed that it could neither interfere with the slave trade, at least not before 1808, nor take any action affecting the emancipation of slaves. The constitution, in other words, meant what it said. Nevertheless, the House did go on to reserve the right to regulate the trade. In 1794, for instance, following intense pressure from abolitionists, Congress passed legislation prohibiting United States citizens from supplying slaves to foreigners. Similar commitments were also made regarding the humane treatment of slaves during the Middle Passage.[56]

Thanks largely to the efforts of the Pennsylvania Society, the London Committee was kept closely informed of the events unfolding in New York. The result, when it came, was responsible for a subtle shift in the relationship between British and American abolitionists. At a personal level, Sharp and Hoare would continue to support attempts to test the regulatory powers invested in Congress, but increasingly after 1790 the societies in the United States began to look to Britain for inspiration and not vice versa.[57] Moses Brown of Providence made this very point, writing to James Phillips in 1791. With regard to the slave trade, he explained,

the Society for Abolishing Slavery in Phila, New York, this place, Connecticut and several other places, have prepared addresses to revive before Congress their Interposition in stopping the Slave Trade as far as in their power & we have reason to hope they will do it, but their next meeting is not till the 11th*mo* next, before when we hope to hear the British Parliament has set the example.[58]

Brown perhaps meant this as a rhetorical device, but there was no denying the growing importance attached to the British movement in the United States.

The Committee first turned its attention to European involvement in the slave trade early in 1788, within weeks of the organisation of the Société des Amis des Noirs. Mindful that the 'arguments in its favour founded on a competition of supposed National Interest, will be removed by the reformation becoming general', on 5 March the Committee called upon Clarkson and Dillwyn to prepare 'a selection of such arguments & Tracts as being translated into the French, Spanish, Portuguese, Dutch & Danish Languages as may appear most likely to answer the purpose'.[59] There the matter rested until June 1789, when an offer to undertake the translation work came from Benjamin Frossard at Lyon. Frossard was a man of large reputation, a philosopher and cleric who held an honorary degree from Oxford University and was also a member of the Manchester Literary and Philosophical Society. (Significantly, it was another member of this society, Thomas Walker, who first brought Frossard to the Committee's notice in April 1788.) Frossard set to work almost at once and by the end of the year had a manuscript ready for the Committee, which finally went to press early in 1790, but the long delay undoubtedly hampered efforts to create a following among Britain's maritime partners.[60]

In the meantime, the Committee fell back on some more orthodox methods. Early in 1789, for instance, a box containing bound copies of Clarkson's *Essay on the Inhumanity of the Slave Trade* was sent through William Eden, British ambassador extraordinary at Madrid, to the King of Spain, the Comte D'Aranda, and the Marquis del Companes. A similar box was also sent to the Chevalier de Pinto in Portugal.[61] But without grass-roots support and organised societies to provide a basis for mutual co-operation the Committee was unable to build on these initiatives. The situation in France offered reason for greater encouragement. Earlier attempts by Wilberforce to reach some sort of agreement with the French, in 1787, had admittedly met with little success.[62] The organisation of the Amis des Noirs, however, followed by the

storming of the Bastille on 14 July 1789, provided British abolitionists with fresh grounds for optimism. The London Committee
almost immediately opened a correspondence with the new
society, welcoming the appearance of an organisation that sought
to put French abolitionists on an equal footing with their colleagues in Britain and the United States.[63] For the moment at least,
the proceedings of the Amis des Noirs could be looked upon as yet
another sign of progress and, as such, worthy of notice in the
British press. The society also provided abolitionists with a vital
channel of communication, first with Louis XVI's ministers and
then with figures like Lafayette and Brissot de Warville, principal
actors in the events that threatened to engulf France after 1789.

Despite appearances, however, the Amis des Noirs bore very
little resemblance to its English cousin, either in terms of personnel or public support. For one thing, too many of its members,
including Condorcet and Mirabeau, were caught up in the French
Revolution and preoccupied with things other than the slave trade.
As a consequence, the society had a weak organisational structure,
relying on the radical press, notably *Le Patriote Français*, to put its
message across. Finally, the impetuosity of many French abolitionists, notably their apparent readiness to do away with slavery
itself, provoked a violent response from pro-slavery interests,
alienating many would-be supporters of abolition. When in the
spring of 1789 the Amis des Noirs lobbied *bailliages*, urging them
to instruct their deputies in the Estates General to support
measures for the abolition of slavery and the slave trade, only a
small minority, about eight per cent, rallied to the cause, a
disappointing result which fell some way short of the upsurge in
public support that many on both sides of the Channel had hoped
for.[64]

Clarkson was to be made painfully aware of the shortcomings of
the Amis des Noirs when he visited Paris in July 1789 with the
intention of trying to induce the French Constituent Assembly to
take up the question of the slave trade. Clarkson grew so disillusioned with the society, its inactivity and lack of effectiveness,
that, armed with a French translation of his *Impolicy* and thousands of copies of the plan and sections of a slave ship, he at last
decided to lobby members of the Assembly himself.[65] But interests
in favour of the trade mobilised quickly and even friends to the
cause were forced to admit that the Assembly was unlikely to act

'unless England would concur in the measure'. Clarkson left Paris at the end of the year a bitterly disappointed man, frustrated that he should have had no better success and conscious that only a 'promise of speedy abolition' from Pitt's ministry would possibly induce the French to join the movement.[66] Further disappointment was to follow when on 8 March 1790 the French government announced that it had no intention of interfering with the slave trade and, further, would prohibit all agitation that in any way threatened French interests in the Caribbean.[67]

This setback, followed within a matter of weeks by the decision of the United States Congress to uphold the trade, rocked the movement back on its heels. The message was clear. If international action against the slave trade was to be forthcoming, then the British would have to set the example.

Understandably, the London Committee would now become increasingly preoccupied with events at Westminster. Evidence on behalf of the trade finished about the middle of April 1790. Two months later, in June, Pitt decided to go to the country, a move that caused fresh doubts in abolitionist circles. The election, however, proved a resounding success for Pitt and for his supporters.[68] Quick to seize the initiative, in September the Committee arranged for one copy of Clarkson's *Impolicy* and one copy of his *Efficiency* to be sent to every new member of Parliament. These were followed in February 1791 by more copies of the plan and sections of a slave ship.[69] Not long afterwards the Commons' hearings drew to a close. In March Wilberforce and others set about preparing a digest or abridgement of the evidence presented against the trade, which reached members of the House just in time for the debate on 18 April. Here again, it was the Committee that took responsibility for seeing the abridgement through the press; in all, 1,500 copies were printed and distributed in less than two weeks, a monumental effort that tested even the ingenuity of James Phillips.[70] But despite all of these efforts, and another bravura performance from Wilberforce, the motion was defeated, this time by 163 votes to 88.[71]

The size of this defeat prompted Wilberforce, who by this time was himself a member of the Committee, to propose launching another petition campaign, but this time on a much larger scale.[72] Everything indicated that public support for abolition was still strong. In July 1790 the Committee had launched a new fund-raising drive which brought in over £2,000.[73] Help also came from an unexpected quarter in the shape of William Fox's *Address to the People of Great Britain, on the Propriety of Abstaining from West India Sugar and Rum* (1791). This short address, published at a time of soaring sugar prices, proved an immediate and startling success. Estimates vary but 70,000 copies were said to have been printed in only four months, running through some fourteen or fifteen impressions.[74] Fox's pamphlet, and a host of pirated versions, inspired a nationwide boycott of West Indian sugar which at its peak involved some 300,000 families. The *Leeds Intelligencer* reported on 13 January 1792 that in Birmingham 'upwards of a thousand families have left off the use of sugar'. Even the King and Queen Charlotte were said to have joined the boycott, a scene visualised by James Gillray in his political satire, *Anti-Saccharrites,—Or—John Bull and his Family leaving off the Use of Sugar.*[75]

Many people, particularly those in fashionable circles, found an acceptable substitute in the shape of East Indian sugar. When Katherine Plymley visited Josiah Wedgwood and his family at Etruria in May 1791 she found that 'none of them eat sugar as the quantity they have sent for from the East Indies was not then arrived'.[76] By the end of the year so-called 'free sugar' was being imported into Britain in increasing quantities, leading to calls in some quarters for the East India Company to be put on the same footing, as regards duties and drawbacks, with its West Indian competitors. The directors of the company made their own representations to the Treasury in March 1792, arguing that the importation of East Indian sugar upon equal terms with other colonial producers was not only essential to the relief of the British consumer, who was being made to pay for a sudden and unexpected shortage of West Indian sugar, but 'the prosperity of the public revenue, and the preservation of the sugar trade'. The threat to West Indian planters and merchants was obvious. Eager to hold on to their privileges, they offered little resistance when at last, in May 1792, the House of Commons intervened to peg the price of West Indian sugar, precipitating an immediate slump in the market.[77]

In this roundabout way non-consumption did have an impact, but as a form of economic sanction designed to strangle West

Indian trade and force planters to put an end to the slave trade it proved singularly ineffective. Nevertheless, the boycott hinted at a depth of popular feeling that, once harnessed, might yet prove decisive. Clarkson, a firm advocate of non-consumption, wrote (and privately distributed) a short letter on the subject in January 1792, drawing attention to Fox's *Address* and pointing out the merits of abstinence as a stimulus to petitioning. 'There can be no doubt', Clarkson told local correspondents,

> but that every one in your part of the world, who refuses West India produce after the perusal of this little tract, will be forward to support the petitions which you and your friends are endeavouring to obtain. In fact, when I have reflected upon the extraordinary effects produced by the Address, I have considered that those, who were distributing it, were in reality (though perhaps very undesignedly) paving the way for signatures to the different petitions which we have all of us at heart.[78]

Some of Clarkson's colleagues were more cautious, fearing that the boycott might harm the cause by linking abolition with popular agitation and the spectre of the mob. But the excitement and interest aroused by non-consumption was impossible to ignore and, as Clarkson predicted, throughout 1791–92 it played a vital role in generating support for petitions against the slave trade.

At every level the campaign of 1792 was a particular triumph for the Committee's organisational skill. Work began in earnest within days of the Commons defeat of 1791. On 26 April the Committee asked Clarkson to prepare an abstract of Wilberforce's abridgement of the evidence against the trade, which went to press the following July. Over 5,000 copies were printed at this stage and a cheap edition followed in November.[79] These abstracts were intended for general distribution; the Committee's minutes are quite clear on this point. Clarkson himself distributed large quantities on his tour of the north of England in October, November, and December 1791. Arrangements were also made for extracts to appear in the London and provincial press. Katherine Plymley noted in her diary on 21–2 October that Clarkson and her brother, Joseph, 'talk'd of putting extracts from the abstract of the evidence in the Shrewsbury Paper', adding that 'extracts were to be put in as many county Papers as cou'd be'.[80] Often these advertisements were supported by local subscribers, but the London Committee also played its part, taking a column in Woodfall's *Diary*, for instance, at half a guinea a week.[81]

The abstracts, together with copies of the recent Commons debate, were intended to prepare the way for the petition campaign that was to follow. The Committee's strategy was set out in the detailed instructions given to William Dickson prior to his tour of Scotland in January 1792. Timing was evidently considered critical. No one was to organise a petition until told to do so by the Committee in London. In the meantime, local agents and correspondents were to go on circulating pamphlets as before. 'They themselves know what is the object of their own labours', Dickson was advised,

> but it is *not necessary to state it to the public* who, if they know that the reason of their being desired to read was to obtain signatures to petitions would not read at all. Let them be content to go on informing the minds of the people, till the day arrives when it will be proper to *disclose* the *design*. By this time, their minds having been prepared, it will be no difficult thing to prevail on them to petition.

This course of action also recommended itself because 'if petitions were *professed* to be the object, the news wd soon transpire, & if it were to get to the ears of the planters, Slave merchts & West India merchts they wd endeavour to counteract the object, by getting counter-petitions from the same places'.[82]

For the moment the Committee was happy to bide its time. Local agents were first alerted in December 1791. Precise details followed in January 1792 when the Committee informed correspondents that Wilberforce was likely to give notice of his intention to bring in a Bill for the abolition of the trade on or about 6 February, which was to be their signal to prepare petitions. At the last minute, however, Wilberforce decided that his notice should follow rather than precede the petitions, leaving the initiative firmly with the Committee.[83] The campaign finally got under way in February 1792. Part of the intention was clearly to embarrass the House of Commons with the level of public support for abolition. Clarkson, for one, was confident that over 200 petitions would be forthcoming from England alone. 'By no means let the People of Brough add their Names to those of Appleby', he warned Thomas Wilkinson at Penrith on 1 March 1792. 'The two Petitions must be perfectly distinct. It is on the number of Petitions that the H. of Commons will count'.[84] The Committee also tried to exercise as much control as possible over the shape and content of the campaign. Petitions were to be confined exclusively to the abolition of the slave trade and 'all appearance of unnecessary petitions from the same place [was] to be avoided'. 'The more spirited the Pets. are the better', Dickson was told, 'but in *general* terms'. Above all, it was considered 'impossible to be too earnest in pressing the distinction between emancipation and abolition'.[85]

Some petitioners clearly chose to ignore these instructions. The presbytery at Aberdeen was reported to have signed and sent off a petition that was '*verbatim* the same with their pet. in 1788, & contained a prayer that Parlt wd relieve the slaves in W.I.'.[86] The real threat to abolition, however, came from events over which the Committee had no control, namely, the French Revolution and the slave rebellion in Santo Domingo. The rising tide of revolutionary violence caused widespread panic among the propertied classes during 1791–92, so much so that the London Committee had to proceed with great caution; Dickson advised a group of abolitionists in Portsoy 'to [be] beware of any allusion to the French Revolution, or even to liberty'.[87] Wilberforce, for his part, found it 'absolutely necessary' to keep clear of the subject.[88] But still the rumours persisted. In some quarters the petition campaign itself was looked upon as nothing more than a calculated ploy, a 'pretence' to disguise the 'deep designs' of men dismissively referred to as 'the JACOBINS of ENGLAND'.[89]

The slave rebellion in Santo Domingo of 1791 gave resonance and meaning to the association between abolition and revolution. In Perth Dickson found that one local resident, while sympathetic to abolition, was 'terrified for insurrections'.[90] Understandably, the Committee was eager to refute the charge that abolition of the trade, or even abolitionist activity, might in any way lead to the destruction of West Indian property. Santo Domingo, abolitionists countered, had not been caused by 'the friends of the blacks in France', but by 'the pride and obstinacy of the whites who drove them to their fate, by an impolitic and foolish dissention with the mulattoes, and with each other'.[91] Determined to give such views as wide a hearing as possible, in February 1792 the Committee printed and distributed 1,000 copies of Clarkson's essay on the causes of the insurrection, and that same month published an advertisement in the London and provincial papers restating its original aim and purpose, namely, the 'Abolition of the Trade to the Coast of Africa for Slaves'.[92] But for many Santo Domingo would remain synonymous with abolition, a potent symbol of violence, instability, and unrest.

It is a measure of the strength of abolitionist support that the London Committee and its agents were able to overcome these obstacles. In all, 519 petitions were presented to the Commons, 'the largest number ever submitted to the House on a single subject or in a single session'.[93] While the industrial north continued to provide the most vocal support for abolition, every English county was represented in 1792, in addition to which Scotland made a massive contribution, thanks largely to the efforts of William Dickson. By contrast with 1788 this was truly a nationwide campaign, an extraordinary achievement that spoke volumes for the Committee's energy and perseverance. Successful as the campaign was, however, its sheer size invited comment and scrutiny. In Parliament Liverpool's Colonel Tarleton argued that many of the petitions were fraudulent, or, worse still, the work of deluded fanatics ('the Sectaries of the Old Jewry'). In some villages and towns, Tarleton claimed,

> mendicant physicians and itinerant clergymen, have exercised almost unexampled zeal and industry ... to extort names from the sick, the indigent, and the traveller: in others, the grammar-schools have received ceremonial visits, from the indefatigable emissaries of the Abolitionists; and the boys have been indulged with the gladsome tidings of a holiday, provided they would sign their own, and the names in the neighbourhood.[94]

Possibly, the Committee misjudged the mood of the Commons; after all, petitioning on this scale was always likely to cause alarm in the minds of men with one eye on events in France. But the campaign could not be ignored and it undoubtedly exerted considerable leverage in the ensuing debate, which saw the House resolve by 230 votes to 85 that the trade ought to be *gradually* abolished.[95] Nevertheless, even this concession fell some way short of the 'immediate and utter abolition' that Wilberforce and the Committee had hoped for. Once again, the Committee's annual report lamented, 'the opposition of Interest and the plans of Policy, have prevented our Success'.[96] Despite these misgivings, however, the Committee moved quickly to capitalise on the Commons vote. On 8 May 1792, after a long silence, contact was re-established with the Amis des Noirs in Paris. Three weeks later it was agreed to go further and prepare a French translation of the 1791 debate on Wilberforce's motion, with a view to giving it as wide a circulation as possible.[97]

After lengthy discussion 1 January 1796 was fixed as the date for the abolition of the slave trade. The Lords, however, rejected the Commons' resolution and on 5 June 1792 voted to postpone the business until the following session, when they would proceed by calling evidence to their own bar. Abolitionists suffered further humiliation in 1793 when the Commons refused to revive the subject of the slave trade, thus effectively reversing the resolutions of the previous year.[98] By this stage the members of the Committee were clearly exasperated. On 20 June an emergency meeting was held to take into consideration the state of the proceedings in Parliament. The outcome was a decision to 'recommend to the Friends of the Abolition of the Slave Trade to abstain from the use of West Indian sugar and rum'. Subsequently a draft circular letter was prepared giving details of how the boycott might be best pursued; on 13 August, however, the Committee suddenly drew back from going ahead with the project.[99] Once again, the precise details are unclear, but the likeliest explanation is that Wilberforce, who was present on 20 June and again on 4 July, interceded. The Committee's annual report referred only obliquely to the proposed boycott, confessing that 'so difficult is the situation in which we now find ourselves, that we must (for the present at least) content ourselves with informing you of the present state of the business'.[100]

The readiness of the Committee to embrace the idea of a boycott was the surest indication of just how desperate the struggle had become by 1793. At the same time, however, by failing to seize the initiative the Committee lost momentum and, ultimately, purpose. As the hearings in the Lords spluttered to a halt even the gathering of fresh evidence lost its significance.[101] The result was disintegration and decay. In 1793 the Committee met on no fewer than thirty-three occasions; in 1794 the figure fell to nine. That same year Clarkson withdrew from the fight, his health broken by a punishing round of tours and meetings. Thereafter, the Committee went into steep decline, finally ceasing operations in 1797.[102] In 1804, however, it suddenly sprang back to life, presumably at the instigation of Wilberforce, who was about to revive the question of the slave trade in the House of Commons. By this date twenty-eight of the original Committee were still alive, but only a handful, including Clarkson, Sharp, Harrison, and Richard Phillips, seem to have been ready to resume their labours. These veterans of the cause were now joined by twelve new members, among them James Stephen and Zachary Macaulay.[103]

On the face of it, the revived Committee seemed not dissimilar to its predecessor, but in reality there were some significant differences. Whereas the original Committee had been conceived as a vehicle for opinion building and had directed its attention very largely to the country, the new Committee was primarily a Parliamentary lobby. The obvious intention was to bring as much pressure as possible to bear on members of both Houses, directly or indirectly, and to ensure that the Parliamentary supporters of abolition were always present in strength. So on 23 April 1805 we find the Committee assuring Lord Henry Petty, who had been deputed to challenge Pitt on the subject in the Commons, that at the first sign of opposition it would endeavour 'to procure a full attendance of Members friendly to the principles of this Society'.[104] Petitioning or anything that hinted at popular agitation was clearly dismissed as being too dangerous, and for this reason the Committee seems to have taken less interest than its predecessor had done in maintaining a correspondence with local abolitionists. If the minutes are to be believed, the revived Committee was a more low-key affair; even at a peak in 1805 it met only ten times, a level of activity which surely reflected its narrower focus of attention.

It is almost impossible to judge how successful these tactics were. Undoubtedly, the Committee's activities kept up the pressure on Parliament to abolish the trade, but at the same time the political climate had changed dramatically since 1797. Not only was the Cabinet in favour of the measure but so too were a whole batch of new Irish MPs. Moreover, for the first time there were signs that 'the old Landed Interest in the West Indies', increasingly fearful of the likely effects of Caribbean over-production, was deserting the anti-abolitionist ranks.[105] Nevertheless, the situation was still a volatile one and, as the Committee clearly appreciated, a favourable result was only likely to come about as a result of careful management. As it was, the Committee was forced to wait a year while the Attorney General steered through Parliament his Foreign Slave Trade Bill, and right to the last there was every prospect that the Lords would vote against abolition, or, just as damaging, resort to delaying tactics.[106] Even when victory finally came in 1807 the outcome was far from certain.

The evolution of the London Committee from a sophisticated reform organisation into a low-level lobby should not blind us to its central importance in any history of the mobilisation of public opinion against the slave trade. The Committee's relationship with Wilberforce and the other Parliamentary supporters of abolition is well documented, even if it is not always fully understood. Less widely recognised is its role as a shaper of public opinion, both at home and abroad. In its original guise the Committee was instrumental in creating a constituency for abolition. It did this by swamping the country with books and pamphlets and, in the case of advertising and subscription lists, adjusting to the demands of a rapidly expanding consumer society. In the process, the Committee established an organisational structure which, in turn, made mass petitioning possible on an unprecedented scale. This structure did not suddenly emerge in 1792, however; it was the result of years of painstaking effort. The Committee, in other words, provided a rallying point for opponents of the slave trade, its activities giving the extra-Parliamentary movement coherence, impetus, and, above all, political direction.

Notes

1. Thomas Clarkson, *The History of the Rise, Progress and Accomplishment of the Abolition of the Slave Trade by the British Parliament*, 2 vols., London, 1808, I, pp. 105–7, 116–30; Davis, *The Problem of Slavery in the Age of Revolution*, pp. 218–21.

2. For Wilberforce and the controversy surrounding the publication of *The Life of William Wilberforce* (1838) see Chapter Three.
3. This tendency is particularly evident in the work of Seymour Drescher. See his *Capitalism and Antislavery: British Mobilization in Comparative Perspective*, New York, 1987, esp. pp. 2, 67–88.
4. See Chapter Three.
5. Clarkson, *History*, I, pp. 122–30.
6. Hugh Honour, *The Image of the Black in Western Art*, Cambridge, Massachusetts, 1989, IV, i, p. 314 (n. 121).
7. Biographical files, Friends House Library, London; 'Memoirs of Samuel Hoare', Friends House Library, Box 376/6; Humphrey Lloyd, *The Quaker Lloyds in the Industrial Revolution*, London, 1975, pp. 145–202; *Memoirs of the Life of Richard Phillips*, London, 1841; Matthews MSS, A1/5, Friends House Library.
8. For Clarkson's radicalism and his sympathy and support for the French Revolution see Chapter Three.
9. John Barton to William Roscoe, 6 March 1788, Roscoe Papers, 920 ROS/243, Liverpool Record Office, Liverpool.
10. For Wedgwood see J. Money, 'Birmingham and the West Midlands, 1760–1793', esp. pp. 300–2; Anthony Burton, *Wedgwood: A Biography*, London, 1976, pp. 99–100, 140–3, 194–7, 203, 211–14. For Kippis see *Dictionary of National Biography*, XI, pp. 195–7; Albert Goodwin, *The Friends of Liberty: The English Democratic Movement in the Age of the French Revolution*, Cambridge, Massachusetts, 1979, p. 86. For Forster see *Dictionary of National Biography*, VII, p. 452.
11. Membership of the Committee was initially fixed at a maximum of thirty, but this rule was rescinded in May 1791 to accommodate William Wilberforce, Charles James Fox, William Burgh, Lord Muncaster, and William Smith, the chief parliamentary supporters of abolition. By 1792 the number of members had risen to forty-three.
12. Abolition Committee Minutes, 22 May 1787, Add. MSS 21254, British Library, London. These minutes are arranged in three volumes as follows: Add. MSS 21254 (22 May 1787–26 February 1788); Add. MSS 21255 (5 March 1788–7 July 1791); Add. MSS 21256 (20 July 1790–1819).
13. Phillips had been trading with Wedgwood since at least 1785. See Wedgwood Papers, 24260–66.124, Keele University. Phillips's relationship with Walker is not clear, but it is interesting to note that his (Walker's) name appears on the Committee's original list of subscribers. Wedgwood Papers, 21074.111.
14. See Abolition Committee Minutes, 26 August 1788.
15. In a little over fifteen months the Committee printed and distributed nearly 85,000 pamphlets, reports, circular letters, and subscription lists. Abolition Committee Minutes, 29 July 1788.
16. Abolition Committee Minutes, 24 June, 1, 28 July, 12 August, 4, 18 November 1788, 28 July, 22 September 1789, 16 February 1790, 22 March, 5, 12, 19 April, 17 May, 29 November, 28 December 1791.
17. Ibid., 12 August, 18 November 1788.

18. Ibid., 7, 22 June, 4 September, 27 November, 11 December 1787, 15 January, 12 August, 11 November 1788. Nearly 5,000 subscription lists were distributed up to August 1788 alone.

19. For subscription lists and subscriptions in general see Borsay, *The English Urban Renaissance*, pp. 251–2.

20. Capel Lofft to Samuel Hoare, 23 December 1787, Clarkson Papers, CN 123, Huntington Library, San Marino, California.

21. Abolition Committee Minutes, 2 October 1787 and 1 July 1788.

22. Wedgwood Papers, 21073.111. I am greatly indebted to the Trustees of the Wedgwood Museum, Stoke-on-Trent, Staffordshire, for permission to quote from these papers.

23. Abolition Committee Minutes, 16 October 1787. My italics.

24. Clarkson, *History*, I, pp. 415–16. Clarkson's sermon on the abolition of the slave trade, delivered on 30 October, was the first of its kind in Manchester. Thomas Seddon was scheduled to speak on the same subject on 21 October, but his sermon was later postponed until 30 December. See *Manchester Mercury*, 9 October, 25 December 1787; Drescher, *Capitalism and Antislavery*, p. 213 (n. 26).

25. John Pollock, *Wilberforce*, London, 1977, p. 74.

26. Abolition Committee Minutes, 1, 8, 22 January 1788.

27. See, for example, Drescher, *Capitalism and Antislavery*, pp. 67–88.

28. E. M. Hunt, 'The North of England Agitation for the Abolition of the Slave Trade, 1780–1800', M.A. thesis, University of Manchester, 1959; Lillie Robinson, 'Thomas Walker and Manchester Politics', B.A. thesis, University of Manchester, 1931. While the decision to petition was made late in December 1787 the actual form of a petition was not adopted until 7 January 1788. The Manchester petition finally reached the House of Commons on 11 February, by which date York, Bedford, Hull, Norfolk, the City of London, Ripon, Maidstone, Southampton, Huntingdon, and Birmingham in one form or another had all petitioned Parliament. See *Manchester Mercury*, 1, 8 January, 5, 12, 19 February 1788; *Commons Journal*, XLIII, 1788, pp. 159, 166, 187, 198–9, 200.

29. Drescher, *Capitalism and Antislavery*, pp. 67, 71. See also Anstey, *The Atlantic Slave Trade and British Abolition, 1760–1810*, pp. 263, 265–6. It was the Manchester committee, he argues, 'which sought to give abolitionist pubic opinion a cutting edge by the organisation of petitions to Parliament'.

30. Drescher, *Capitalism and Antislavery*, pp. 70, 210–11 (n. 17).

31. *Manchester Mercury*, 9, 16 October 1787; Clarkson, *History*, I, pp. 415–16; Abolition Committee Minutes, 30 October 1787.

32. Clarkson, *History*, I, pp. 415–16; *Manchester Mercury*, 11 December 1787. Drescher misreads this letter, or, at least, seems to rely on the somewhat garbled version of it in Robinson, 'Thomas Walker and Manchester Politics', p. 14.

33. Abolition Committee Minutes, 11, 18 December 1787, 1 January 1788; *Manchester Mercury*, 18 December 1787.

34. Abolition Committee Minutes, 18 December 1787. The relevant minute

reads: 'A letter from Thos. Cooper and others dated Manchester 11th Dec. 1787 was read, which the Treasurer [Hoare] informed the Committee he had written a short reply to, the Meeting at Manchester being to be held on the 20th'. Such business was normally transacted by the Committee in full session.

35. *Manchester Mercury*, 1 January 1788; John Barton to William Roscoe, 21 January 1788, Roscoe Papers, 920 ROS/239.

36. Abolition Committee Minutes, 22, 29 January, 5, 12, 26 February, 5, 11 March 1788.

37. The words are Wilberforce's in discussing the setting up of 'country committees'. Abolition Committee Minutes, 29 July 1788.

38. For Maidstone see Alan Everitt, 'Country, County and Town: Patterns of Regional Evolution in England', in Peter Borsay, ed., *The Eighteenth-Century Town*, pp. 97, 100.

39. James Ramsey to Samuel Hoare, 29 December 1787, Clarkson Papers, CN 141, Huntington Library.

40. *Commons Journal*, XLIII, 1788, pp. 156ff. and index; Drescher, *Capitalism and Antislavery*, p. 76.

41. See, for example, the petitions from Salisbury and Taunton, *Salisbury Journal*, 24 March 1788, and *Sherborne Mercury*, 21 April 1788.

42. Drescher, *Capitalism and Antislavery*, p. 77.

43. *Commons Journal*, XLIII, 1788, pp. 159ff. and index.

44. Anstey, *The Atlantic Slave Trade*, pp. 265–7.

45. Abolition Committee Minutes, 16 February 1788.

46. Ibid., 6 May 1788.

47. Ibid., 13 May, 24 June 1788.

48. Ibid., 17 March, 21 April 1789. For the plan and sections of a slave ship see Chapter Six.

49. Clarkson, *History*, II, pp. 61–2; Pollock, *Wilberforce*, pp. 72–5.

50. *The Life of William Wilberforce. By his Sons, Robert Isaac Wilberforce [and] Samuel Wilberforce*, 5 vols, London, 1838, I, pp. 225–6.

51. Betty Fladeland, *Men and Brothers: Anglo-American Antislavery Cooperation*, Urbana, Chicago, and London, 1972, pp. 17–26; Davis, *The Problem of Slavery in the Age of Revolution*, pp. 213–32.

52. Fladeland, *Men and Brothers*, p. 40; Abolition Committee Minutes, 5 July 1787.

53. John Barton to William Roscoe, 12 December 1787, Roscoe Papers, 920 ROS/252.

54. Abolition Committee Minutes, 2 October 1787, 20 May, 1, 8 July, 23 September 1788, 20 January 1789. See also James Pemberton to James Phillips, 22 July 1783, Portfolio MS 6/152, Friends House Library; James Pemberton to James Phillips, 18 October 1794 (Temp MSS 508/36/4), 30 May 1796 (Spragg MS Vol. 156/73), 12 February 1799 (Dix MS Vol. 294/20), Friends House Library; Joshua Gilpin to James Phillips, 26 November 1792, Gibson MSS 337/73, Friends House Library.

55. Fladeland, *Men and Brothers*, pp. 43–9, 53; Leon F. Litwack, *North of*

Slavery: The Negro in the Free States, 1790–1860, Chicago and London, 1961, pp. 1–4.

56. Fladeland, *Men and Brothers*, pp. 55–8, 63–9, 72–4. The United States Congress subsequently abolished the slave trade with immediate effect from 1 January 1808.

57. Fladeland, *Men and Brothers*, p. 66.

58. Moses Brown to James Phillips, 5 March 1791, Port 23/44, Friends House Library.

59. Abolition Committee Minutes, 5 March 1789.

60. Ibid., 29 April 1788, 25 June 1789, 12 January, 24 February 1790. For Frossard see *Biographie Universalle*, Supplement, IX, pp. 532–3.

61. Abolition Committee Minutes, 20 January, 24 February 1789.

62. Pollock, *Wilberforce*, pp. 72–5; *The Life of William Wilberforce*, I, pp. 154–8.

63. Abolition Committee Minutes, 8, 29 July, 21 October 1788, 20 January 1789.

64. Davis, *The Problem of Slavery in the Age of Revolution*, pp. 94–9; Daniel P. Resnick, 'The Société des Amis des Noirs and the Abolition of Slavery', *French Historical Studies*, VII, 1972, pp. 558–69.

65. Clarkson, *History*, II, pp. 122–52. Clarkson's *Essay on the Impolicy of the African Slave Trade* was published in 1788.

66. Clarkson, *History*, II, pp. 164–6.

67. Davis, *The Problem of Slavery in the Age of Revolution*, pp. 99–100.

68. Pollock, *Wilberforce*, pp. 96–102.

69. Abolition Committee Minutes, 28 September 1790, 1 February 1791. Clarkson's *Essay on the Comparative Efficiency of Regulation or Abolition, as applied to the Slave Trade* was published in 1789.

70. Abolition Committee Minutes, 12 March, 5, 12, 19 April 1791.

71. Pollock, *Wilberforce*, pp. 102–3.

72. Anstey, *The Atlantic Slave Trade*, p. 273.

73. Abolition Committee Minutes, 20 July 1790, 13 December 1791.

74. Wedgwood Papers, 24738B–32; *Eighteenth Century Short Title Catalogue*, CD-Rom version, 1992.

75. Clarkson, *History*, II, pp. 349–50; *Leeds Intelligencer*, 30 January 1792; Draper Hill, ed., *The Satirical Etchings of James Gillray*, New York, 1976, pp. 102–3 (plate 25).

76. Diary of Katherine Plymley, 1066/1 (20 October 1791), Shropshire Record Office, Shrewsbury.

77. *Times*, 19 December 1791, 13, 19 March 1792; *Gentleman's Magazine*, LXII, 1792, p. 275 (quotation); *Statutes at Large*, XVI, 1792, pp. 229–33; Lowell Joseph Ragatz, *The Fall of the Planter Class in the British Caribbean, 1763–1833*, New York and London, 1928, p. 212.

78. Wedgwood Papers, 24738B–32.

79. Abolition Committee Minutes, 26 April, 5 July, 29 August, 29 November, 28 December 1791.

80. Diary of Katherine Plymley, 1066/2 (21–2 October 1791).

81. *Diary, or Woodfall's Register*, 9, 10, 12, 14, 17, 20 February, 26, 27 March 1792.

82. William Dickson, 'Diary of a Visit to Scotland, 5th January–19th March

1792, on behalf of the Committee for the Abolition of the Slave Trade', Temp. Box 10/14, Friends House Library. All of these comments come in the form of instructions given to Dickson before he left London. They appear to be written in Clarkson's hand. See also Josiah Wedgwood to Thomas Clarkson, 18 January 1792, Wedgwood Papers, microfilm edition, E.18990.26; Josiah Wedgwood to Rev. Mr Plymley, 2 July 1791, Wedgwood Papers, microfilm edition, E.18998.26.

83. Abolition Committee Minutes, 13 December 1791; Wedgwood Papers, 24739.32 (circular letter of January 1792); Joseph Woods to William Matthews, 4 March 1792, Matthews MSS, A/5, Friends House Library.

84. Thomas Clarkson to Thomas Wilkinson, 1 March 1792, Wilkinson MSS 114/3, Friends House Library.

85. Dickson, 'Diary of a Visit to Scotland'.

86. Ibid. (entry for 21 February).

87. Ibid. (entry for 14 February).

88. Diary of Katherine Plymley, 1066/3 (22–30 October 1791).

89. *A Very new Pamphlet indeed! Being the Truth; addressed to the People at Large. Containing some Strictures on the English Jacobins, and the Evidence of Lord M'Cartney, and Others, before the House of Lords, respecting the Slave Trade*, London, 1792, p. 3.

90. Dickson, 'Diary of a Visit to Scotland' (entry for 5 February).

91. *A Short Address to the People of Scotland, on the Subject of the Slave Trade. With a Summary View of the Evidence delivered before a Committee of the House of Commons, on the Part of the Petitioners, for its Abolition*, Edinburgh, 1792, pp. 29–30. The same question was debated by the Coach-makers' Hall Society in Foster's Lane, Cheapside, in November and December 1791. See *Diary, or Woodfall's Register*, 23 November, 1 December 1791.

92. Abolition Committee Minutes, 31 January, 14 February 1792.

93. Drescher, *Capitalism and Antislavery*, p. 80.

94. *The Debate on the Motion for the Abolition of the Slave Trade, in the House of Commons, on Monday the Second of April*, 1792, London, 1792, p. 84.

95. Pollock, *Wilberforce*, pp. 114–16.

96. Abolition Committee Minutes, 19 June 1792.

97. Ibid., 8, 29 May 1792.

98. Pollock, *Wilberforce*, pp. 122–3; Clarkson, *History*, II, pp. 461–3; *The Life of William Wilberforce*, I, p. 350.

99. Abolition Committee Minutes, 20 June, 4, 9, 30 July, 13 August 1793.

100. Ibid., 20 August 1793.

101. Clarkson, *History*, II, pp. 464, 468.

102. Ibid., pp. 469–71. The Committee met twice in 1795, twice in 1796, and twice in 1797. See Abolition Committee Minutes.

103. Abolition Committee Minutes, 29 April 1805.

104. Ibid., 23 April 1805.

105. Pollock, *Wilberforce*, pp. 187–9, 199–214; Anstey, *The Atlantic Slave Trade*, pp. 321–42.

106. Anstey, *The Atlantic Slave Trade*, pp. 343–90.

Chapter Three

THOMAS CLARKSON

PERHAPS the most important member of the London Committee, certainly until his retirement in 1794, was Thomas Clarkson. Yet today Clarkson remains a sadly neglected figure, eclipsed by his friend and co-worker, William Wilberforce.[1] The two men could not have been more different. Where Wilberforce was slight and angular, Clarkson was tall and well-built; where Wilberforce was confident, articulate, and at ease in the best of company, Clarkson was brusque and rather awkward; where Wilberforce moved effortlessly in the world of the club and the Commons chamber, Clarkson preferred the company of his Quaker friends. But these things alone do not account for Clarkson's relative obscurity. Had he followed Wilberforce and sought a political career, then things might have turned out differently. Neither does it help that he destroyed most of his papers. The problem, however, is also in part historiographical. In the nineteenth century Wilberforce's sons, Robert and Samuel, launched an attack on Clarkson that sought to play down his contribution to the abolition of the slave trade, reserving pride of place to their father. As so often happens in these cases, some of the mud stuck. For many historians Clarkson remains the maverick of British anti-slavery, a hack with an exaggerated sense of his own importance.[2] Nothing could be further from the truth.

The early details of Clarkson's life are easily related. He was born in Wisbech in 1760, the son of a local schoolteacher. He attended St Paul's, went up to St John's College, Cambridge, in 1779, and graduated with honours in 1783.[3] It was a distinguished record, but not one that obviously marked Clarkson out for the path he was about to follow. For his real life began with his momentous decision to devote himself to the abolition of the slave trade. The story is well known but bears repetition nonetheless. Clarkson was first introduced to the slave trade by Peter Peckard, Vice-Chancellor of Cambridge University, who in 1785 set it as the subject of the Latin prize for senior bachelors. Clarkson had already the year before won the prize for middle bachelors and was keen to add to his list of academic honours— indeed, believed it was expected of him.[4] On his own admission, Clarkson was then 'wholly ignorant' about the slave trade. As he researched into the subject, however, he found that he became increasingly agitated:

> It was but one gloomy subject from morning to night. In the day-time I was uneasy. In the night I had little rest. I sometimes never closed my eye-lids for grief . . . I always slept with a candle in my room, that I might rise out of bed and put down such thoughts as might occur to me in the night, if I judged them valuable, conceiving that no arguments of any moment should be lost in so great a cause.

What began as a 'trial for academical reputation' became something altogether more ambitious, namely, a design to produce a work 'which might be useful to injured Africa'.[5]

Clarkson won the prize for senior bachelors, but by now the slave trade 'almost wholly engrossed' his thoughts. Returning from Cambridge to London, he paused in sight of Wades Mill in Hertfordshire. It was here that he began to conceive the idea of trying to do something to bring the trade to an end. Reaching London, he determined to translate and expand his prize-winning essay with a view to publishing it. This was in November 1785. Early the following year an old family friend, Joseph Hancock, introduced Clarkson to the bookseller, James Phillips. It was a chance encounter, but one that was to prove yet another turning-point. For not only did Phillips agree to publish Clarkson's essay, which appeared in June 1786, he also introduced him to William Dillwyn, Granville Sharp, James Ramsay, and his cousin, Richard Phillips. Here was a world until then entirely unknown to Clarkson. He began to realise that he was not alone, after all.[6]

Up to this point, Clarkson had been destined for a career in the Church; he had ambitions and 'a thirst after worldly interest and honours'. His prospects, he believed, were 'brilliant'. Yet at the same time he could not help but ponder the significance of his meeting with James Phillips or the chain of events that had led to his increasing preoccupation with the slave trade. As Clarkson himself put it: 'My mind was overwhelmed with the thought that . . . the finger of Providence was beginning to be discernible; that the day-star of African liberty was rising, and that probably I might be permitted to become a humble instrument in promoting it'. For months he turned the subject over in his mind. Then, at last, during a visit to James Ramsay at Teston in the summer of 1786, he announced his intention to devote himself full-time to the cause.[7] From this moment on Clarkson, in effect, became a professional reformer.

Together with Richard Phillips, Clarkson now set about devising an appropriate strategy. The collecting of evidence went on as before. He visited slave ships in the port of London, taking careful notes as he went along; indeed, tried to 'see all who had been to Africa'.[8] In the meantime, Clarkson began lobbying members of Parliament. The *Essay* formed a central part of this strategy, but it was also decided that Clarkson should wait on MPs personally. One of these MPs was William Wilberforce, who in all likelihood had already heard of Clarkson from his friends James Ramsay and Sir Charles and Lady Middleton. Clarkson's own account of this meeting, surely one of the most important events in the history of British anti-slavery, takes up just one page of his *History*. The two men talked about the slave trade and about Clarkson's *Essay*. Wilberforce asked for more evidence, wanted sources, and even expressed an interest in being kept informed of Clarkson's progress 'from time to time'. But there was as yet nothing to suggest that he was willing to take up the issue in the House of Commons, or so Clarkson thought.[9]

Nevertheless, Clarkson was sufficiently encouraged to go on lobbying Wilberforce, even at the expense of ignoring other MPs altogether. He was now effectively a go-between, meeting regularly with Wilberforce, sometimes at Wilberforce's own house, and reporting back to his Quaker friends in the City.[10] As the months passed by Wilberforce's importance to the future of the movement became apparent. But still Clarkson hesitated. He seemed reluctant to press Wilberforce, perhaps fearing that Wilberforce might yet frustrate all of his hopes. Wilberforce, for his part, had probably already made up his mind to introduce a motion calling for the abolition of the slave trade. He had discussed the subject with Ramsay and the Middletons at Teston in the autumn of 1786, and again with Pitt at Holwood on 12 May.[11] All of this was unknown to Clarkson. It was not until later in May, at a dinner organised by his friend, Bennett Langton, that he finally got the signal he had been looking for. Yes, Wilberforce said, he had 'no objection to bringing forward the measure in Parliament, when he was better prepared for it, and provided no person more proper could be found'.[12]

Within days Clarkson and his friends had organised the Society for the Abolition of the Slave Trade and, with it, the London Committee.[13] Catherine Clarkson liked to claim that her husband had been 'the means of forming the Committee', a view echoed recently by Ellen Wilson.[14] It was, rather, a collective decision, taken in the full knowledge that Wilberforce was ready to support the cause in Parliament. Clarkson admitted as much himself. He had proposed a 'union' of some sort shortly after his first meeting with Wilberforce, only to find that his fellow labourers, Dillwyn, James Phillips, Woods, Harrison, and Lloyd, 'had had their eyes upon me, and, from the time they had first seen me, had conceived a desire of making the same use of me as I had now expressed a wish of making of them, but that matters did not appear ripe at our first interview'. No firm decision was made at this stage. Instead, it was agreed to go on meeting every week, so as to monitor Clarkson's progress, 'by which we might all judge of the fitness of the time of calling ourselves an united body'.[15] By May 1787, clearly, that time had arrived.

It is important to be clear about the origins of the London Committee because only then can we understand how it functioned. This was not Clarkson's committee, any more than it was Wilberforce's committee. It was, obviously, a co-operative effort. Dillwyn, James Phillips, Woods, and the other members of the original Quaker committee, offered Clarkson moral and financial support, organisational skills, and, above all, legitimacy. Clarkson, for his part, offered the Committee his energy, his enthusiasm, and his time. He also provided an important channel of communication with Wilberforce and the other Parliamentary supporters of abolition. But theirs was a partnership; each was essential to the other. Clarkson likened the Committee to a human body, 'made up of a head and of various members, which had different functions to perform'. It followed that 'as every limb is essentially necessary for the completion of a perfect work; so in the case before us, every one was as necessary in his own office, or dependent as another'.[16]

Clarkson's own special role or 'office' warrants closer scrutiny. It is clear, for instance, that he was removed from much of the everyday business—correspondence and so on—which inevitably fell to Samuel Hoare, as treasurer, and James and Richard Phillips, Dillwyn, and Harrison. He was also frequently absent from meetings. Clarkson attended just four out of twenty-one meetings in 1787, as few as nine out of thirty meetings in 1790, and twelve out of thirty-one in 1791.[17] Only during 1788 was he in anything like regular attendance, taking an active part in the Committee's publication programme, as well as lobbying MPs, and arranging the evidence presented before the Privy Council. The next year, however, he was absent for six months in Paris and in 1790 and again in 1791 he was away from London for long periods of time. Nevertheless, even during his absences he remained in close contact with the Committee, sometimes writing as regularly as once or twice a week. In no sense of the term was Clarkson a free agent and neither was he treated as such.[18]

Clarkson's real impact was felt in the provinces. In 1787 he visited the major slave ports. This was followed in 1788 by a tour of the south coast of England; in 1790 by a tour of Scotland and the northern parts of England; and in 1791 by a tour of Shropshire, the north, and north-east of England. In all, it is estimated that he travelled 35,000 miles, mostly by night.[19] These tours enabled Clarkson to judge for himself the strengths and weaknesses of the abolitionist cause. They enabled him to meet the men who were involved in the movement at the local level, who sat on committees and organised subscriptions. Clarkson, as a result, became the public face of abolition. His very presence gave the movement authenticity and meaning. He was the 'ostensible person', who, as the Committee's representative, could be turned to for advice, support, and encouragement.[20] It was a demanding role (indeed, it finally broke Clarkson), but one that was vital to the Committee's success in mobilising public opinion against the slave trade.

Clarkson's main objective on these tours, especially those of 1787 and 1788, was to collect more evidence against the slave trade, locate witnesses, and, if possible, arrange for them to be brought to London. He meticulously recorded the dimensions of slave ships, searched muster rolls to document the frightening mortality rate among seamen engaged in the trade, and interviewed ships' surgeons, engineers, soldiers, and officers in the navy.[21] His obvious intention was to master the subject completely: the method of procuring slaves on the west coast of Africa; their treatment during the Middle Passage; and, finally, their reception and sale in the British West Indies. Clarkson was also unflagging in his efforts to collect information about Africa itself, its natural resources, and its potential as a (legitimate) trading partner. Clarkson's 'Africa box', containing examples of African produce (cotton, spices, gum rubber, and different kinds of wood), became yet another propaganda tool, designed to convince sceptics that there was, after all, an alternative to the slave trade.[22] The Sierra Leone experiment, an early colonisation scheme sponsored by Sharp, Wilberforce, and Clarkson among others, was part of the same strategy.[23]

In this way Clarkson rapidly became a leading authority on the slave trade. Collecting evidence, however, was only part of his brief. He was also an organiser. We can see this as early as 1787. Visiting Bridgwater on 20 July he called upon 'Alderman Sealy and the Mayor Mr Crandon' to discuss petitions and the distribution of his *Summary View*. Five days later, Clarkson was in Monmouth. 'After Dinner', he records in his journal, 'I wrote a Note to Dr Davis, Mayor of the Town, relative to the Intention of my Visit. He desired to see me. I went accordingly, conversed with him on the Subject, told him every Thing that had been done, and what was intended to be done. He promised a Petition should be made, whenever we wrote for it'.[24] More visits followed, to Gloucester, Worcester, Chester, and, finally, to Manchester, where Clarkson delivered a sermon to a packed congregation, including a group of forty or fifty blacks.[25] On this tour, in other words, Clarkson was actually preparing the way for the petition campaign of 1788, in the process establishing links with local activists, as well as men like Sealy, Crandon, and Davis.

The following year Clarkson was given the task of organising local committees on the south coast of England. Here again, in Poole, Exeter, and Plymouth, his mere presence acted as a stimulus to local activity. Clarkson's visit to Exeter in November, for instance, was the occasion of a large public meeting at the Guildhall, chaired by the mayor, Richard Jenkins.[26] On the same tour he also spoke to a meeting in Tiverton, helping to focus attention on a subject that until recently had aroused little public concern. 'What ought not to escape notice on this occasion', remarked the *Exeter Flying Post*, 'is, that many of the principal inhabitants were, a few months since, either averse or indifferent to the cause'. But having read some of the tracts lately published, 'conversed with persons well acquainted with the subject, and heard the sermon before mentioned', they were convinced of their duty, 'and, like honest men and Christians, not only relinquished their prejudices, but, setting an example to persons in similar situations, made more than ample amends for any lukewarmness in a cause they *now* consider as interesting not only to every Englishman, but every one who bears the name of MAN'.[27]

Later still, in 1790 and 1791, Clarkson was responsible for reviving flagging spirits and preparing the way for yet another petition campaign. By now he was in regular correspondence with a vast network of local and regional contacts. But it is easy to see how a personal visit, however brief, could help to make the Committee's intentions clear. In this sense, Clarkson's tour of 1791 was of critical importance, not just in organising and reorganising local committees, but in establishing a point of contact. We can see this clearly in Shrewsbury, where Clarkson's visit in October 1791 coincided with a number of new local initiatives, including the publication of extracts from the *Abstract* in the local press.[28] It is true that Clarkson could be impetuous, awkward, and obsessive. Nevertheless, there is no doubting the contribution he made outside Parliament, both as an organiser and as an orchestrator. Energetic and resourceful, Clarkson provided a vital link between London and the provinces, enabling the London Committee to tap a vast reservoir of public feeling.

This alone might have been enough to secure Clarkson's reputation. But at the same time he was a prolific author. The *Essay*, published in 1786, was followed by Clarkson's *Summary View* (1787), his *Essay on the Impolicy of the African Slave Trade* (1788), *An Essay on the Comparative Efficiency of Regulation or Abolition, as applied to the Slave Trade* (1789), and *Letters on the Slave Trade* (1789). In addition, he was responsible for the *Abstract of the Evidence Delivered before a Select Committee of the House of Commons* (1791), as well as several shorter pieces on the abstention campaign and the slave rebellion in Santo Domingo. Obviously, Clarkson's vast knowledge placed him in an ideal position to produce these works. And what he lacked in literary flair he more than made up for in a logical, orderly mind that was ideally suited to the organisation and arrangement of vast amounts of information. It was a remarkable achievement, particularly given Clarkson's other commitments.

As we have seen, these various publications formed the basis of the Committee's opinion-building activities. The figures are startling. Besides over 15,000 copies of Clarkson's *Summary View*, the Committee printed and distributed over 5,000 copies of his *Essay*, 2,000 of his *Impolicy*, 2,000 of his *Comparative Efficiency*, and 10,000 of the *Abstract* (including 3,000 copies of a cheap edition).[29] In this way, Clarkson's name became synonymous with the abolition of the slave trade. It is striking, for instance, that the Committee did not publish or distribute any of Wilberforce's Commons speeches (although they did publish Pitt's speech in the 1788 debate); perhaps more striking still that Wilberforce's first publication on the subject, his *Letter on the Abolition of the Slave Trade*, did not appear until 1807. Here again, Clarkson was the 'ostensible person'. Indeed, no other member of the Committee contributed as much to the growing literature on the slave trade. No other member of the Committee, with the possible exception of Wedgwood, did as much to popularise abolition or to give it intellectual authority.

This, in short, was Clarkson's special 'office'. Whether collecting evidence, organising committees and petitions, lobbying members of Parliament, or producing books and pamphlets, he added an extra dimension to the Committee's activities. Its only full-time member, he was willing and able to devote himself to the abolition of the slave trade in a way that would have been unthinkable for businessmen like Hoare, Phillips, and Lloyd. And the Committee, of course, reaped the benefits. When Clarkson took up the cause in 1786 he made a very special commitment. He never deviated from that path, seldom rested, never gave up hope. He was, as Coleridge said, 'the moral Steam-Engine, or the Giant with one Idea'.[30]

What sort of a person was Thomas Clarkson? Very few people, one suspects, ever really got that close to him. Although Clarkson had a wide circle of acquaintances, he had very few close personal friends, and no private life to speak of. To some extent, of course, this went with the territory. Constantly busy, often in the same place for only a matter of days, he had neither the time nor the energy to pour into personal relationships. But at the same time there was a brusqueness about Clarkson, a tendency to be obsessive and over-serious, that made him a difficult person to warm to. People admired him, wondered at his enthusiasm and his perseverance, but not many seem to have actually liked him. 'Guileless', 'impetuous', 'tactless', 'humourless': these are just some of the adjectives that spring to mind when biographers attempt to describe Clarkson.[31]

Katherine Plymley, the sister of Joseph Plymley (later Corbett), perhaps had as good an opportunity as anyone to observe Clarkson. Katherine, it needs to be said, was already prejudiced in Clarkson's favour. Privately, she admitted that 'whatever his external appearance or manners had been it wou'd not have lessened my idea of him'. But to her relief she found Clarkson 'amiable and courteous in manner, above the middle size, well made and very agreeable in his person with a remarkable mildness of voice and countenance'. Yet even Katherine had been unprepared for the 'indefatigable perseverance' with which Clarkson pursued the abolition of the slave trade. As she noted in her diary on 20 October 1791: 'He seems to forget himself in his desire to promote the good of others and all this is done with such regularity & calmness that he does not appear harried'.[32]

During his short visit to Shropshire Katherine would become more familiar with Clarkson's 'regularity'. Each day was carefully planned, every hour and minute put to good use. When he was not meeting her brother's friends and discussing 'business', he was writing letters or walking in the garden, pausing only to chat at supper. He was, in fact, overbearingly regular and punctual. Katherine records a revealing incident when her brother came down late one morning. After a while Clarkson began to fidget. 'If I had known Mr Plymley wou'd not have been quite exact I cou'd have written some letters', he at last told Katherine. Katherine obligingly 'ran for a table & desk . . . [and] When he sat down to write . . . he said "now we shall gain time if you will seal the letters"'.[33] This was the pattern of Clarkson's life: to live was to work.

Katherine obviously marvelled at such industry in a young man who was, after all, still only thirty-one years of age. But others felt that Clarkson sometimes let his enthusiasm run away with him.

Lord Brougham was particularly anxious on this point. 'I am sure I have seen you write twenty letters about getting something done at a particular time', he chided Clarkson late in life, 'when, upon the least reflection, you must certainly have seen that it did not signify many straws whether or not it was done at all, and not a single straw whether it was done one day or another'.[34] The charge was fairly made. Clarkson needed to be active, needed to feel that he was pushing forward the great cause, needed to know that he had done all that he could. What began as a duty became a compulsion, the ruling passion of his life.

It was Clarkson's singleness of purpose that led to what some saw as his impetuosity. This was a source of tension from the first. When in August 1787 Clarkson wrote asking permission to take Alexander Falconbridge with him to Liverpool, his colleagues on the London Committee reacted nervously. For one thing, they were uneasy about retaining witnesses at this stage in the business. For another, they knew little or nothing about Falconbridge or his character. Samuel Hoare tried to be as diplomatic as he could. 'The little experience I have already had of mankind has excited much caution on forming my opinions from first appearances', he warned Clarkson, 'and I hope the zeal and animation with which thou hast taken up the cause will be accompanied with temper and moderation, which can alone insure its success'.[35] John Barton echoed these sentiments. As he confessed to William Roscoe: 'I am really affraid [sic] he will at times be deficient in caution, as well as incur much expense, perhaps unnecessarily'.[36] It was not just the expense, however. Barton obviously feared that Clarkson might actually do 'us' (the Committee, the cause) real harm.

Clarkson got his way over Falconbridge, but for many the doubts lingered. And with good reason. While he was in Bristol in 1787 Clarkson became so incensed at the treatment of seamen employed in the slave trade that he decided to take one case, the murder of William Lines, to court. Against considerable odds he won. This was only the start of the matter, however. Some months later the same case was brought before the Lords of Admiralty. But by now two of the principal witnesses had been spirited away, while the other two were working somewhere in South Wales. Hurriedly, Clarkson sent a messenger to bring them to London; then he decided to set out himself, crossing the river Severn in a fearsome storm, risking his own life in the process. The witnesses were at last found but all to no avail: the case had already been heard and the chief mate, Vicars, acquitted.[37] Clarkson had been warned that something of the sort might happen. Yet he had insisted on proceeding against Vicars. He had insisted on making himself heard.

The more conservative members of the London Committee fretted about these 'hasty prosecutions'.[38] They also fretted about Clarkson's radicalism and his sympathy for the French Revolution. We know surprisingly little about Clarkson's early political views or his political education. His monumental *History* is silent on issues like the suffrage or electoral reform, and there is nothing to suggest that he came to abolition through political radicalism (as Sharp had done, for instance). Yet, like many of his generation, he was inspired by the French Revolution, both as an idea and as an event. Clarkson's personal visit to Paris in 1789, and his meetings with leading revolutionaries, with Brissot de Warville, Mirabeau, and Condorcet, reinforced this identification with the principles of the revolution.[39] Nothing deterred him, not even the rising tide of revolutionary violence in France. Even as late as November 1792 he was still confident that an 'Excellent Republic will be established on ye Ruins of Despotism & arbitrary Power'.[40]

Clarkson made no secret of his sympathy for the French Revolution. Here again, Katherine Plymley's diary is revealing. At dinner one evening the conversation turned to the revolution. Clarkson spoke animatedly on the subject. He openly defended Paine—indeed, thought that 'he may have colour'd higher and not gone beyond the truth', and reiterated his belief that the sentiment of the nation was behind the Revolution:

> . . . in the tour he made last year, he heard but little said of the French revolution, and of the few he did hear speak of it, most seem'd to blame it and to think it wou'd not succeed, but this year [1791] he found a very great change. It was become a subject of general conversation, and among those he convers'd with he thought it was generally mention'd with approbation.[41]

On this occasion Clarkson found himself among friends. At Shrewsbury the next day, however, his audience turned out to be men of 'high monarchical principles'. Not surprisingly they concluded that Clarkson was a 'revolutionist'. Indeed, they became so alarmed that Katherine's brother 'found himself oblig'd to call on several persons to assure them how far Mr C was from wishing a revolution in this country'.[42]

Later, when the two men met in Chester, Plymley advised Clarkson to avoid the subject of the Revolution, for fear that it would make his (Plymley's) task of organising petitions that much more difficult. Clarkson readily concurred. Yet in doing so it is quite clear that he had been oblivious to the danger:

> Mr C said it is singular that almost the first word Mr Wilberforce said to me when I met him at Mr Gisbornes was this—O, Clarkson I wanted much to see you to tell you that I have found it absolutely necessary to keep clear from the subject of the French Revolution and I hope you will. Your dining at the Revolution dinners in London has been talked of . . . [43]

In time Clarkson did learn to curb his enthusiasm for the French Revolution. He grew more cautious about speaking out in public, more circumspect, but the damage had already been done. William Dickson, touring Scotland early in 1792, found that at Glasgow several abolitionists were 'afraid C's honest zeal wd hurt our cause', alluding especially to his 'letter on Sugar and on F.R.'.[44] In private, moreover, Clarkson continued to support the revolution, even approaching several of his friends for contributions to a fund for the National Assembly. And then in the autumn of 1792 he was recognised by the French Convention, along with Wilberforce, Joseph Priestley, Tom Paine, and George Washington.[45] The embarrassment of abolitionists was complete.

It is easy to dismiss Clarkson as politically naive, as guileless, or simply irresponsible. But when it came to the Committee's own tactics he could be remarkably astute. Clarkson, for instance, was one of the first to exploit the potential of Wedgwood's famous cameo of the kneeling slave, and used it extensively on his tour of southern England in 1788. He also understood about political cunning, deceit, and manipulation. As we have seen, the petition campaign of 1792 involved months of careful planning, the real object being disguised or even denied.[46] Clarkson helped to organise that campaign and even drafted the very detailed (and explicit) instructions given to Dickson in 1792. With a clear end in sight, like this, Clarkson was at his best: practical, energetic, and persistent. No one knew more about the petitioning process or took greater pains to ensure that petitioners responded promptly to the Committee's directions. He was, in effect, the perfect campaign manager.

We can make the same point in a rather different way. Later, following his retirement from the cause, Clarkson decided to live in the Lake District. The move was again carefully planned. He made detailed inquiries about livestock, crops, trees, and bushes. Katherine Plymley was asked to help design a suitable cottage and suggest furnishings.[47] It was all somehow typical of the man and essential to our understanding of him. Clarkson's relationship with Coleridge, whom he met through the Wordsworths, was marked by the same commonsense approach and the same eye to business. Coleridge at this time had a number of projects in mind: a new periodical, the *Friend*; a printing press; and a volume of poems. Clarkson warmed to the idea of the *Friend* and even agreed to collect subscriptions for Coleridge. He also suggested a number of alterations to the prospectus, most of them calculated to 'sell' the periodical to his Quaker friends.[48]

Launching a new periodical, like orchestrating a petition campaign, was second nature to Clarkson. He had all the calculations at his fingertips and knew about newspaper duties, costs, and the importance of subscribers.[49] But when Coleridge began to lose interest in the project and pursue other ideas, Clarkson became increasingly concerned. 'I do not like you turning Printer', he complained in February 1809. 'Who is to vend your works, when you print them?—the Booksellers—and these will have a decided Prejudice against you–nay, they will combine against you; and if they should, your Books will lie upon your own shelves'.[50] Clarkson was similarly at a loss to understand why Coleridge wanted to prepare a volume of poems when the *Friend* was barely off the ground. Clarkson advised him to give up the idea: 'Establish this, and you may afterwards establish what you please. Why will you lose the Independence of your mind by being under Obligations when there is no necessity—Give up this Publication for the present—Give it up as you did your Printing Press'.[51]

The insistent tone of these letters suggests why it was that many people found Clarkson offputting. He could be courteous, thoughtful, and painstaking in his efforts to help others. But he could also be insensitive, domineering, and tactless. Clarkson clearly did not understand Coleridge, any more than he understood Coleridge's reluctance to be tied to the routine of editing a monthly periodical. He was not, one suspects, a man of large insights. He tended to treat people as cyphers, as signatures on petitions. This was all very well as long as they were doing what he wanted them to do. But when they hesitated, as Coleridge did, he grew irritable and impatient. Coleridge, for his part, understood Clarkson perfectly. He recognised his resolve, his energy, and his benevolent nature; indeed, praised all of these qualities.[52] Yet at the same time he recognised (even if he did not identify with) the obsessive and overbearing side to his nature: the fretting, the bullying, the 'indefatigable perseverance'.

And Clarkson was obsessive. Once he had settled on something (whether it was the *Friend* or the abolition of the slave trade) he was determined to see it through. He was afraid of nothing. At Liverpool he received threatening letters and was assaulted in the streets, on one occasion narrowly escaping with his life.[53] Yet Clarkson never shrank from his duty. He went on collecting evidence, pursuing witnesses, and organising petitions. One of the most arresting images in the *History* is that of Clarkson and Falconbridge discussing abolition in the 'King's Arms' in Liverpool. 'Day after day we beat our opponents out of the field', he writes, 'as many of the company acknowledged, to their no small mortification, in their presence. Thus, while we served the cause by discovering all that could be said against it, we served it by giving numerous individuals proper ideas concerning it, and of interesting them in our favour'.[54] It is a remarkable passage and one that speaks volumes about Clarkson's tenacity, his energy, and, above all, his courage.

If anything, the physical dangers to Clarkson increased. When he visited Liverpool again in 1792 he was forced to enter the town by night (there would be no more debates in the 'King's Arms').[55] These tours brought other pressures, too. As Clarkson explained, writing to Matthew Montagu in August 1793: 'Travelling on this Subject I am considered as the ostensible Person. Mr Wilberforce is unknown, for he has had no dealings personally with them. Our Committee escape for the same Reason, & therefore I am the Person applied to, who can bear it the least'. There is no question that Clarkson brought some of these pressures on himself. But for many abolitionists up and down the country he was their only link with the Committee in London. And so men (and women) applied to him for money and for places, for relief and for support. Clarkson estimated that he had personally expended more than £1,500 in this way, much of it on retaining witnesses. 'I knew no Alternative', he complained wearily. 'To offend I dare not, knowing their Services might be wanted at a future time'.[56]

In time the tours, the long hours, and the constant anxiety began to take their toll. When Clarkson visited the Plymleys in 1791 he was already in poor health.[57] By the spring and summer of 1793 he was on the verge of complete nervous and physical collapse. 'I am suddenly seized with Giddiness and Cramps', he told Montagu.

> I feel unpleasant Ringing in my Ears. My Hands frequently tremble. Cold Sweats suddenly come upon Me. My Appetite becomes all at once ravenous, & if I am not almost immediately gratified, I am ready to feint. I find myself weak, easily fatigued, & out of Breath. My Recollection is also on the Decline.[58]

At last he was forced to retire, seeking refuge in the Lake District and the gentler pursuits of the gentleman farmer. He was, quite literally, exhausted, in body and mind.

For five years Clarkson had poured all his energies into the abolition of the slave trade. It had been a superhuman effort. But perhaps no one fully appreciated how much he had been affected by his labours, not even Clarkson himself. When Clarkson said that he agonised over some of the barbarities he encountered on his tours, when he said they 'harassed' his constitution, he did not exaggerate.[59] He was, it seems, 'naturally gloomy' and perhaps given to bouts of depression. Henry Crabb Robinson once observed of Clarkson that 'as soon as he is satisfied that any measure *ought* to succeed, it is not possible to convince him that it *cannot*'.[60] But because he believed so passionately in what he was doing, he found it all the more difficult to cope with disappointment and defeat. Clearly, this is what happened in 1793. The reverse in the House of Lords and then the Commons rocked Clarkson back on his heels and precipitated a nervous collapse. He had been buoyed up by the prospect of victory: defeat left him drained of all emotion. It was a sad exit, but one that in the circumstances was not entirely unexpected.

In all, Clarkson spent nearly ten years in the Lake District. During this period he married, had a son, also Thomas, and befriended the Wordsworths, the Southeys, and the Coleridges. His health improved. He turned his mind to other projects, starting work on his *Portraiture of Quakerism* (1806). He seemed relaxed and contented. But then in the summer of 1803 his wife, Catherine, fell seriously ill, so ill, in fact, that she finally left the Lake District, returning first to her parents at Bury St Edmunds and then moving to Bristol to be near Dr Beddoes. Clarkson stayed on at the family's home in Eusemere a few months longer, but the 'Lake Years' were effectively over. The cottage and farm were sold to Lord Lowther in 1804.[61]

Clarkson's move south to Bristol and then to London coincided with the revival of the London Committee on 23 May 1804 and, with it, the start of a fresh Parliamentary campaign. He resumed his labours as before, undertaking a tour of England in 1805 to collect yet more evidence.[62] But the Committee, and the cause, had changed appreciably since 1794. As we have seen, the reorganised Committee was, in effect, a Parliamentary lobby shaped very much in Wilberforce's image. And with the passage of time new leaders had emerged, among them Zachary Macaulay and James Stephen. Inevitably, it took time for Clarkson to adjust to these changes. Macaulay and Stephen were strangers to him. Indeed, Clarkson appears to have had very little contact with either Wilberforce or any other of the members of the Committee between 1793 and 1804. All of this was bound to have an effect. Whereas he had once been a driving force, Clarkson now found himself on the periphery and perhaps even shut out of the deliberations which finally led to the Commons victory of 1807.

Clarkson's growing isolation in the final years of the campaign is, of course, reflected in his two-volume *History*. In a book running to over 1,100 pages, only about ninety deal with the period 1804 to 1807. Macaulay and Stephen, for instance, are mentioned only once by name.[63] The oversight was not intentional. Clarkson set out to write a personal history, with the inevitable result that he tended to concentrate on his own involvement in the movement and his own labours. Yet for this very reason the *History* alienated many of the younger generation. Even Wilberforce was moved to say that the book 'though so far accurate as that nothing is said . . . which is not true and still more is not *intended* to be so, yet [it] by no means conveys a just conception of all that deserves commemoration'.[64] In particular, he felt that justice had not been done to his brother-in-law, James Stephen, a view shared by many in the Clapham Sect, among them Robert and Samuel Wilberforce and Stephen's own son, James.[65]

Nevertheless, Wilberforce's common sense and his obvious regard for Clarkson ensured that for the moment the matter rested there. Wilberforce's death in 1833, however, cleared the way for a revisionist attack on Clarkson and his *History*. Almost immediately, Robert and Samuel began a life of their father, which finally appeared in 1838. The Wilberforces' disagreement with Clarkson was simple. His *History*, they argued, created the impression that Clarkson had 'originally engaged' their father in the cause and that Wilberforce had subsequently become 'a sort of Parliamentary agent, of whom you availed yourself'.[66] The *Life* sought to set the record straight. With remarkable ingenuity, it traced Wilberforce's interest in the abolition of the slave trade to a letter written to a York newspaper when he was only fourteen years of age. Clarkson, meanwhile, was recast in the role of Wilberforce's agent (hence his visit to Paris in 1789). And, as for the London Committee, the Wilberforces claimed that 'from the first' their father had 'directed' its endeavours.[67]

But it was the tone of the *Life* that caused greatest offence. Clarkson and his *History* were dismissed at the first opportunity:

> Of this book it is necessary to declare at once, and with a very painful distinctness, that it conveys an entirely erroneous idea of the Abolition struggle. Without imputing to Mr Clarkson any intentional unfairness, it may safely be affirmed that his exaggerated estimate of his own service has led him unawares into numberless misstatements. Particular instances might be easily enumerated, but the writers are most anxious to avoid any thing resembling controversy on this subject. Contenting themselves, therefore, with this declaration, they will henceforth simply tell their own story, without pointing out its contradictions to Mr Clarkson's 'History'.[68]

The Wilberforces also made great play of two minor incidents: Clarkson's obvious irritation with Wilberforce when his brother, John, failed to win a naval promotion; and an embarrassing episode involving an annuity for Clarkson, where again he proved more of a hindrance than a help.[69] By concentrating on these incidents, as opposed to Clarkson's connection with the London Committee, the *Life* came close to dismissing his significance altogether. As Griggs puts it: 'One is led to believe that Wilberforce thought of Clarkson as a man undoubtedly honest and persevering, but as an odd sort of person who occasionally proved of considerable value'.[70]

Clarkson had already been given fair warning of what to expect from the Wilberforces, but even he was caught off balance by the vehemence of their attack.[71] Two charges seem to have particularly bothered him. One of these concerned his relationship with Wilberforce. Clarkson vigorously denied any claim to have first introduced Wilberforce to the subject of the slave trade. More than that, he was willing to concede that in all probability Wilberforce would have taken up the cause without his intervention. But he did intervene and Clarkson continued to insist that in 1787 Wilberforce still knew 'very little about the slave trade or Africa'. The question was not 'in whose heart benevolent feelings were first excited'; rather, 'who first put the shoulder to the wheel, who first conceived the project and acted upon it of rousing a whole nation to a sense of the national iniquity'. Clarkson claimed this distinction for himself, pointing again to his labours in 1785 and 1786.[72]

The other charge concerned the function of the London Committee. Naturally, Clarkson denied any suggestion that Wilberforce had 'directed all of their endeavours'. Wearily, he went over the early history of the Committee, describing its work, and drawing attention to the enterprise (and independence) of its members. There was very little new here—Clarkson had set it all out in his *History*—but he did put a new gloss on his own role in the organisation of the Committee. In effect, he now implied that he had been the prime mover, prevailing on men like Sharp and Sansom to join the five members of the original Quaker committee.[73] It was a large claim, but one that was vital to Clarkson's defence and his reputation. For in divorcing Clarkson from the Committee, by skipping over the fact that he had been a member of the Committee at all, the Wilberforces were able to make good their claim that Wilberforce, and not Clarkson, had been the driving force outside Parliament.

Clarkson set out to defend himself in his *Strictures on a Life of William Wilberforce* (1838), edited by Henry Crabb Robinson, who added a preface and supplement. But the controversy was not over yet. There was another broadside (possibly intended as a retraction) from the Wilberforces in their *Correspondence of William Wilberforce* (1840), and although they later expunged all of the offending passages from an abridged version of the *Life* (1843), the whole business left a bitter taste, dividing a large section of the Victorian intellectual world into two hostile camps: the Wilberforces and James Stephen, on one side; Robinson, Southey, and Wordsworth, on the other.[74] Clarkson, for his part, was clearly bewildered by the behaviour of Robert and Samuel Wilberforce. Initially, he put their hostility down to ignorance and a misguided belief that their father had been the guiding genius of the early abolitionist movement. Only later did he begin to understand the depth of feeling against him among members of the Clapham Sect, and even then he may not have fully appreciated just how hostile men like James Stephen were.[75]

Today this whole affair strikes us as trifling and, in truth, rather sad. As Griggs observes: 'it is not Clarkson *versus* Wilberforce but Clarkson *and* Wilberforce'.[76] Each had his own proper 'office' in the early abolitionist movement; Wilberforce's was inside Parliament, Clarkson's outside. Clarkson said as much himself. In chapter eleven of the *History* he paused to reflect on the course of events up to 1787, the organisation of the London Committee, and his own relationship with Wilberforce. 'What', he asked,

> could I myself have done if I had not derived so much assistance from the committee? What could Mr Wilberforce have done in Parliament, if I, on the other hand, had not collected that great body of evidence, to which there was such a constant appeal? And what could the committee have done without the Parliamentary aid of Mr Wilberforce?

Here again, Clarkson used the trope of the human body, stressing not competition but mutuality and interdependence.[77]

This leaves the question of Wilberforce's relationship with the Committee. If Wilberforce did not have a direct hand in the organisation of the London Committee, he certainly had an input into its deliberations, even before he became a member himself in April 1791. Two examples spring to mind. In the summer of 1788 the Committee put forward a proposal to hold a general meeting in London on 7 August. Almost immediately the scheme was abandoned, following a letter from Wilberforce 'containing many forcible Arguments against it'. Wilberforce again intervened over the (country) committee idea, advising Clarkson and his colleagues 'to avoid giving any possible occasion of offence to the Legislature by forced or unnecessary Associations'.[78] The Committee was obviously guided by Wilberforce and, as far as one can tell, quick to take appropriate action. But this was not quite the same thing as leadership. Wilberforce did not initiate policies, at least not where the Committee's opinion-building activities were concerned, any more than he had a hand in the organisation of petitions. Rather, he acted as a buffer, steering the Committee away from areas of possible conflict.

Later, of course, Wilberforce played a full part as a member of the Committee. His attendance at meetings was erratic, but he was closely involved in two important decisions, one relating to the planning and organisation of the petition campaign of 1792, the other to non-consumption.[79] The first of these, the petition campaign, was in all likelihood Wilberforce's idea, although the details were again left to the Committee. Non-consumption was a more complex issue. It is safe to assume that Wilberforce had doubts about the boycott of West Indian sugar and rum, at least as a 'public' policy. Yet he seemingly endorsed the decision to go ahead with the boycott and was conspicuously absent when on 13 August the whole scheme was abruptly abandoned.[80] Indeed, one is left with the distinct impression that throughout this affair the Committee (Wilberforce included) was feeling its way. Wilberforce undoubtedly determined the outcome of the debate, but, to judge from the minutes, it was a more close-run thing than historians like to imagine.

Wilberforce, in other words, helped to shape the political education of the London Committee. He not only provided leadership in Parliament, but gave Clarkson and his colleagues a sense of what was possible. Wilberforce, for his part, looked to the Committee for organisation, as well as information. It is true that he kept up a massive correspondence and had his own regional contacts, among them William Mason and Thomas Gisborne.[81] But these contacts were never extensive enough to sustain a nationwide campaign. For that Wilberforce needed the London Committee. This emerges very clearly from the movement at the grass-roots level. Most local activists, the men who organised committees, collected funds, and distributed books and pamphlets, had little or no contact with Wilberforce. Instead, they worked through the London Committee, or, failing that, looked to Clarkson for guidance.[82]

This, ultimately, is what the Wilberforces failed to grasp. They assumed that the London Committee had always been a Parliamentary lobby and, as such, answerable to their father. This may have been true of the period after 1804, but it was clearly not the case between 1787 and 1793. In its original guise the London Committee was the prototype of the nineteenth-century reform organisation. It was part of a broad popular movement which attracted thousands of Britons. Which, of course, brings us back to Clarkson. The 'office' that he chose for himself was not an easy one; neither was it particularly glamorous. But as long as petitions were the focus of the campaign, inside and outside Parliament, then figures like Clarkson were vital to the success of the early abolitionist movement.

Clarkson was never a popular figure. He was too serious, too obsessive, too tactless. Yet he has a special place in the history of British anti-slavery. In his own day Clarkson was rightly regarded as a patriarch, the 'unwearied Friend of Afric's injured race'.[83] He was as celebrated in the United States as he was in England. Henry Wright assured Catherine Clarkson in 1845 that 'in the estimate of American Abolitionists, & of all our numerous *free* colored people', her husband was 'more intimately & *endearingly* associated with the holy cause of Anti-Slavery than any or all of those, who, in this kingdom [England] took part in it'.[84] Nor did he exaggerate. In 1846 a group of New York blacks met to commemorate the abolition of slavery in the British West Indies and listen to an address by Alexander Crummell. Crummell was later to emerge as one of the leading black intellectuals of the nineteenth century, and it is telling that his subject on this occasion (and, indeed, his first venture into print) should have been a eulogy on the life of Thomas Clarkson.[85]

Perhaps the most revealing tribute came from Wilberforce, who, at a public meeting in London in 1830, spoke affectionately of 'those happy days' when the two men had first begun their labours together.[86] Clarkson and Wilberforce were never that close but theirs was a special relationship, created out of a common interest and a common sense of purpose. Wilberforce was wittier and more brilliant, a patrician who could count William Pitt among his closest friends. But in Clarkson he found the perfect foil, a plain and unostentatious man who was willing to devote himself full-time to the cause. If not quite the leader of the movement outside Parliament, Clarkson did as much as anyone to give abolition focus and direction. He was that rarity in the eighteenth century, a professional reformer. And through his researches and his tours, his books and his pamphlets, he helped to push Britain into the abolitionist era. For that alone he deserves our respect and our admiration.

Notes

1. While the literature on Wilberforce is voluminous, only two biographies of Clarkson have appeared in the last fifty or more years: Earl Leslie Griggs, *Thomas Clarkson: The Friend of Slaves*, London, 1936; and Ellen Gibson Wilson, *Thomas Clarkson: A Biography*, London and New York, 1990.
2. See, for instance, the picture of him that emerges in John Pollock's *Wilberforce*, esp. pp. 55-8.
3. Griggs, *Thomas Clarkson*, pp. 23-4; Wilson, *Thomas Clarkson*, pp. 4-9. Clarkson's father, John, died when Clarkson was only six years of age. Clarkson appears to have taken after his mother, who, according to Griggs, was a woman of 'great energy of character'.
4. Griggs, pp. 24-5; Wilson, pp. 9-10; Clarkson, *History*, I, pp. 205-6.
5. Clarkson, *History*, I, pp. 207-9.
6. Ibid., pp. 210-17.
7. Ibid., pp. 216, 224-30.
8. Ibid., pp. 233-42.
9. Ibid., pp. 241-2; Griggs, pp. 33-4; Pollock, *Wilberforce*, p. 55; Robin Furneaux, *William Wilberforce*, London, 1974, p. 71.
10. Clarkson, *History*, I, pp. 249-51.
11. Ibid., pp. 251-2; Pollock, pp. 52-5; Furneaux, pp. 71-2.
12. Clarkson, *History*, I, pp. 252-4.
13. Ibid., pp. 254-8.
14. Catherine Clarkson to William Wordsworth, 1838 (?), Wordsworth Papers, Wordsworth Library, Grasmere; Wilson, p. 18.
15. Clarkson, *History*, I, pp. 245-8.
16. Ibid., pp. 271-2.
17. These figures are abstracted from the Abolition Committee Minutes. As a point of comparison, Harrison attended twenty out of twenty-one meetings

in 1787, James Phillips eighteen, and Samuel Hoare and Richard Phillips seventeen each. In 1790 William Dillwyn attended twenty-six out of thirty meetings, and Harrison and James Phillips twenty-five.

18. It is interesting to note, for instance, that on his tour of the south coast of England in 1788 Clarkson was specifically requested to give an account of his progress 'every fortnight'. And later he was recalled to London at the express desire of the Committee, which had one eye on the proceedings of the Privy Council. See Abolition Committee Minutes, 26 August, 4 November 1788.

19. Thomas Clarkson, *Strictures on a Life of W. Wilberforce by the Rev. W. [R.] Wilberforce and the Rev. S. Wilberforce. With a Correspondence between Lord Brougham and Mr Clarkson; also a Supplement containing remarks on the Edinburgh Review of Mr Wilberforce's Life*, London, 1838, p. 79. For details of Clarkson's various tours see his *History*, I, pp. 292–441; II, pp. 2–11, 194–9, 346–52.

20. Thomas Clarkson to Matthew Montagu, 28 August 1793, (Elizabeth) Montagu Papers, MO 710, Huntington Library, San Marino, California.

21. Clarkson, *History*, I, pp. 298–302, 310–19, 322–30, 338–42, 349–67, 371–90.

22. Ibid., pp. 302–3, 373, 379. For Clarkson's 'Africa box' see Thomas Clarkson to Thomas Wilkinson, 21 December 1806, Wilkinson MSS 14/41, Friends House Library, London.

23. For Sierra Leone and the Sierra Leone Company see Clarkson, *History*, II, pp. 342–5; Griggs, pp. 65–8; Pollock, pp. 109–13, 226–7; Christopher Fyfe, *A History of Sierra Leone*, London, 1962.

24. Clarkson's Journal, 1787 (entries for 20, 25 July), Clarkson Papers, St John's College, Cambridge. See also Clarkson, *History*, I, pp. 321, 347–8.

25. Clarkson, *History*, I, pp. 368–71, 418.

26. *Exeter Flying Post*, 1 November 1788.

27. Ibid., 13 November 1788. 'What afforded particular pleasure', the same report went on, 'was the harmony of different descriptions of men, the gentlemen of the establishment, with the dissenters, forgot all their distinctions, and only seemed anxious who should be most zealous in a cause equally interesting to both'.

28. See Chapter Two.

29. Again, these figures are abstracted from the Abolition Committee Minutes. See, in particular, the entries for 12 August 1788, 28 July 1789, 26 April and 29 November 1791.

30. Quoted in Griggs, p. 26.

31. Griggs, pp. 17, 29–30, 81; Wilson, p. x.

32. Diary of Katherine Plymley, 1066/1 (20 October 1791) and 1066/3 (22–30 October 1791).

33. Ibid., 1066/2 (21–2 October 1791).

34. Clarkson, *Strictures on a Life of W. Wilberforce*, p. xiii.

35. Abolition Committee Minutes, 7 August 1787.

36. John Barton to William Roscoe, 15 August 1787, Roscoe Papers, 920 ROS/ 247. Barton continued to cast a critical eye over Clarkson's progress. See also Barton to Roscoe, 28 September 1787, 920 ROS/248.

37. Clarkson, *History*, I, pp. 358–64, 426–35. Clarkson's account of this incident is revealing. He does not consider the wider issues involved in the case, or, indeed, the position (and reputation) of the London Committee. Instead, he simply records that: 'I saw the necessity of bearing up against the disappointment, and I endeavoured to discharge the subject from my mind with the following wish, that the narrow escape which the chief mate had experienced, and which was entirely owing to the accidental circumstances now explained, might have the effect, under Providence, of producing in him a deep contrition for his offence, and of awakening him to a serious attention to his future life' (p. 435).

38. Thomas Clarkson to Matthew Montagu, 28 August 1793.

39. Clarkson, *History*, II, pp. 123–66; Griggs, pp. 51–9.

40. The words are those of Elihu Robinson, one of Clarkson's Quaker friends, quoted in Wilson, p. 79.

41. Diary of Katherine Plymley, 1066/1 (20 October 1791). Clarkson is also reported to have said of Edmund Burke: 'Mr Burke must be mad, this is the favourable light to place his conduct in, if he is not mad he is worse'.

42. Ibid., 1066/3 (22–30 October 1791).

43. Ibid.

44. Dickson, 'Diary of a Visit to Scotland' (entry for 18 January 1792). The previous day Dickson had had to defend Clarkson against charges that at Liverpool he 'gave grog to the sailors, who said afterwards they had given him stories long as main-top-bowling'.

45. Griggs, pp. 58–9; Wilson, pp. 78–9.

46. See Chapter Two.

47. Griggs, pp. 83–4; Wilson, pp. 88–90.

48. Thomas Clarkson to Samuel Taylor Coleridge, 12 August, 6 December, 7 December 1808, 20 January 1809, Wordsworth Papers, Wordsworth Library, Grasmere. For Clarkson's relationship with the Coleridges, the Southeys, and the Wordsworths see Griggs, pp. 102–11; Robert Gittings and Jo Manton, *Dorothy Wordsworth*, Oxford, 1985, pp. 108–11, 164, 182–4, 211–12; Pamela Woof, ed., *Dorothy Wordsworth: The Grasmere Journals*, Oxford, 1991, pp. 30, 47–8, 50, 53, 54–7, 76–7, 83–4.

49. In all, Clarkson collected fifty-three subscriptions for the *Friend*. See Clarkson to Coleridge, 17 February, 4 March, 2, 25 April 1809, Wordsworth Papers.

50. Clarkson to Coleridge, 17 February 1809.

51. Clarkson to Coleridge, 19 June 1809.

52. Writing to Francis Jeffrey, editor of the *Edinburgh Review*, in July 1808 Coleridge explained: 'I do not hold Clarkson's fame dear because he is my friend; but I sought and cultivated his acquaintance, because a long and sober inquiry had assured me, that he had been, in an awful sense of the word, a benefactor of mankind: and this from the purest motives unalloyed by the fears and hopes of selfish superstition–and *not* with that feverish power which fanatics acquire by crowding together, but in the native strength of his own moral impulses. He, if ever human being did it, listened exclusively to his conscience, and obeyed its voice at the price of all of his

youth and manhood, at the price of his health, his private fortune, and the fairest prospects of honourable ambition'. Quoted in Griggs, p. 97.

53. Clarkson, *History*, I, pp. 409–10.

54. Ibid., p. 388.

55. Diary of Katherine Plymley, 1066/2 (21–2 October 1791). According to Katherine, Clarkson believed that if he went into Liverpool by day 'they would kill me, certainly kill me'. Later, her brother told her that 'Mr C had had several letters to tell him his life would be in danger should he be seen there'.

56. Clarkson to Montagu, 28 August 1793.

57. Diary of Katherine Plymley, 1066/2 (21–2 October 1791). 'Tho far from being thin', Katherine thought Clarkson had 'the look of very delicate health'. She goes on, quoting Clarkson: 'I can't be long together without eating, if I cou'd not have taken the liberty of asking for some cold meat today at one o'clock I shou'd have been quite ill by three'.

58. Clarkson to Montagu, 28 August 1793.

59. Clarkson, *History*, I, p. 408. See also Griggs, pp. 62–3.

60. Wilson, pp. 1, 11–12.

61. Griggs, pp. 79–90.

62. Abolition Committee Minutes, 29 April, 14 May, 9 July 1805; Clarkson, *History*, II, pp. 502–3.

63. Clarkson, *History*, II, p. 490.

64. Quoted in Wilson, p. 119.

65. Catherine Clarkson later explained that her husband had 'scarcely ever seen Mr Stephen's face till after the African Institution was formed'. See Catherine Clarkson to Wordsworth, 1838 (?); Wilson, p. 119. This is a slight exaggeration, although Clarkson and Stephen were clearly not well acquainted. For instance, the two men were both present at meetings of the London Committee on 6 June 1804, 23 April 1805, and 2 June 1806. See Abolition Committee Minutes.

66. Clarkson, *Strictures*, p. 7. This charge was originally made in a letter from Robert Wilberforce dated 18 July 1834. Later, in their *Life*, the Wilberforces retreated from this position, admitting that Clarkson *himself* had never claimed to have 'engaged' Wilberforce in the cause. See *The Life of William Wilberforce*, I, pp. 146–7.

67. *The Life of William Wilberforce*, I, pp. 9, 151–2, 228–32.

68. Ibid., p. 141.

69. Ibid., II, pp. 38–44, 51–5.

70. Griggs, p. 174.

71. Clarkson, *Strictures*, pp. 7–12; Catherine Clarkson to Wordsworth, 1838 (?); Griggs, pp. 170–1.

72. Clarkson, *Strictures*, pp. 30–46.

73. Ibid., pp. 63–83; Catherine Clarkson liked to claim that her husband had been 'the means of forming the committee & of applying to Mr W etc etc'. See Catherine Clarkson to Wordsworth, 1838 (?).

74. In 1807 Wordsworth had referred to Clarkson as the 'first [to] lead that enterprise sublime'. Later, in a new edition of his sonnets, published in 1838,

Wordsworth added the following note: 'This honour has, I am told, been denied to Mr Clarkson by the Sons of Mr Wilberforce, in the account of his life lately published by them ... Although in fact who might be first and who might be second, where such rare and high qualities were put forth by both labourers, is of little moment; yet, in case Mr C. should not himself think it worth while to take up the matter, I shall avail myself of some future occasion to make public the grounds of evidence upon which I first entertained, and still retain, the belief that I am not in error in having spoken as I have done through every part of this humble tribute to the virtues of my honoured friend'. See William Wordsworth, *Sonnets*, London, 1838, p. 148. Catherine Clarkson appears to have been particularly keen to enlist Wordsworth's help in this controversy. See Catherine Clarkson to William Wordsworth, 1838 (?), 30 September, 10 November 1838, Wordsworth Papers.

75. Clarkson, *Strictures*, pp. 7–11. Catherine was obviously in no doubt that James Stephen was behind the Wilberforces' attack on her husband. See Catherine Clarkson to William Wordsworth, 10 November 1838.

76. Griggs, p. 181.

77. Clarkson, *History*, I, pp. 271–4.

78. Abolition Committee Minutes, 1, 15, 29 July 1788.

79. The London Committee met over a hundred times between April 1791 and April 1796. In all, Wilberforce attended twenty-three of these meetings, eight between 21 December 1791 and 28 February 1792, and five between 29 January and 4 July 1793. Again, these figures are abstracted from the Abolition Committee Minutes.

80. Abolition Committee Minutes, 20 June, 4 July, 13 August 1793.

81. This emerges very clearly from the *Life*. See, for example, I, pp. 335–41.

82. See, for example, Granville Sharp to William Elford (chairman of the Plymouth committee), 29 December 1791, Clarkson Papers, Moorland-Spingarn Research Center, Howard University, Washington, D.C.

83. The phrase comes from J. T. Shewell's *Tribute to the Memory of Cowper*, quoted in Griggs, p. 191.

84. Henry C. Wright to Catherine Clarkson, 25 October 1845, Clarkson Papers, Moorland-Spingarn Research Center, Howard University.

85. Alexander Crummell, *The Man, the Hero, the Christian! A Eulogy on the Life and Character of Thomas Clarkson, delivered ... December 1846*, New York, 1847. Another edition, published in London, appeared in 1849. For Crummell see Wilson Jeremiah Moses, *Alexander Crummell: A Study of Civilization and Discontent*, New York, 1989; J. R. Oldfield, *Alexander Crummell (1819–1898) and the Creation of an African-American Church in Liberia*, Lewiston, New York, 1990.

86. Catherine Clarkson to Wordsworth, 1838 (?).

Chapter Four

COMMITTEES AND PETITIONS

IN recent years historians of British anti-slavery have become increasingly preoccupied with the provinces and the dynamics of popular abolitionism. And yet we still know very little about organised activity at the local level. In particular, little attention has been paid to the committee system, at least outside Manchester. How did it operate? How active were local committees, what exactly did they do, and what was the nature of their relationship with the London Committee? Secondly, we have only incomplete accounts of the petitioning process, that is, the way in which petitions were organised, and, as yet, no attempt has been made to study the language of petitions. Perhaps this neglect has something to do with the size of the task and the intractability of the sources. Nevertheless, with patience it is possible to recapture something of the intensity of the movement at the local level, its structure and its organisation.

At the heart of organised anti-slavery was the committee system. The earliest committees were set up to orchestrate the petition campaign of 1788. Typically, these committees assumed the task of collecting subscriptions and managing the petitions, which usually meant seeing to it that they were made available for signing and, ultimately, that they reached local MPs in time to be presented to the House of Commons. Frequently, as in the case of Sheffield and Manchester, the committees also had responsibility for drawing up the form of the petitions themselves. Some committees, as a result, were quite substantial affairs, dominated by activists like Thomas Walker and Thomas Cooper; the committees at Manchester, Bristol, Norwich, Birmingham, Nottingham, and Sheffield obviously fell into this category.[1] In other instances, the committees appear to have consisted of *all* the subscribers, any five of whom had power to 'dispose of the Money subscribed, for the Purpose intended; and to manage the Business'.[2] It was not unusual, therefore, for some local committees to survive only a matter of months, that is, as long as it took to get the petitions to London.

Later, when it became obvious that abolitionists were in for a long and hard struggle, the London Committee turned its thoughts to organising local committees on a more permanent basis, the obvious model being Manchester.[3] It was with this in mind that Thomas Clarkson was requested to undertake a tour of the south coast of England in the summer of 1788. Clarkson began his journey in Kent in July. After less than a month, however, he was back in London. The Committee minutes provide few details, but they make it clear that the reason was 'the difficulties which have occurred to [Mr Clarkson] during his late Journey of exciting a sufficient degree of public attention to form Committees'. This setback prompted the Committee to adopt a different plan—'by writing letters to those places where there [was] any probability of Country Committees being useful either to gain information or to add to the Funds of the Society'.[4] Clarkson, however, had greater success when he resumed his tour of the south coast in September, being instrumental in setting up committees in Poole and Plymouth.[5]

The London Committee met with a particularly favourable response in Exeter. In 1700 Exeter had been an important centre of the woollen trade and, outside London, one of the largest towns in the country. Competition from Yorkshire woollens, however, and the increasing importance of Dartmouth as a local port of registration, had seen Exeter decline quite dramatically during the course of the eighteenth century, losing ground to the industrial north and to neighbours like Plymouth.[6] The development of a broader service- and consumer-based economy to some extent cushioned the impact of Exeter's declining status, but the frustrations were obvious in a town with a strong dissenting tradition. Shopkeepers and representatives of the emerging professions, many of whom were Nonconformists, inevitably resented the influence of an elite, the City Chamber, in local politics, and, as time went on, grew louder in their demands for greater accountability; a Constitutional Society for the Redress of Grievances was organised in 1782. Growing middle-class radicalism was also reflected in the town's support for John Wilkes. Exeter's recorder, Serjeant Glynn, was one of Wilkes's most enthusiastic supporters and when in 1774 Wilkes was finally released from prison 'Exeter celebrated with illuminations and peals on the church bells'.[7]

Given this set of circumstances, it is not surprising to learn that Exeter petitioned strongly against the slave trade in 1788 or that many of its inhabitants now welcomed the committee idea.[8] The impetus came from Samuel Milford, a Unitarian, the son and son-in-law of serge makers, and co-founder in 1786 of the Exeter City Bank.[9] At a public meeting held on 10 June 1788 Milford and twenty-nine others organised a local Exeter committee 'to unite with the Society in London . . . [and] to take such measures from time to time, as may appear to them likely to promote this benevolent intention'.[10] All of these men, as one might expect, were representatives of Exeter's growing middle class and included in their number influential figures like Richard Hall Clarke, another banker, and Joseph Saunders, a prosperous woollen draper. A large number were also Nonconformists. At least eight were Quakers, among them Saunders, Thomas Sparkes, a druggist, Samuel Cross, a grocer, and John Dymond, a linen draper.[11] A further three, Thomas Morgan, James Manning, and Timothy Kenrick, were dissenting ministers.[12]

Between July 1788 and January 1789 the Exeter committee met no fewer than eight times, usually at the City Bank.[13] A large part of its activities involved fund-raising. By 1789 £362 6s. had been collected in and around Exeter, details of all the contributions being published in the *Sherborne Mercury*.[14] Here again, subscription lists appear to have been used quite deliberately to stimulate interest in abolition. The highlight of the committee's activities, however, was a general meeting at the Guildhall on 1 November 1788 convened by the mayor and addressed by Clarkson and Robert Paul, junior, 'who had been in the trade upwards of fifteen months [and] gave an account of what dreadful inhumanities he had been witness to during his continuance therein'. After an 'able' speech from Clarkson, the meeting closed with a series of resolutions, pointing out the enormities of the slave trade and reaffirming the committee's determination 'to put an end to the kidnapping, the depredations, the massacres, which are daily perpetrated on the innocent inhabitants of Africa; in short, to prohibit any further commerce in human flesh to that country'.[15]

The Exeter committee continued to meet through 1790 and 1791, albeit sporadically, and seems to have survived more or

less intact until the petition campaign of 1792.[16] Important as
Exeter was, however, it was rapidly eclipsed in the south-west of
England by the Plymouth committee, organised in November
1788. Unlike Exeter, Plymouth experienced rapid growth during
the eighteenth century and by 1801 was comfortably the eighth
largest town in England. It was also the centre of a wider regional
community that reached into north Cornwall and beyond.[17] For
these reasons the London Committee was especially anxious to
establish a presence in the area. Clarkson's visit in November
provided just the stimulus that was needed, but here again there
was an important local driving force in the shape of William
Elford, a partner in the banking firm of Elford, Tingcombe and
Clark, a friend of William Pitt, and later to become MP for
Plymouth. Elford and his colleagues, who included his son,
Jonathan Elford, and his business partner, John Tingcombe,
were to prove one of the most active and innovative of all local
committees, in the process helping to put Plymouth on the
provincial map as an important centre of abolitionist activity.[18]

Again, the Plymouth committee met regularly through 1788 and
early 1789, but its activities were altogether more ambitious than
those of the Exeter abolitionists. Not content with raising money,
which it did in significant amounts, the committee also sought to
influence the local (and national) debate through its own publications.[19] The most famous of these, of course, was the plan and
sections of a slave ship, 1,500 copies of which were ordered to be
'struck off and distributed gratis' on 29 December 1788. The
committee also arranged with one of its members, John Bidlake,
Headmaster of Plymouth Grammar School, to publish his *Slave-
Trade: A Sermon preached at Stonehouse Chapel* (1789). Bidlake
was an influential figure and his sermon, printed locally by
Haydon and Son, quickly ran through two impressions, the
proceeds from this and a similar piece by Robert Hawker, Vicar
of Charles Parish, going to the committee, which advertised both
publications extensively in the local press.[20]

The Plymouth committee, moreover, had its own corresponding
members, including William Prideaux of Modbury and the Rev.
Samuel Blatchford of Ford, Kingsbridge.[21] To judge from advertisements in the *Sherborne Mercury*, it was also successful in
attracting subscriptions from as far afield as Liskeard, St Austell,
and St Germans in Cornwall. More important still, given

Plymouth's connections with the sea, was the information that the committee was able to collect regarding the slave trade: a very early notice of its activities, for instance, thanks two men, James Brown and Thomas Bell, masters in the Royal Navy, for the 'very important intelligence they have already communicated, and for their offers of future intelligence'. Contacts of this kind gave the committee a unique vantage point. When rumours persisted that Clarkson had exaggerated the 'abuses and cruelties practised in the prosecution of this trade', William Elford intervened to assure readers of the *Sherborne Mercury* that 'the whole tenor of the extensive evidence, which their situation has enabled them to collect on the subject, corroborates and supports Mr Clarkson's accounts in the most positive and ample manner'.[22]

Exeter and Plymouth do not usually figure very prominently in histories of British anti-slavery, but here was evidence of energy, enthusiasm, and considerable ingenuity. How many other committees sustained this level of activity it is impossible to say.[23] Many existed only in name—this was certainly true of Birmingham and Nottingham, for instance—and even recognised centres like Manchester flagged badly after 1789. The Commons defeat of 1791, however, coincided with renewed interest in abolition. Several towns, among them Shrewsbury, held meetings to 'thank the members who had voted in favour of the object of their petition'. In Manchester a similar meeting on 23 May pledged 'never to desist in our endeavours till the people of Great Britain have wiped away this scandal from the Christian name'.[24] Thereafter, details of subscriptions began to appear regularly in the local press, while considerable space was also devoted to the progress of the boycott of West Indian sugar and rum. And with another petition campaign in prospect, the country committees again came back to life, along with some new committees that appeared for the first time.

Perhaps the most active of these new committees was the one established in Newcastle-upon-Tyne late in 1791. Newcastle was an old regional centre that unlike Exeter had managed to hold its own during the eighteenth century. One of the reasons for this was undoubtedly its broader economic base; Newcastle had a long history as a coal exporter, but it also had strong links with the glass industry, as well as salt and pottery.[25] Vigorous and wealthy though it was, however, the town was no stranger to labour disputes and had been badly shaken by the Wilkite agitation. Here again, there was a strong link between radicalism and dissent; Newcastle had one of the largest dissenting communities in the north of England, made up principally of Unitarians and Scots Presbyterians.[26] For all this, the town's response to abolition had been strangely muted. Only the corporation had petitioned in 1788; there had been no public meetings, no popular agitation, and, as far as one can tell, very little discussion of the subject at all in the local press.

Nevertheless, when Clarkson visited Newcastle in 1791 he met with a warm reception, not least from Thomas Allason, Vicar of Haddon-on-the-Wall, William Turner, a schoolmaster and minister of the wealthy Hanover Square Unitarian Chapel, and William Batson, a prosperous corn merchant.[27] Here, as it turned out, was the nucleus of the Newcastle committee that met for the first time in November of 1791. At this stage there was very little to be done except distributing tracts. Accordingly, at a second meeting on 20 December the committee took the decision to reprint and distribute 2,000 copies of the *Abstract* of the evidence against the slave trade. Significantly, no mention was made of petitions; encouraged no doubt by Clarkson, the committee studiously avoided the issue, offering only that 'nothing more will be necessary [to do away with the slave trade] than a plain Statement of Facts, by Persons who speak, not from Hearsay, but from actual Knowledge; and who were subject to be cross-examined by those who were interested to detect Misrepresentations'.[28]

Later, at a meeting on 13 January 1792, the committee revealed its true intentions. The result was a series of resolutions that provide a fascinating insight into organised activity at the local level. Arrangements were made to send one copy of the *Abstract* to each of the following: local sheriffs and justices of the peace; the mayors and aldermen of the corporations of Newcastle, Durham, and Berwick-upon-Tweed; the Master and Brethren of Trinity House and the Stewards of the several incorporated companies in Newcastle; and 'the officiating Minister of every Parish Church, the Minister of each Dissenting Congregation, the Stewards of the several Societies of Methodists, and the Clerks of the People called Quakers'. In addition, each copy of the *Abstract* was to be accompanied by a card from the Newcastle committee expressing their hope 'that a more thorough knowledge of the subject will produce a general disposition to join in a respectful Petition, or Petitions, to Parliament, for the entire abolition of this inhuman traffic'.[29]

In other parts of the country the petition campaign involved trying to breathe new life into committees that had long been inactive. Take the case of Nottingham. In 1788 management of the Nottingham petition had been put in the hands of a committee that included, among others, George Walker, the mayor, Joseph Lowe, and John Hawksley, a local druggist. Thereafter, it seems to have done very little. Seven of the original sixteen members, however, served on the 'new' Nottingham committee that was organised at a general meeting at the Change Hall on 22 December 1791.[30] The same level of continuity is evident in the case of the Birmingham committee, where again seven names appear on both lists, among them Charles Lloyd, the Quaker banker and philanthropist.[31] Some of these committees were obviously hurriedly revived to 'manage' local petitions, leaving little time to do much by way of distributing tracts or opinion-building; here, one suspects, a great deal often depended on individual rather than collective action. Others, like the Edinburgh committee, were far more energetic, orchestrating campaigns that clearly required careful thought and preparation.

The Edinburgh committee seems to have stirred into life during the spring of 1791. A general meeting was held in May to applaud the efforts of Wilberforce and the other Parliamentary supporters of abolition, and William Dickson visited the town later in the year, by which date the committee's chairman, Campbell Haliburton, was already in contact with the Committee in London.[32] Haliburton, it appears, was especially anxious to exploit the potential of the plan and sections of a slave ship and, at his request, the blocks were sent to Edinburgh in October, bound up with copies of Clarkson's *Abstract*. Soon both items were familiar sights north of the border. Katherine Plymley noted in her diary in February 1792 that 'the committee at Edinburgh have been very active . . . They have sent an abstract of the evidence to every clergyman throughout Scotland—they paste up a plan of a Slave ship wherever they think it will be seen by many, and desire the clergy to spread the abstract as far as possible'.[33] The committee was also responsible for *A Short Address to the People of Scotland, on the Subject of the Slave Trade* (1792), a thirty-page pamphlet which included extracts from Clarkson's *Abstract*, together with lines from William Roscoe's poem *The Wrongs of Africa*, as well as *Slavery: An Essay in Verse* (1792) by Captain J. Marjoribanks.

Similar initiatives came from other parts of Scotland. In 1791, for instance, the Glasgow committee printed and distributed *An Address to the Inhabitants of Glasgow, Paisley and the Neighbourhood*, which in a novel departure had stitched into it a copy of the plan and sections of a slave ship (a rare example, still intact, can be found in the Bodleian Library, Oxford). Elsewhere in the country, sermons and addresses were timed to coincide with the petition campaign, the obvious intention being to swell the number of likely signatures.[34] In the Welsh borders Joseph Plymley and the Shrewsbury committee worked tirelessly to organise petitions, Plymley himself riding hundreds of miles to collect signatures and generally promote the cause.[35] And, as ever, there was Clarkson spurring on the local committees as he toured the north of England in 1791, organising new committees, and distributing more copies of his *Abstract*. At times the pace was hectic, the excitement infectious. Newcastle, it seems, was gripped by abolition fever. Even the local playhouse caught the mood; *The West Indian*, *The Padlock*, and *Oroonoko* were all performed at the Theatre Royal during the early months of 1792.[36]

The country committees played an indispensable role in creating an anti-slavery consensus and, just as important, they provided the London Committee with a firm organisational base. Not least of their achievements was their success in raising funds. The records are sadly incomplete, but in 1788 alone the committees at Bristol, Sheffield, and Norwich all sent donations of £100 to London; Exeter, hardly an obvious centre of abolitionist activity, contributed £315.[37] Donations continued to come in from Birmingham and Norwich during the early months of 1789, while smaller sums were expended locally on advertising, pamphlets, and the management of petitions.[38] Subscriptions, ranging anywhere from 1s. 6d. to a guinea, were generally made to local banks or through the committees themselves. Religious and political affiliations obviously played a part here, as did business contacts, but committees also made extensive use of the local press. Advertisements and subscription lists were a common sight in provincial newspapers during the petition campaigns of 1788 and 1792; the *Newcastle Courant*, for instance, published weekly lists throughout the 1792 campaign, even if it meant printing only one or two names.[39] Here again, the role of social emulation is important. Newspapers provided a medium through which the public could test the social acceptability of abolition, its influence, and its political complexion.

Newspapers were also important because they enabled abolitionists to reach a wider public (significantly, there is no evidence that local committees corresponded with one another). The obvious example here is Manchester, which used the provincial press to dazzling effect in 1787–88 to announce its decision to petition the House of Commons.[40] Thereafter, the device was widely imitated. Most petition meetings arranged to publish their proceedings in the local press and many went further and inserted them in one or other of the London papers. The resolutions adopted at a meeting in Leeds on 24 January 1788, for instance, were published in 'the Leeds and York papers, the St James Chronicle and the London Packet'.[41] Publicity of this kind helped to create a 'competitive humanitarian market' in which abolition became inextricably linked with matters of civic pride. 'Let us not, my friends, be backward in so laudable a business', 'Clericus' told readers of the *Leeds Intelligencer* in 1788. 'This borough hath not been the last in other generous and humane designs. Let it not on this occasion be said, that we want either religion or humanity'. In a similar manner, Daniel Holt, editor of the *Newark Herald*, sought to interest his readers in the 1792 campaign by appealing to the progress already made in Birmingham, Leicester, and Loughborough, all near neighbours.[42]

The committee system, it is clear, transformed abolition into an important political force. Some of the committees, as we have seen, were remarkably resourceful, producing their own publications, lobbying local ministers and justices of the peace, and distributing thousands of prints and pamphlets. Others inevitably assumed a lower profile, but no obvious pattern emerges here; Plymouth, in its way, proved every bit as influential as many of the committees in the industrial north, Manchester included, and much the same can be said for Edinburgh or Glasgow. Important as local committees were, however, the real impetus came from London, not the provinces. This was as true of fund-raising and information-gathering as it was of petitioning. Throughout, the agenda was set by the London Committee and communicated to the provinces in a series of circular letters, reports, and requests for fresh subscriptions. The local committees, in effect, were treated as agents of the metropolitan group and, as far as one can tell, that is the function they performed.

Of course, the real purpose behind organised activity at the local level was the preparation of petitions to Parliament. Petitioning itself was not unusual; on the contrary, it was 'a normal avenue of popular political expression'. At the same time, however, it does appear to have gained momentum during the second half of the eighteenth century. The Middlesex election affair and the crisis in the American colonies both resulted in petitioning on a broad scale. Indeed, James Bradley estimates that 'at least 40,000 Englishmen were involved in popular agitation over America in the period 1775–8'.[43] Parliamentary reform also generated widespread support in the form of petitions to Parliament, creating a flurry of activity in 1783–84. And in Birmingham and the West Midlands the General Chamber of the Manufacturers of Great Britain (1785) demonstrated how petitioning could be utilised to give coherence to 'the manufacturing interest' as a new force in British politics.[44] By the late 1780s, in other words, petitions were being turned to with increasing regularity as a means of giving expression to middle-class concerns.

Petitions against the slave trade were usually one of three kinds. In the first place, there were the petitions emanating from universities, guilds, presbyteries, and provincial synods. In 1788 over twenty per cent of petitions fell into this category, among them the Manufacturers of Earthenware in Staffordshire and the universities of Cambridge, Aberdeen, and Glasgow. Four years later, in 1792, the number of these petitions rose to forty-seven (about ten per cent of the total), thanks in large part to the enthusiastic response from Scottish guilds and presbyteries.[45] Responsibility for organising and managing petitions of this kind presumably fell to the members of the guild or society concerned; certainly, they were generally too small to warrant setting up anything as formal as a business committee, as was the case with county and town petitions. Often it required only one local activist to provide the necessary momentum. In

Leicestershire, for instance, fifty clergymen led by Thomas Greaves, Rector of Broughton Astley, defied the archdeacon to petition Parliament in 1792, arguing that 'when the zeal of a large portion of the laity for abolishing the odious traffic in our fellow creatures seems to have revived with additional fervour . . . silence on our part would be a dereliction of our duty as Men, as Britons, and as consistent Ministers of the Gospel'.[46]

Then there were the petitions emanating from counties. In 1788 and again in 1792 the number of these petitions was relatively small, barely reaching double figures. The problem here, one assumes, was that county petitions were difficult to organise, involving careful planning and co-ordination. To take one example, in 1788 copies of the Nottinghamshire petition were circulated to ten different towns around the county, responsibility for which was left in the hands of a committee of fifteen under the chairmanship of the Hon. Henry Stanley. The committee met for the first time on 13 March, but it was not until 25 June that the Nottinghamshire petition finally reached the House of Commons.[47] Three months was an unusually long time to take over a petition and it was this sort of calculation that undoubtedly deterred many in 1792, particularly given the secrecy surrounding the second, larger campaign. Numbers were an important consideration here, as well, hence the emphasis on towns, although the London Committee insisted that 'petitions from Towns will not render those from Counties unnecessary'.[48] Nevertheless, it is perhaps not accidental that only four English counties petitioned Parliament in 1792—Shropshire, Derbyshire, Northumberland, and Staffordshire—together with Pembroke, Cardigan, Hereford, Monmouth, Montgomeryshire, Dumfries, Banff, and Stirling.[49]

Far more numerous were the town or borough petitions. But here again, there were important distinctions. In some towns the corporation petitioned, in others the 'inhabitants', in others again privileged groups (nobility, magistracy, freemen, 'principal inhabitants'), or any combination of the above. In 1788, for instance, some seven or eight corporations petitioned Parliament in their own right, while a further twenty-five petitioned jointly with other groups, together representing about thirty per cent of all petitions. In 1792 this figure fell to sixteen per cent, although in a handful of cases the mayor, bailiff or portreeve, as the head of the corporation, acted alone and joined the petition movement.[50] At the same time, the number of petitions which came from 'inhabitants' only increased from twenty-five per cent to just over fifty per cent. Drescher puts the 1792 figure somewhat higher.[51] In sixteen cases, however, those petitioning are described in the *Commons Journal* as the 'principal inhabitants' of their respective towns and parishes. Twenty-two petitions, moreover, refer explicitly to electors, magistrates, or freeholders, as well as 'inhabitants', while no less than fifty-five refer explicitly to clergymen and gentlemen. Put another way, over one third of the borough petitions in 1792 involved 'some corporate or special status group', to say nothing of those inhabitants' petitions which may well have included privileged citizens.[52]

In large part, the increasing number of inhabitants' petitions can be attributed to the sheer size and scale of the 1792 campaign. By contrast with 1788 many of the areas petitioning in 1792 were little more than villages or small hamlets, places like Chesham in Buckinghamshire and St Just in Cornwall.[53] Local politics also played a part in determining who petitioned in these circumstances. In Exeter, for instance, the City Chamber refused to petition in 1788, or, indeed, to join with the 'Mayor, Gentlemen, Clergy and other Inhabitants', because 'they thought it a presbyterian Trick'.[54] The linkage between abolition, dissent, and radical politics would continue to alienate many at the local level, particularly those with one eye on events in France. Moreover, as corporations up and down the country rushed to condemn the revolution and express their loyalty to King and Parliament, abolition understandably took on a very different complexion. Nevertheless, it would be misleading to conclude that abolition necessarily divided corporations and 'inhabitants', or that it was necessarily perceived as an anti-corporation issue. Admittedly, there were disputes, but many more corporations petitioned Parliament in 1792 than was the case in 1788, a large number, sixty-two in all, petitioning jointly with other groups, and eighteen petitioning in their own right.[55]

Typically, with county and town petitions the petitioning process began with a requisition from local citizens to the sheriff (county) or mayor (town) to hold an appropriate meeting. In most cases this was a formality, but opposition did sometimes occur, especially during the 1792 campaign. At Wenlock in Shropshire, for instance, Joseph Plymley found himself facing a possible rebellion led by George Forester, formerly the local MP. Forester, it seems, had 'set his face against the abolition' and Plymley had to work very hard to rally the local burgesses before the meeting at last went ahead on 6 March.[56] At Hertford, meanwhile, the mayor refused to lend the townspeople the use of the town hall, and abolitionists encountered similar obstacles in Monmouth.[57] William Burgh confessed to Wilberforce in December 1791 that as far as obtaining a petition from Yorkshire was concerned a great deal would depend on the sheriff, adding that,

> some prudence will be requisite to prevent the discussion of other subjects being brought before the assembled County for the sake of splitting interests etc. Our Enemies I know are always on the watch to do this mischief; if they have not the Wisdom I will give them full Credit for all the malice and Venom of the Serpent.[58]

As Burgh's comments suggest, opposition was sometimes carried through to petition meetings themselves. At Malton, in Yorkshire, 'a letter was read from the great proprietor of the town to the people convened there for the purpose of Petitioning, dissuading his tenants from such a measure'.[59] Animosities also surfaced at Tiverton in 1792, where the Town Clerk, Beavis Wood, opposed the petition idea on the grounds that 'the *sudden* abolition proposed would not be safe or prudent'. The battle lines in Tiverton were clearly drawn, those sponsoring the petition, among them George and Martin Dunsford, being identified with a group of seditious Jacobins and local 'anti-Corporators'. 'I did not attend the Committee', Wood noted in his journal on 20 February, 'as I know the trim of the parties concerned, and that it would be difficult if not impossible to remove any impression or opinion they had taken'. A petition was at length proposed, signed, and sent to Dudley Ryder, the local MP, but here again the corporation stood aloof, refusing to join the 'Mayor, Clergy and other respectable Inhabitants of Tiverton'.[60]

Petition meetings could also be disrupted by squabbles among abolitionists themselves. Usually, the task of drafting and presenting the form of a petition was entrusted to the local committee or some other interested party. The authority of these men to direct proceedings did not always pass unchallenged, however. In Sheffield, for instance, William Mason reported that three petitions had been produced at the first meeting in 1792 and that 'disputes ran high concerning which was to be preferred'. During the same campaign, Mason was himself involved in a heated confrontation at Rotherham, where a Quaker by the name of Payne brought in 'a violent Paper not in the least couched in petitionary terms'.[61] Nevertheless, disputes of this kind were unusual. Most meetings, it seems, were orderly, businesslike, and good-natured. At Durham in 1792 the mayor was followed on the platform by William Hoar, 'who very pathetically and with great ability and perspicuity showed the cruelty, impolicy, injustice and immorality of this inhuman traffic. The subject then underwent a very able and temperate discussion and the business was conducted with perfect unanimity'. Dickson reported from Edinburgh on 6 March that 'when the Dean of Faculty spoke a pin might have been heard to drop—not a whisper but when plaudits made the whole place resound'.[62]

Petition meetings usually took the form of a series of resolutions that were printed verbatim in the local press. It is easy to overlook the significance of these resolutions, but they were, in fact, an important part of the petitioning process. At Carlisle in 1792, for instance, the town meeting began with a series of eight resolutions, among them the following:

1. That the exercise of the Slave Trade has a necessary tendency to encourage and perpetuate the vicious usages and institutions which prevail in that country [Africa], and to obstruct other commercial intercourse with the inhabitants, as well as an improvement in their moral character and civil condition.

2. That the sufferings of the Slaves in the Middle Passage are inseparable from the Trade.

3. That it is contrary to uniform experience, and to the known laws of nature, that any class of human beings who are properly treated, and placed in a climate suiting their constitution, should not be able to keep up their numbers.

4. That consequently to prohibit the future importation of Slaves is only to lay the Planters under a necessity of forming and executing proper dispositions and regulations in favour of the Negroes already in those islands, which dispositions and

regulations, without such necessity, we conceive will not be formed, or if formed, will not be executed.[63]

Significantly, it was not until the ninth resolution that the meeting got to the subject of a petition.

Elsewhere, resolutions appear to have been used as a safety valve to deal with potentially embarrassing situations. At Rotherham, William Mason managed to persuade Payne that his 'violent Paper' would be better served as a resolution and 'withdrew in a committee to arrange it in that mode'. The result, which Mason considered 'still too flaming', is worth quoting in full, providing as it does an insight into official thinking (in what was a sensitive political climate), as well as the dynamics of popular abolition.[64] 'Although we have had the Mortification to find that similar Petitions to the present have been ineffectual', the resolution began,

> we are determined to persevere in our Application to our Representatives, with an additional Fervour, in Hopes that they may finally enact a Law for that most benevolent Purpose, and by so doing, clear the Land from the Guilt of Blood; nor suffer History to record that the Parliament of Great Britain was the Advocate of Slavery, at the Time when the Virtue of the People demanded its Annihilation.[65]

Once a meeting had agreed on the form of a petition it was left open for signature, usually at the town hall or exchange. Sometimes petitions were also left in coffee houses and local inns. Copies of the 1788 Nottinghamshire petition, for instance, could be found at the 'White Lion' in Nottingham, the 'Kingston's Arms' in Newark, the 'Swan Inn' in Mansfield, the 'Crow' in Retford, the 'George' in Worksop, the 'Saracen's Head' in Southwell, the 'Red Lion' in Tuxford, the 'Hugh Pole Inn' in Ollerton, the 'Angel' in Blythe, and the 'King's Arms' in Bingham.[66] In other cases, signatures were received at local shops, hotels, banks, and printing offices.[67] The whole process might take only a matter of weeks. Many of the petitions prepared in 1792 seem to have reached Parliament within a fortnight, creating intense pressure at the grass-roots level, particularly during the later stages of the campaign. Manchester, in 1788, let its petition circulate for nearly a month, while, as we have seen, the

Nottinghamshire petition took longer still, but in most areas of the country the excitement was over almost as soon as it had started.[68]

Not content with petitioning, some local inhabitants went further and 'instructed their Members to support [abolition] by their votes'. The *Diary* reported in April 1792 that 'in many parts of the country parties are forming to support those only in the next Sessions as their Representatives, who will do their utmost to exterminate this greatest of all human evils'. We can see this most clearly in Tewkesbury, formerly the seat of Sir William Coddrington, who himself had large interests in the West Indies. When in 1792 Coddrington's nephew, Captain Dowdeswell, offered himself for election, the people apparently insisted 'on his promising his vote for abolition' before they would give him their support. Dowdeswell prevaricated, whereupon the townspeople declared themselves in favour of his rival, Captain Lloyd. This was enough to force Dowdeswell's hand, or so it would seem. Within days he published a letter in the local newspaper agreeing to support abolition, thereby securing himself the seat. It was a small episode, but further proof of the growing assertiveness of the provincial middle classes.[69]

Some idea of the intensity of the campaign at the local level emerges from the diaries of Katherine Plymley. Katherine's brother, Joseph, Curate of Leebotwood and Longnor, was an early convert to the cause and in 1788 had been instrumental in securing petitions from each of the archdeaconries of Shropshire.[70] Later, in 1790, he had been introduced to the members of the London Committee through Dr Baker and thereafter 'continued from time to time doing all in his power for the cause by inserting arguments in papers, conversing with company on the subject and by subscribing himself and procuring subscriptions from many [others]'.[71] The campaign of 1792 found Plymley a busy man. Late January and the early part of February were taken up preparing requisitions for local and county meetings and sorting out the difficulties at Wenlock. Once these were out of the way, Plymley turned his attention to drawing up petitions for the 'County, Town [Shrewsbury], Ludlow, Bridgnorth and one for the Franchises of Wenlock'. He also played a vital role in the meetings themselves, orchestrating proceedings at Shrewsbury on 17 February and arranging for Mr Egdon, the mayor, to second the county petition.[72]

Plymley's efforts did not end there, however. The next day, 18 February, he went to Shrewsbury 'for the purpose of obtaining more names to the petition'.[73] Over the next few weeks this would become a familiar pattern. Plymley was in Shrewsbury again on 25 February, this time collecting signatures for the county petition. Significantly, Katherine kept a meticulous record of the progress of both campaigns. On 23 February she noted that 300 people had signed the Shrewsbury petition and 100 the county petition. A week later the county petition had grown to 360 names and on 10 March Katherine reported with evident satisfaction that the final figure was 464, including fifty-seven clergymen.[74] Plymley's diary is invaluable because it reveals how important figures like her brother were at the local level. These were the men who made petitions possible, particularly in the more remote areas of the country. Katherine recognised this herself when she wrote in her diary on 17 February: 'the meetings today though very respectfully attended yet fully evinced the necessity and good effect of my Brother's zeal and activity, for there were but few appear'd with whom he had not some previous intercourse either in person or by letter; and as few as those he had conversed with were absent'.[75]

Agents like Plymley obviously tried to control every stage of the petitioning process, from drafting petitions to collecting signatures. As far as possible, they also tried to control who signed local petitions. The London Committee, for its part, was concerned only that petitioners should be 'respectable', an important word in the abolitionists' vocabulary. In practice, this meant excluding certain groups, among them women and, in some cases, illiterate labourers.[76] Elsewhere, it seems likely that no one under the age of fifteen was allowed to sign, although, as one observer admitted, 'there is scarce any preventing boys or at least improper people from signing'.[77] Frequently, decisions had to be made on the spot. Approached by Dr Beddoes about the propriety of organising a petition from Shifnal, Joseph Plymley at first hesitated, fearing that petitions from 'such small towns' might be 'ridiculed', as indeed they were.[78] The problem was a very real one, namely, how best to weigh the zeal of local inhabitants (whoever they were) against the wider interests of the movement, as dictated by the Committee in London.

As we have seen, the respectability of petitions was to become a major issue in 1792. Colonel Tarleton, for one, claimed that 'the magistrates of the places whence these extraordinary Petitions have originated, have seldom been approached'. 'The Town Halls', he went on, 'have still more rarely had these Petitions displayed in them, in order to await the deliberation, the decision, or the signatures of the grave, respectable, and informed part of the community'.[79] Others went further, questioning the authority and competence of the inhabitants of 'small market towns . . . to dictate to our Parliament what is proper to be done in this affair'. As a correspondent in the *Gentleman's Magazine* put it in 1792: 'a petition from Manchester, or such places, or from a county at large, may be supposed to be formed by gentlemen who are competent to judge; but are men, who never read more than the provincial paper, and whose *summum bonum* is getting drunk at an ale-house, are they fit people to decide on the existence of our Western possessions?' Here, for many, was the crux of the matter, the proper relationship between London and the provinces and between 'gentlemen' and butchers, miners, and barbers.[80]

Of course, respectability is a relative term. As we have seen, privileged groups (nobility, clergy, magistrates, and so on) did, in fact, support the abolition of the slave trade in large numbers. Needless to say, there were abuses, even abolitionists recognised that. But given the size and scale of the 1792 campaign the wonder is that they did not occur more often. All of which brings us back to the question of organisation. What emerges very clearly from both campaigns is the effectiveness of agents and country committees in shaping and directing the movement at the grass-roots level. Critics may not have liked what they saw, but in 1788 and again in 1792 men like Plymley showed that at relatively short notice it was possible to mobilise public opinion on an unprecedented scale, not just in England (or the industrial north), but across the country, in England, Scotland, and Wales. Theirs was a remarkable achievement, a demonstration of strength, solidarity, and growing middle-class independence.

The petition campaigns of 1788 and 1792 have figured so largely in the recent historiography of British anti-slavery because they are the only means we have of measuring popular support for abolition. The numbers involved are, indeed, startling. In 1792 3,865 people signed the Edinburgh petition 'on the spot at different tables all with the most admirable decorum'. The final figure was 10,885, exceeded only by the 15,000 to 20,000 reported to have signed the Manchester petition.[81] In all, some 400,000 people may have put their names to petitions in 1792, but just as important as the size of the campaign was its range and diversity. In Northumberland, for instance, even market towns like Belford (400 signatures), Wooler (400 signatures), and Alnick (600 signatures) organised petitions, adding their voices to the gentlemen and ship owners of North and South Shields. Cornwall also rose up in 1792, not just mining towns like Redruth, but small villages, too: St Mawes, Grampound, Tregony, East Looe, and St Germans (all Parliamentary seats).[82]

Any estimate of this kind is necessarily tentative, but 400,000 petitioners would represent about thirteen per cent of the adult male population of England, Scotland, and Wales in 1791 (assuming, of course, that most petitioners were males over the age of fifteen).[83] Taking the same measure, Exeter's 1,000 or more petitioners in 1788 represented about sixteen per cent of its adult population; Sheffield's 2,000 petitioners about twenty-two per cent of its adult male population. It is not inconceivable, therefore, that in some parts of the country between a quarter and a third of the adult male population petitioned Parliament. In Manchester in 1792 the figure was possibly as high as fifty per cent.[84] By any standard (and estimates based on the number of male household heads would inflate these figures still further) this was a movement of quite staggering proportions.

Numbers are one thing. Petitions can also tell us a great deal about the mental outlook of those men (and women) who supported abolition of the slave trade in the late eighteenth century. But first a word of caution. Petitions were frequently the work of a small handful of activists, those men most closely associated with the movement at the local level—figures like Plymley, for instance. The London Committee, moreover, also had an input into the shape and form of petitions, most notably during the campaign of 1792. As a guide to popular feeling on abolition, therefore, petitions have obvious limitations. But, taken together with the resolutions passed by public meetings up and down the country, they do shed important light on anti-slavery discourse during this period, its content, character, and, above all, its relevance to middle-class concerns.

To begin with, most petitions addressed the slave trade as a religious issue. Petitioners frequently referred to the trade as 'unchristian', meaning that it was either 'repugnant', 'reproachful', or 'inconsistent with the Profession of the Christian religion'.[85] The clergy within the Archdeaconry of Leicester, for example, felt bound,

> as Ministers of that Holy Religion which inculcates universal love, humbly to remonstrate against a traffic, which is a constant violation of the most essential duties of Christianity—and which, if continued under the sanction of the British Legislature, may be expected to bring down upon this country the severest judgement of Heaven.[86]

The slave trade also had a significance for the Church's wider mission and the progress of Christianity in general, a popular theme in the late eighteenth century. The inhabitants of Leeds could not 'but lament the invincible prejudices of these unenlightened Heathen, against our common Christianity, which must arise in their Minds, from the cruelty and injustice of those Christian States who are the authors of their present misery'.[87] Britain, in other words, was setting herself against God's divine purpose, inviting yet more displeasure.

Religious considerations dovetailed neatly with what we might call a broader humanitarian response. All petitioners were agreed that the slave trade was 'inhuman' or 'fundamentally unjust and enormously oppressive'.[88] Many went further, evoking images that sought to give expression to middle-class anxieties. The Devon petition of 1788, for instance, began with a passionate denunciation of 'that iniquitous, cruel and infamous traffic carried on between Africa and America—by dragging our fellow creatures from everything dear to them into slavery'.[89] The language used here is revealing. Slaves were frequently referred to as 'our fellow creatures'; abolitionists, in turn, liked to describe themselves as 'friends to humanity'. Similarly, it was not uncommon to draw out the cruelty of the slave trade in this way, the breaking up of families, the practice of 'purchasing harmless Men, Women and Children, to sell in British Dominions for Slaves'.[90] The trade, in short, was offensive. The inhabitants of Birmingham spoke for many when they told Parliament that while they had 'the commercial interests of this kingdom very deeply at heart', they could not conceal their 'detestation of any commerce which always originates in violence and too often terminates in cruelty'.[91]

As human beings, of course, slaves were entitled to rights and liberties. The slave trade, according to the inhabitants of Plymouth, was an 'invasion of the natural rights of mankind'. 'To traffic with the personal liberty of our Fellow-Creatures is equally abhorrent to the Laws of God and Man', echoed the 1788 Nottingham meeting.[92] Such sentiments, drawing as they did on rationalist thought and the contemporary debate on Parliamentary reform, had a powerful hold over middle-class Britons, but by 1792 they had begun to assume a very different resonance and meaning. As a consequence, the petition campaign of that year contained relatively few references to liberty or to the rights of man. Nevertheless, some petitioners did try to negotiate these obstacles as best they could. The inhabitants of Topsham, for instance, could not help expressing their conviction that the 'exercise of the African Slave Trade [was] injurious to the natural and inherent rights and privileges of mankind', but did so, they were at pains to point out, as 'loyal subjects of these kingdoms'.[93]

The slave trade, then, violated the principles of religion, humanity, and liberty. As was to emerge with greater clarity from the 1792 campaign, it was also impolitic. The inhabitants of Halifax, to take one example, put it forward as their belief that 'by wholesome Laws and humane Treatment of the Negroes already in the islands, the Cultivation of the West India Estates would be effected at a less Expense, without any Importations [of slaves]'.[94] Like other petitioners, they also drew attention to the ruinous effect of the trade on the health and lives of British seamen, and pointed out the obvious advantages of setting up a reciprocal trade with Africa 'in the various Produce and Manufactures of both Countries, on Terms far more advantageous to Great Britain'.[95] Several petitions, like those from Stafford and Leicester, even identified the slave trade as the 'fundamental cause' of insurrections in the West Indies. 'The late insurrection at St Domingo proves only "That a slave watches his opportunity to get free"', echoed the inhabitants of Carlisle, adding that 'the existence of this principle cannot, without extreme injustice, be ascribed to the discussion and transactions which have passed upon the subject in England'.[96]

The trade stood condemned, but so, too, did the nation. For many petitioners, the continued existence of the slave trade was quite literally a 'National disgrace'.[97] In the words of the Halifax meeting of February 1788, it was 'unworthy the Character of Britons to support Commerce by Slavery'. Why? Because Britain was the 'most liberal Nation on Earth'.[98] The slave trade, argued the inhabitants of Plymouth, was 'directly opposite to that inherent love of freedom which characterises this nation. We, who are jealous, to the most sensible degree, of any encroachment of our own rights, ought by all means to discourage every infringement of the happiness of others'.[99] Abolitionists played on this theme constantly. During the 1792 campaign, for instance, Britain was described time and time again as a 'free and enlightened nation', a phrase that became almost a taunt to prompt Parliament into taking action against the slave trade. It followed that abolition would somehow reflect glory on the British people. Abolition, according to the *Leeds Intelligencer*, would 'raise the true glory and honour of the British empire to an infinitely higher pitch than all the victories of a Marlborough, a Hawke, or an Alexander could ever achieve'. 'Let none be afraid of espousing the cause of the Negro', proclaimed an editorial in the *Newark Herald* in 1792, "tis the cause of mercy, 'tis the cause of our country—and sooner or later it shall succeed'.[100]

Abolition of the slave trade, in other words, was inextricably linked with the character and destiny of the British nation itself. Such an appeal would have been unthinkable before 1783. But the loss of the American colonies forced Britons to think about themselves and about their failings: 'They had been corrupt and presumptuous, and they had warred against fellow Protestants. And they had been duly punished'.[101] It only remained now to make an act of atonement. America also provided petitioners with an example of a rather different kind. The revolution, after all, had been about ideas and principles, not least of which were liberty and equality. Seen in these terms, abolition was a way for Britons to redress the balance, to reaffirm their commitment to liberty at a time when Americans seemed to have gained the upper hand. Such concerns, considerations of prestige and national character, help to explain broad, middle-class support for abolition, its momentum, and, indeed, its relevance. As Linda Colley argues: 'after the American war anti-slavery was increasingly seized on as a means to redeem the nation, as a patriotic act'.[102]

What gave added impetus to this debate were contemporary ideas about progress. According to David Spadafora, a doctrine of general, indefinite progress gained rapid ascendency in England after 1760.[103] Material progress was the most obvious and visible evidence for the popularisation of such beliefs, but so, too, were population growth, the progress of liberty, and changing attitudes towards animals, children, women, the insane, and the sick. Until the American war there was perhaps no pressing reason to question how the slave trade fitted in with such ideas of general progress, but thereafter it assumed a particular significance. As we have seen, many petitioners during the campaigns of 1788 and 1792 implied that the trade was not only immoral but also curiously outmoded, an affront to human sensitivity, and an impediment to future progress. The inhabitants of the Isle of Wight went further, expressing their conviction that, freed of the slave trade, the diffusion of science, the 'influence of every humanising art, and especially the all-healing blessings of our mild religion' would reach 'an exaltation and extent which the prepossessed and illiberal have never had in contemplation'.[104]

Here, in other words, was a discourse which identified petitioners with progress, change, sensitivity, and compassion, with what we might call 'modernity'. (The slave trade, by implication, was associated with everything that was old, corrupt, and decaying.) As we have seen, such ideas already enjoyed wide currency among the middle and lower middle classes. Nevertheless, it was unusual to find them expressed in so coherent and forceful a manner. Viewed in this light, the petitions were further evidence not only of a quite remarkable shift in social attitudes, but of a growing political assertiveness. The same was true of the committee system. More transitory perhaps than some of the political clubs of the 1760s and 1770s, country committees nevertheless helped to break down narrow sectarian bounds, bringing together different elements from within the urban middle classes. Such societies conferred on their members considerable prestige and political power. Put another way, the campaigns of 1788 and 1792 were part of a much broader movement, described by Brewer and Money and others, which saw the middling sort breaking away from 'the constraints of patrician political patronage and control' and asserting themselves more and more in the public sphere.[105] They were, in short, part of the 'making' of the British middle class.

Notes

1. For the Manchester committee see *Manchester Mercury*, 1, 8, 15 January 1788; Drescher, *Capitalism and Antislavery*, pp. 67–88.

2. See, for example, *Nottingham Journal*, 9 February 1788 (Chesterfield meeting).

3. Abolition Committee Minutes, 12 August 1788.

4. Ibid., 26 August 1788.

5. Clarkson, *History*, II, pp. 4–7.

6. Wrigley, 'Urban Growth and Agricultural Change', pp. 42–3, 47, 78–9; Robert Newton, *Eighteenth-Century Exeter*, Exeter, 1984, pp. 65–7. Wrigley estimates that the population of Exeter increased from 16,000 c. 1750 to just 17,000 in 1801.

7. Newton, *Eighteenth-Century Exeter*, pp. 76–83; W. G. Hoskins, *Two Thousand Years in Exeter*, pp. 84–5.

8. *Exeter Flying Post*, 14 February, 13, 20 March 1788; *Sherborne Mercury*, 31 March 1788. Over a thousand people were reported to have signed the Exeter petition in 1788.

9. Newton, *Eighteenth-Century Exeter*, pp. 65–6.

10. *Sherborne Mercury*, 29 May, 16 June 1788.

11. Select Monthly Meetings of the East Division of Devon, held at Exeter, 1776–1783, Devon Record Office, Exeter, 874 D/M2–6; Minute Books of Monthly Meetings of the East Division of Devon, held at Cullompton, Spiceland, etc., 1785–1792, Devon Record Office, 874 D/M23; *Exeter Pocket-Journal*, 1791; *Universal British Directory*, 1798.

12. Allan Brockett, *Nonconformity in Exeter, 1650–1875*, Manchester, 1962, pp. 140–1, 147–9, 153–9. Morgan, Manning, and Kenrick were all Presbyterians. Manning's brother, George, a wealthy merchant, was also a member of the Exeter committee.

13. *Sherborne Mercury*, 31 July, 24, 31 October, 6, 10, 24 November 1788, 12 January 1789; *London Chronicle*, 2–4 December 1788.

14. See, in particular, *Sherborne Mercury*, 24 November 1788.

15. Ibid., 6 November 1788.

16. Ibid., 19 August 1790, 28 July 1791.

17. Wrigley, 'Urban Growth and Agricultural Change', pp. 42–3.

18. *Sherborne Mercury*, 8 December 1788. For Elford see *Dictionary of National*

Biography, VI, p. 600. Elford was successively Mayor of Plymouth (1797), Recorder (1798–1833), and MP (1796–1806).

19. Between December 1788 and February 1790 over £130 was raised locally by the Plymouth committee. Of this sum, £100 was sent to London, £5 12s. expended on collecting evidence, and a further £3 14s. 6d. on advertising. See *Sherborne Mercury*, 8, 22 December 1788, 5, 19 January, 16 February 1789, 1 February 1790.

20. *Sherborne Mercury*, 5, 19 January, 2 February, 2 March 1789.

21. Ibid., 8 December 1788, 19 January 1789.

22. Ibid., 8 December 1788, 1 February 1790.

23. A great deal, obviously, depended on the efforts of figures like Milford and Elford, the local chairmen. These were the men who were responsible for sustaining the movement at the local level, carrying much of the burden of collecting funds, and providing a vital link between London and the provinces. Some, like Milford, welcomed these new responsibilities, but others became distracted or involved with other projects.

24. Diary of Katherine Plymley, 1066/4 (30 October 1791–9 February 1792); *Newcastle Courant*, 11 June 1791.

25. Wrigley, 'Urban Growth and Agricultural Change', pp. 42–3, 78–9; R. J. Morris, 'Voluntary Societies and British Urban Elites, 1780–1850: An Analysis', in Peter Borsay, ed., *The Eighteenth-Century Town*, pp. 340–1.

26. James E. Bradley, *Religion, Revolution and English Radicalism: Nonconformity in Eighteenth-Century Politics and Society*, Cambridge, 1990, pp. 255–6.

27. Clarkson, *History*, II, pp. 351–2; Friends House Library, MS Vol. 294 (329); *Universal British Directory*, 1798. For Turner and the Hanover Square congregation see Bradley, *Religion, Revolution and English Radicalism*, pp. 255–6; John Seed, 'Gentlemen Dissenters: The Social and Political Meanings of Rational Dissent in the 1770s and 1780s', *Historical Journal*, 28, 1985, pp. 302–3.

28. *Newcastle Chronicle*, 17, 24 December 1791.

29. *Newcastle Courant*, 21 January 1792.

30. *Nottingham Journal*, 16 February 1788; *Newark Herald*, 28 December 1791; Clarkson, *History*, II, p. 352. The seven men concerned were: Rev. Mr Bigsby, Francis Evans, George Walker, John Hawksley, Samuel Storer, Francis Hart, and Robert Denison.

31. *Aris's Birmingham Gazette*, 7 January 1788, 6 February 1792. For Charles Lloyd see *Dictionary of National Biography*, XI, pp. 1288–9. Another member of the Birmingham committee was Samuel Garbett, one of the prime movers behind the General Chamber of the Manufacturers of Great Britain. See J. Money, 'Birmingham and the West Midlands, 1760–1793', esp. pp. 297–302.

32. Abolition Committee Minutes, 31 May, 29 August 1791.

33. Ibid., 25 October 1791; Diary of Katherine Plymley, 1066/4 (30 October 1791–9 February 1792).

34. See, for example, *Sherborne Mercury*, 27 February 1792 (meeting at

Ashburton); *Newcastle Courant*, 18 February 1792 (meeting at North Shields).

35. For Plymley see Section 2 below.
36. *Newcastle Courant*, 28 January, 4 February, 3 March 1792.
37. Abolition Committee Minutes, 19 February, 1 April 1788; *Morning Chronicle*, 23 December 1788; *Sherborne Mercury*, 24 November 1788.
38. Abolition Committee Minutes, 14 April 1789.
39. See, for example, *Newcastle Courant*, 14, 21, 28, January, 4, 11, 18, 25 February 1792.
40. Drescher, *Capitalism and Antislavery*, pp. 67–70.
41. *Leeds Intelligencer*, 5 February 1788. See also *Newark Herald*, 28 December 1791 (Nottingham meeting).
42. Drescher, *Capitalism and Antislavery*, p. 76; *Leeds Intelligencer*, 22 January 1788; *Newark Herald*, 15 February 1792.
43. Bradley, *Religion, Revolution and English Radicalism*, pp. 317–19.
44. Money, 'Birmingham and the West Midlands, 1760–1793', pp. 297–301.
45. These figures and those that follow are abstracted from the *Commons Journal*, XLIII, 1788, and XLVII, 1792.
46. *Gentleman's Magazine*, LXII, 1792, p. 230; *Commons Journal*, XLVII, 1792, p. 612.
47. *Nottingham Journal*, 15 March 1788; *Commons Journal*, XLIII, 1788, p. 601.
48. Wedgwood Papers, 24739.32 (circular letter of 19 January 1792).
49. *Commons Journal*, XLVII, 1792, pp. 558 (Banff), 565 (Shropshire), 579 (Pembroke and Hereford), 589 (Cardigan and Staffordshire), 601 (Stirling), 622 (Montgomeryshire), 627 (Dumfries, Derby, Northumberland, and Monmouth).
50. Again, these figures are abstracted from the *Commons Journal*, XLIII, 1788, and XLVII, 1792. For municipal corporations see Sidney and Beatrice Webb, *The Manor and the Borough*, 1908, rpt., Hamden, Connecticut, 1963, esp. pp. 306–20.
51. Drescher seems to indicate that only about fifteen per cent of petitions in 1792 were restricted to privileged groups (nobility, corporation, freemen, etc.). This would imply that the balance, eighty-five per cent, emanated either from the 'inhabitants' of towns and parishes, or from 'participants in voluntary associations without political privileges' (guilds, presbyteries, etc.). See Drescher, *Capitalism and Antislavery*, p. 74 (table 4.1).
52. Throughout, I have been careful to rely on the 'titles' listed in the main body of the *Commons Journal*. Those listed in the indices are often incomplete or abbreviated and therefore misleading. See Drescher, *Capitalism and Antislavery*, pp. 74–5.
53. *Commons Journal*, XLVII, 1792, pp. 542 (Chesham), 579 (St Just).
54. Henry Ley to John Ley, 2 April 1788, Devon Record Office, 63/2/11/2/38.
55. These figures are abstracted from the *Commons Journal*, XLIII, 1788, and XLVII, 1792.
56. Diary of Katherine Plymley, 1066/4 (30 October 1791–9 February 1792). George Forester (1735–1811) was MP for Wenlock 1758–61, 1768–80,

1785–90. His cousin and heir, Cecil Forester, was elected to the seat in 1790. See Lewis Namier and John Brooke, *The House of Commons, 1754–1790*, London, 1964, II, p. 450.

57. Drescher, *Capitalism and Antislavery*, p. 220 (n. 65).

58. William Burgh to William Wilberforce, ? December 1791, Wilberforce MSS C.17, fol. 20, Bodleian Library, Oxford.

59. Quoted in Drescher, *Capitalism and Antislavery*, p. 220 (n. 65).

60. John Bourne, ed., *Georgian Tiverton: The Political Memoranda of Beavis Wood, 1768–98*, Devon and Cornwall Record Society, new series, 29, Torquay, 1986, pp. 125–6; *Commons Journal*, XLVII, 1792, p. 565.

61. *The Life of William Wilberforce*, I, pp. 339–40.

62. *Newcastle Courant*, 3 March 1792; Dickson, 'Diary of a Visit to Scotland' (entry for 6 March 1792).

63. *Sheffield Register*, 17 February 1792.

64. *The Life of William Wilberforce*, I, p. 339.

65. *Sheffield Register*, 17 February 1792.

66. *Nottingham Journal*, 15 March 1788. Again in 1788, copies of the Manchester petition were left open for signature at eleven local public houses, as well as 'Mr Harrop's, printer, Market-place, and Mr Falkner's, stationer'. See *Manchester Mercury*, 8 January 1788.

67. *Aris's Birmingham Gazette*, 4 February 1788, 13 February 1792; *Newcastle Courant*, 11 February 1792. An opponent of abolition at Ipswich claimed that the local petition there had been 'taken from the Hall, and carried about the Town. Gentlemen were accosted in the streets, to sign'. See *Diary, or Woodfall's Register*, 30 March 1792.

68. *Manchester Mercury*, 1, 8 January, 5, 12, 19 February 1788; *Commons Journal*, XLIII, 1788, p. 220.

69. *Diary, or Woodfall's Register*, 2 April 1792.

70. Diary of Katherine Plymley, 1066/3 (22–30 October 1791). For Plymley, later Corbett, see *Victoria County History, Salop*, London, 1968, VIII, p. 110; *Alumni Cantabrigiensis*, Part 2, V, p. 142.

71. Diary of Katherine Plymley, 1066/3 (22–30 October 1791). Plymley was elected an Honorary Corresponding Member of the London Committee in 1791. See Abolition Committee Minutes, 5 July 1791.

72. Diary of Katherine Plymley, 1066/4 (30 October 1791–9 February 1792) and 1066/5 (9–24 February 1792).

73. Ibid., 1066/5 (9–24 February 1792).

74. Ibid., 1066/5 (9–24 February 1792), 1066/6 (24 February–5 March 1792), 1066/7 (5–12 March 1792).

75. Ibid., 1066/5 (9–24 February 1792).

76. Drescher, *Capitalism and Antislavery*, p. 219 (n. 58).

77. Dickson, 'Diary of a Visit to Scotland' (entry for 25 February 1792).

78. Diary of Katherine Plymley, 1066/5 (9–24 February 1792).

79. *The Debate on the Motion for the Abolition of the Slave Trade*, p. 86.

80. *Gentleman's Magazine*, LXII, 1792, p. 228. For similar comments see *Diary, or Woodfall's Register*, 28 February 1792.

81. Dickson, 'Diary of a Visit to Scotland' (entry for 6 March 1792); *Newcastle Courant*, 31 March 1792; *Diary, or Woodfall's Register*, 27 March 1792.

82. Drescher, *Capitalism and Antislavery*, pp. 82, 219 (n. 59); *Newcastle Courant*, 3, 17 March 1792; *Times*, 20, 26, 31 March 1792.

83. This calculation assumes that about one third of the population of England, Scotland, and Wales in 1791 was male and over the age of fifteen. See E. A. Wrigley and R. S. Schofield, *The Population History of England, 1541–1871: A Reconstruction*, Cambridge, Massachusetts, 1981, pp. 208–9 (table 7.8), 216 (table 7.4). I am most grateful to Richard Wall of the Cambridge Group for the History of Population and Social Structure for his help in interpreting these figures.

84. For the population of Exeter see *Annals of Agriculture, and other useful Arts*, London, 1797, VIII, p. 634; for Sheffield see Frederick Morton Eden, *The State of the Poor*, London, 1797, p. 864; for Manchester see E. A. Wrigley, 'Urban Growth and Agricultural Change', pp. 42–3. Again, all calculations are based on the assumption that about one third of the population of these towns was male and over the age of fifteen.

85. See, for example, *Aris's Birmingham Gazette*, 5 March 1792 (Burton-upon-Trent meeting); *Leicester Journal*, 9 February 1788 (Leicester petition); *Leeds Intelligencer*, 5 February 1788 (Leeds meeting) and 27 February 1792 (Bradford petition).

86. *Gentleman's Magazine*, LXII, 1792, p. 230 (petition).

87. *Leeds Intelligencer*, 5 March 1792 (petition).

88. See, for example, *Leeds Intelligencer*, 26 February 1788 (Halifax petition); *Aris's Birmingham Gazette*, 4 February 1788 (Birmingham meeting); *Leicester Journal*, 3 February 1792 (Leicester petition).

89. *Sherborne Mercury*, 31 March 1788.

90. *Aris's Birmingham Gazette*, 4 February 1788 (Birmingham meeting).

91. Ibid., 11 February 1788 (Birmingham petition).

92. *Sherborne Mercury*, 24 March 1788 (petition); *Nottingham Journal*, 16 February 1788 (meeting).

93. *Sherborne Mercury*, 12 March 1792 (petition).

94. *Leeds Intelligencer*, 27 February 1792 (petition).

95. Ibid. See also *Sheffield Register*, 24 February 1792 (Sheffield meeting).

96. *Leicester Journal*, 3 February 1791; *Aris's Birmingham Gazette*, 27 February 1792; *Newcastle Courant*, 18 February 1792 (Carlisle meeting). See also *Sheffield Register*, 24 February 1792 (Sheffield meeting).

97. *Aris's Birmingham Gazette*, 27 February 1792 (Birmingham petition); *Sheffield Register*, 24 February 1792 (Sheffield meeting).

98. *Leeds Intelligencer*, 19 February 1788.

99. *Sherborne Mercury*, 24 March 1788 (petition).

100. *Leeds Intelligencer*, 29 January 1788; *Newark Herald*, 15 February 1792.

101. Colley, *Britons*, p. 353.

102. Ibid., p. 354.

103. David Spadafora, *The Idea of Progress in Eighteenth-Century Britain*, New Haven, 1990, pp. 211–12, 223, 231–8.

104. *Gentleman's Magazine*, LVIII, 1788, p. 312 (petition).

105. Brewer, 'Commercialization and Politics', p. 200. See also J. Money, *Experience and Identity: Birmingham and the West Midlands, 1760–1850*, Manchester, 1977; Seed, 'Gentlemen Dissenters: The Social and Political Meanings of Rational Dissent in the 1770s and 1780s', esp. pp. 322–3.

Chapter Five

ABOLITION AT
THE GRASS-ROOTS LEVEL

IN organisational terms the agitation over the slave trade rested on a system of committees and local agents working in close co-operation with abolitionists in London. This much is clear. But what about those people who came forward to support the movement at the grass-roots level, to contribute funds and sign petitions? Who were they? Sadly, none of the petitions from either the campaign of 1788 or the campaign of 1792 has survived. Nevertheless, we do have access to subscription lists, some of them published by the London Committee, others scattered in local newspapers. We can also learn a great deal about the intentions of abolitionists, that is, who they were trying to reach, from literary sources, and poetry and children's literature in particular. Using this kind of information, it is possible to reach beyond organisation and to focus, instead, on personalities, on the men, women, and children who gave the early abolitionist movement its distinctive character.

Grass-roots support for abolition was predominantly white and predominantly middle-class. There were, of course, prominent blacks who became involved with the movement. One thinks immediately of figures like Olaudah Equiano. An ex-slave who travelled widely and was at one time or another a servant, a hairdresser, a miner, and a ship's steward, Equiano 'emerged in his forties, as a capable and energetic publicist; a fluent writer and speaker, a campaigner prepared to travel wherever he was invited to present the abolitionist cause'.[1] He described some of these experiences in his enormously successful *Interesting Narrative of the Life of Olaudah Equiano, or Gustavus Vassa, the African* (1789). In 1791 Equiano spent more than eight and a half months touring Ireland. The following year he visited Scotland and spoke to meetings in Manchester, Nottingham, Sheffield, Cambridge, Durham, Stockton, and Hull. At the same time, he wrote articles and reviews for the *Public Advertiser* and was personally acquainted with Granville Sharp, Sir William Dolben, Thomas Hardy, first Secretary of the London Corresponding Society, and the Belfast abolitionist, Thomas Digges.[2]

Equiano, like other black leaders in Britain, among them Ottobah Cugoano, author of *Thoughts and Sentiments on the Evil and Wicked Traffic of the Slavery and Commerce of the Human Species* (1787), saw abolition as 'the next link in the chain by which . . . [blacks] could haul themselves out of degradation to dignity'.[3] The Somersett case of 1772 had not, as many thought, emancipated all black slaves in Britain. Rather, it had set a limit of sorts on the ability of masters to take slaves out of the country, that is, against their will. As Walvin and Fryer point out, slavery remained a reality in Britain until well into the 1790s and beyond; it was still being discussed in the courts as late as the 1820s.[4] This was why black Britons responded so positively to the emergence of the early abolitionist movement. If the trade was abolished, and with it colonial slavery, then slavery in Britain would have to be abolished; more than that, blacks would have to be guaranteed their legal rights.

To judge from newspaper reports, a group of twenty or more black abolitionists ('Sons of Africa') were active in and around London during the late eighteenth century.[5] We can only guess at the level of involvement elsewhere in the country. But when Clarkson spoke in Manchester in 1787 forty or fifty blacks were in the audience.[6] Others may well have contributed funds or even signed petitions. Help also came from an unexpected quarter in the shape of black African visitors to Britain. The *Lady's Magazine* reported in October 1791 that 'Prince John, the African prince, is arrived here from Sierra Leone. His business to this country appears chiefly to be respecting the slave trade'.[7] And, indeed, Prince John may have been among the 'several natives of Africa, of noble rank' who later that year participated in the debate on the Santo Domingo slave insurrection at the Coachmakers' Hall Society in London.[8] Here was testimony of a very different kind: immediate, compelling, and, above all, authentic.

Important as these 'black voices' were, however, the real impetus came from the (white) provincial middle classes. A key factor here was religion and religious Nonconformity, in particular. In numerical terms Dissent suffered a decline during the eighteenth century, but in many towns it remained an important and influential force. There were large dissenting communities in Nottingham, York, Newcastle, Exeter, and Manchester, for instance, as well as in small market towns like Devizes and Tiverton.[9] Nonconformists, moreover, though technically excluded under the terms of the Test and Corporation Acts, were gaining widespread acceptance in British society. James Bradley estimates that 'altogether Dissenters at some point in the eighteenth century sat on corporations of at least twenty-eight Parliamentary boroughs, or one in five of every borough in which they had established meetings'. They also held government posts as excise officers and local tax collectors and were free to take up the law. There are frequent references to dissenting attorneys in local records, and Bradley has found examples of dissenting judges, high sheriffs, and justices of the peace.[10] In short, Nonconformists 'were able to penetrate almost all levels of the political system', although such mobility did not prevent them from continuing to seek repeal of the Test and Corporation Acts; indeed, it may have heightened their sense of 'symbolic and psychological exclusion'.[11]

Whether excluded or not, dissenters (and dissenting clergy, in particular) remained profoundly suspicious of anything that touched upon either their independence or their self-respect. As Bradley says, 'they experienced oppression descending upon them from the city corporation, the Anglican Church, the Quarter Session, and the rich and titled'.[12] Dissenters, as a result, were frequently to be found in the ranks of local anti-corporation parties. They adopted a similar attitude with regard to the central government, embracing a range of radical causes that included support for John Wilkes in the Middlesex election affair and conciliation with the American colonies. Bradley has documented the linkage between radicalism and dissent in great detail, even speculating on the possible continuities between the petitioning movements of 1769 (Wilkes) and 1775 (America) and the urban protests of the 1790s.[13] Yet he has little or nothing to say about the agitation over the slave trade. This is all the more surprising because abolition generated widespread support among dissenters, attracting many of the same people who had been involved in the petitioning movement of 1775.

The Quaker network, in particular, made a vital contribution to anti-slavery activity at the grass-roots level, notably in the southwest of England, where its influence reached from Poole in Dorset to Falmouth in Cornwall. Elsewhere, it was Unitarians or Presbyterians who took the lead, organising committees, raising and contributing funds, promoting petitions. Some idea of abolition's wide sectarian appeal emerges from extant subscription lists. Among those who contributed funds to the London Committee in 1788, for instance, were a large number of Baptist congregations in Leicestershire, Derbyshire, and Warwickshire.[14] In Newcastle in 1791–92 subscriptions came from local Methodists as well as two Congregational chapels, the one in the Postern, the other at High Bridge Street.[15] Nonconformists also petitioned Parliament in their own right. Here again, the Quakers are the obvious example, but in 1788 they were joined by the Protestant Dissenters of Devizes and the presbyteries at Glasgow, Aberdeen, Edinburgh, and Kircudbright.[16] Scottish dissenters were in even greater evidence in the 1792 campaign, sending over twenty petitions to Parliament, among them petitions from the presbyteries at Dundee, Inverness, Garioch, and Paisley.[17]

An important lead came from dissenting clergy. One of these was William Turner, who helped to organise the local Newcastle committee in November 1791.[18] Perhaps better known is George Walker, who served on the Nottingham committee between 1788 and 1792. Walker, minister of the Presbyterian High Pavement Chapel, had opposed the war with America and was a fervent supporter of Parliamentary reform, drafting the petition that went up to Parliament from Nottinghamshire in 1780. In Walker's case, abolition was part of a political philosophy that linked the Wilkite agitation of the 1760s with the radicalism of the 1790s. A warm friend of revolutionary sentiment abroad, in 1790 he sponsored yet another petition from Nottingham, this time calling for peace with France.[19] Many other dissenting clergy supported abolition. Of the twenty-three ministers who entered subscriptions to the Exeter committee in 1788, at least half were Nonconformists.[20] Two members of the Plymouth committee, Philip Gibbs and Herbert Mends, were dissenting ministers, as were two members of the Birmingham committee, John Ryland and the English radical, Joseph Priestley.[21] Finally, Gilbert Wakefield is another prominent dissenter who lent his support to abolition, joining his friend, George Walker, on the Nottingham committee in December 1791.[22]

But it was not only dissenting clergy who involved themselves in the movement. Anglicans also played their part. Five bishops subscribed to the London Committee in 1788, among them John Hinchcliffe, Bishop of Peterborough, who had supported conciliation with the American colonies in 1775, and Richard Watson, Bishop of Llandaff.[23] At the local level, the Deans of Gloucester and Bristol were both members of the Bristol committee, while the Dean of Lichfield signed the requisition for the Staffordshire (petition) meeting in 1788.[24] Other examples spring to mind. An influential voice on the Plymouth committee was that of John Bidlake, chaplain to Earl Ferrers, a leading Evangelical, and Headmaster of Plymouth Grammar School. At Cambridge, meanwhile, Peter Peckard, Master of Magdalen College, produced two sermons on the slave trade in 1788, returning to the subject again in his *National Crimes the Cause of National Punishments*, published in 1795.[25] And if the Protestant Dissenting Ministers petitioned Parliament in 1788 so, too, did the Anglican Clergy of Leicester and the Diocese of Chester.[26] More revealing still is the number of clergy who appear to have joined with corporations and local inhabitants in sending petitions to Parliament in 1788. Nearly fifteen per cent of the petitions fell into this category, including those from Exeter, Cambridge, Grantham, Colchester, Leek, Blackburn, and Staffordshire.[27] Who the 'clergy' were in these circumstances we cannot be sure, but that they included a significant number of Anglicans seems indisputable.

Abolition, moreover, cut across Anglican loyalties. An important impetus came from the Clapham Sect, those Evangelicals who gathered around William Wilberforce and Henry Thornton. Key figures in this group were the MPs Samuel Thornton and William Morton Pitt, the author Hannah More, and Mary Middleton, who was instrumental in persuading Wilberforce to take up the abolition of the slave trade.[28] On the fringes of the Clapham Sect and certainly sympathetic to its aims and objectives was Beilby Porteus, Bishop of London. A close friend and supporter of Hannah More, Porteus published a pamphlet on the slave trade in 1784 and was later to become president of the Society to Effect the Enforcement of His Majesty's Proclamations against Vice and

Immorality (1788), one of many reforms launched by Evangelical Anglicans.[29] Wilberforce and his friends, who included William Mason and Thomas Gisborne in the Midlands and the north of England, respectively, were part of a movement that grew steadily in influence during the late eighteenth century. By 1792 there were perhaps as many as sixty Evangelical clergy scattered about the country, not to mention a significant number of prominent lay converts.[30] Committed as they were to an ambitious programme of national (moral) reform, these men and women opened the way for a dialogue with Nonconformists, forging alliances that were to prove of crucial importance at the local level.

The role of religion and religious affiliations in explaining abolitionist activity emerges very clearly from subscription lists. So, too, does the movement's middle-class origins in trade and business. The Exeter list of 1788 contains, in all, over 250 names and is one of the largest of its kind. Of those easily identifiable in newspapers and local directories approximately twenty-five per cent were shopkeepers (druggists, milliners, linen drapers, grocers). A further sixteen per cent were merchants, among them George Manning, John Waymouth, Samuel Churchill, and William Kennaway, while twenty-two per cent were small manufacturers (weavers, tailors, dyers).[31] Abolition, in other words, penetrated deep into the middling ranks. Indeed, some of these people may have been close to artisans in status, a point that again needs to be borne in mind when tracing the emergence of what some historians have called the 'new radicalism'. James Bradley notes the involvement of this same group, the lower middle class, in the petitioning movements of 1769 and 1775.[32]

It is instructive to compare Exeter with Nottingham, a bustling county town that was also a major centre of the hosiery industry.[33] Here, in a sample of ninety-three subscribers, approximately twenty-five per cent were shopkeepers. By far the greatest number, however, were manufacturers. Nearly half of the sample (forty-six in all) fell into this category, including twenty hosiers and three cotton spinners. William Butcher of Butcher and Whitfield, John Fellows, and William Dearman of Dearman and Walker, another important firm of hosiery manufacturers, all contributed funds to the local Nottingham committee in 1788. But again the whole range of middling people was represented in the Nottingham list. Among those subscribing in 1788 were two shoemakers, a cutler, a breeches-maker, a stonemason, and a joiner and cabinetmaker. Two other features of the Nottingham list are particularly striking. One is the absence of 'gentlemen' (nineteen appear in the Exeter list). The other is the relatively small number of clergymen, eight in all, representing less than five per cent of subscribers.[34]

Another group represented in subscription lists is the emerging professions. In Nottingham no fewer than eight doctors contributed funds, among them John Attenburrow, John Bigsby, and Thomas Barnett.[35] Lawyers also joined the movement. At least two attorneys, both Quakers, sat on the Plymouth committee and another, Francis Evans, was a member of the Nottingham committee in 1788 and again in 1791.[36] Perhaps we should not be surprised at this level of activity. As Roy Porter and Jonathan Barry have shown, the professions generally played an important role in provincial cultural life during the eighteenth century, often taking the lead in the establishment of intellectual institutions—book clubs, libraries, and scientific, literary and philosophical societies.[37] Frequently the same men were involved in a wide range of local projects. William Turner, for instance, besides being a prominent abolitionist was one of the principal figures behind the organisation of the Newcastle Literary and Philosophical Society (1793); George Walker and Gilbert Wakefield formed a literary club in Nottingham during the 1780s; Priestley, meanwhile, was a member of the Birmingham Lunar Society.[38]

These associations (and how many others?) helped to fix abolition within a broader Enlightenment culture that, in turn, was recognisably 'modern'. They gave it status and respectability. Equally important at the local level was the influence of the press. A sympathetic editor might print advertisements at reduced fees or, better still, add his own voice to the movement. Daniel Holt, for example, who was later to be imprisoned for publishing two reform pamphlets (one of them by John Cartwright), lent his weight to the 1792 campaign, intervening at regular intervals through the pages of the *Newark Herald*.[39] Perhaps the best known newspaper printer who supported abolition was William Woodfall. As Clarkson explained in 1791, Woodfall's usual price for a column in his *Diary* was half a guinea, but he had 'made an offer to engage for a column every day at 5 shillings on the side of

Abolition and desir'd the rest may be consider'd as his mite to the subscription'.[40] Other newspaper printers who subscribed to the movement were Robert Trewman, printer of the *Exeter Flying Post*, and George Burbage, printer of the *Nottingham Journal*.[41]

Many booksellers also supported abolition. In Newcastle William Charnley and Edward Humble, junior, both subscribed to the local committee in 1791–92. (The same list also includes a subscription from Ralph Beilby and Thomas Bewick, the engravers.)[42] At Exeter four booksellers came forward with contributions, among them William Grigg and Shirley Woolmer, both dissenters, and Gilbert Dyer, who ran a circulating library in the High Street.[43] These men, like newspaper printers, were ideally placed to influence the public debate over the slave trade. For one thing, their shops were important meeting places where the urban middle classes met to gossip and read the local and national newspapers. For another, they had access to a wide provincial market; in January 1792 Josiah Wedgwood approached his bookseller in Newcastle-under-Lyme about the possibility of 'dispersing' copies of Fox's address on the consumption of West Indian sugar and rum, in this case 'by the hawkers'.[44] Clarkson also seems to have cultivated booksellers, while James Phillips, a leading member of the London Committee, published over forty titles on the abolition of the slave trade between 1783 and 1798.[45]

Abolition, in other words, struck a responsive chord among the provincial middle classes. This is not to deny that other groups played their part. A maidservant, for instance, subscribed to the Plymouth committee in 1789 and elsewhere in the country there are scattered references to artisans who contributed funds and signed petitions.[46] But for the most part the men (and women) who shaped the movement outside Parliament were drawn from the middling ranks. Some of these people were undoubtedly radicals. As we have seen, a strong link emerges at the local level between abolition, Parliamentary reform, and conciliation with the American colonies, notably among dissenting clergy. Abolition, however, was not solely or exclusively a radical issue any more than it was a sectarian (dissenting) issue.[47] Its appeal was eclectic, its constituency broad. Just how broad becomes apparent if we look in greater detail at the involvement of women, and, to a lesser extent, children, in the early abolitionist movement.

The participation of women in the abolition campaign was in large measure yet another consequence of the urban renaissance of the eighteenth century. Urban life brought with it new opportunities for women and new types of paid work. In seaside towns like Brighton, Margate, and Weymouth women might become lodging-house keepers or run coffee houses.[48] Many more were shopkeepers—milliners, grocers, and booksellers. Teaching was another important avenue for middle-class women, especially if they were single.[49] In short, towns enabled a growing number of women to achieve a measure of financial independence and to find roles for themselves that did not necessarily conform to female stereotypes. By definition urban life was also more diverting. It exposed women to new ideas, new sensations, and a new social world, to newspapers and magazines, to balls, assemblies, debates and lectures, and to new kinds of philanthropic endeavour.[50] Of course, not everyone agreed that these trends were necessarily all for the good. But they had an important bearing on the abolition of the slave trade and the ability (and willingness) of women to exert an influence on the movement.

Some indication of the importance attached to female support for abolition emerges from the efforts made to reach and influence women, both individually and collectively. Wedgwood's cameos, for instance, were obviously directed at women as a fashionable sales target.[51] Imaginative use was also made of William Cowper's *The Negro's Complaint*. As Clarkson explains, some of Cowper's friends,

> conceiving it to contain a powerful appeal on behalf of the injured Africans, joined in printing it. Having ordered it on the finest hot-pressed paper, and folded it up in a small and neat form, they gave it the printed title of 'A Subject for Conversation at the Tea-Table'. After this, they sent many thousand copies of it in franks into the country. From one it spread to another, till it travelled almost over the whole island.[52]

From its very title, it is clear that this piece was directed principally at women. Poetry, moreover, was widely recognised as a literary genre that suited feminine sensibilities. Indeed, Roger Lonsdale notes that after 1780 women 'virtually took over, as writers and readers, the territories most readily conceded to them, of popular fiction and fashionable poetry'.[53] Cowper's friends, in other words, knew exactly what they were doing.

More deliberate still in its efforts to reach women—and through them their male relatives—was the Rev. J. Jamieson's *The Sorrows of Slavery: A Poem* (1789). Jamieson quite unashamedly appealed to so-called feminine qualities: compassion, tenderness, sensitivity, benevolence. Black women, he argued in the first part of *The Sorrows of Slavery*, were no different from their white (English) sisters:

> They are not fair like you. But can the hues
> Of Nature various tinge the secret soul?
> Say, does not the alembic of their hearts
> As pure Compassion's genial drop distil
> As your's? Oft do they not o'erflow
> The cisterns of their eye-lids too confin'd?
> Does Grief ne'er wring their heart-strings? Or can Pain
> Make no nerve thrill?

And again:

> Is there no mother here, whose melting heart
> Darts thro' her eyes, when smiling on her babe;
> Who fondly strains her empty breast to yield
> Those drops reluctant famine yet hath spar'd;
> Or feels new pangs more piercing than the first,
> From its fond claspings sever'd by the sword?[54]

Jamieson went on to contrast the plight of black women, taking as his point of departure an 'attack' on a native village in Dahomey. Here again, his images were carefully chosen: women searching frantically for their children as the village is set alight; a daughter snatched from her father's door by 'ruffian hands'; women 'heavy with child' being forced to make the long march from the interior to the sea.[55] But this is as nothing compared to the horrors that await the women on board the slave ship. Part three of the poem tells the story of Calypso, a young mother brutally separated from her only surviving child:

> One night, as on the leaky boards I lay,
> And vainly strove to soothe my crying babe,
> Half chok'd with water dash'd from side to side,

My watchful spoiler, in his sleep disturb'd,
Tore from my arms my helpless innocent;
And—oh! my limbs still quiver, while I tell
The horrid deed—he plung'd it 'midst the stream . . .
He was a Christian, boasted of his name,
And in reply to all my bitter plaints,
My infant curs'd for Heathen unbaptis'd.
Such was his mercy, such the baptism
He gave my babe, and such the powerful means
He us'd to win me to his *better* faith.

(pp. 56–7)

Sold into slavery, Calypso nurses an understandable hatred of Britons and the British nation:

Yes, Britons are our tyrants, while they smile
On those who tyrannize! 'Tis Britain's gold
That bribes our kinsmen us to steal and sell;
'Tis Britain's scourge that slays us; 'tis her rod,
O'er countless billows reaching, to the ground
That smites us down; there her foot tramples us;
Her hand life's pittance snatches from our lips;
Her sword relentless sheds our guiltless blood.

(p. 62)

Jamieson, therefore, moved purposefully from the immorality of the slave trade, its inhumanity and its hypocrisy, to considerations of national honour. And all of this, let it be remembered, in an appeal to British women.[56]

Of course, it was not only men who dealt imaginatively with the subject of the slave trade. Hannah More, Anna Laetitia Barbauld, Helen Maria Williams, Ann Yearsley, and Maria and Harriet Falconar all wrote poems on the subject between 1788 and 1791.[57] Influenced no doubt by More, whose *Slavery: A Poem* appeared in 1788, most of these writers deliberately avoided the sort of graphic descriptions favoured by Jamieson. Instead, they became practised in confronting the horrors of the slave trade (split families, atrocities, rapacious slave traders) in a series of 'unvoiced abstractions'.[58] Harriet Falconar, for instance, describes the trade in these terms:

Angelic maid, thy melting eye may boast
The tear still pour'd o'er Afric's desert coast;
Unhappy land, where hostile av'rice reigns,
And rears her blood-stain'd banners o'er thy plains;
Where stern Oppression's hireling minions rove,
To burst each tender tie of social love;
Inhuman fiend, thy desolating hand
Spread wide destruction o'er the bleeding land.[59]

Other female writers approached the subject indirectly through the abolition campaign itself. Helen Maria Williams's *Poem on the Bill Lately Passed for Regulating the Slave Trade* (1788) praised William Pitt, but urged the 'Senate' to go further to overcome the 'wrongs of Afric's Captive Race'.[60] In a similar vein, Anna Laetitia Barbauld's *Epistle to William Wilberforce, Esq.* (1791) applauded Wilberforce ('Your merit stands, no greater and no less / Without, or with the varnish of success') while at the same time pouring scorn on the 'avarice' and self-interest of his opponents.[61]

Ann Yearsley's *Poem on the Inhumanity of the Slave Trade* (1788) struck a rather different note, however, and indeed may have been intended as a direct challenge to More's poetic sensibilities.[62] Drawing freely on Aphra Behn's *Oroonoko*, Yearsley's poem concerns a young slave, Luco, who is snatched from the bosom of his family somewhere in Africa and sold into colonial slavery. Proud and defiant, Luco at last strikes back and tries to escape. His master's revenge is swift and violent. In the climax of the poem Luco is chained to a tree,

> . . . fuel is plac'd
> In an increasing train, some paces back,
> To kindle slowly, and approach the youth
> With more than native terror. See, it burns!
> . . .
> (Oh, shame, shame
> Upon the followers of Jesus! shame
> On him that dares avow a God!) He writhes,
> While down his breast glide the unpity'd tears,
> And in their sockets strain their scorched balls.
> Burn, burn me quick! I cannot die!' he cries:
> 'Bring fire now close!' The planters heed him not,

But still prolonging Luco's torture, threat
Their trembling slaves around.[63]

Here were scenes to rival anything in Jamieson and it comes as no
surprise to learn that some critics thought Yearsley's poem too
'vigorous and energetic'.[64] Poetry by women was supposed to be
characterised by 'the beautiful, the soft, the delicate'.[65]

Poetry provided eighteenth-century women with an acceptable
(feminine) way of expressing their views on slavery and the slave
trade; it gave them an opportunity to become involved and to
make themselves heard. Women also contributed through their
purses. Thanks to Clare Midgley we now have a better
understanding of the role of women as subscribers to abolition.
The subscription list published by the London Committee in
August 1788 includes the names of over 200 women, that is, about
ten per cent of the total number of subscribers. Among them were
members of prominent Quaker families, the Gurneys of Norwich
and the Frys of Falmouth, as well as such Evangelical Anglican
women as Margaret Middleton, Elizabeth Bouverie, and Lydia
Babington. By and large these were married women who came
from respectable middle-class families. Only three aristocrats
appear in the list: Lady Hatton of Lanstanton, the Dowager
Countess Stanhope, and the Dowager Vicountess Gallway. Most
had no obvious connection with abolition, either by birth or by
marriage, and in coming forward in this manner they were
demonstrating their ability (as individuals) to play an active role
in the movement.[66]

Women also subscribed to local committees. Here again the
obvious example is Manchester, where sixty-eight out of a total
of 302 subscribers were women. Notices of their contributions
appeared prominently in local newspapers. 'Perhaps the most
auspicious Occurrence in the business', noted the *Manchester
Mercury* on 3 December 1787, 'and certainly the most flattering
to its promoters here, is the large and respectable Subscription,
supplied by the Ladies of Manchester'. Some of these women were
the wives and daughters of the men who later organised the local
Manchester committee: Joseph Atkinson, Thomas Bayley, Thomas
Cooper, and William Rigby. Most, but by no means all, were
Nonconformists (Quakers and Unitarians) and a large number
had connections with Manchester's manufacturing interests.[67]

It is tempting to regard Manchester as a special case, but the evidence from other parts of the country suggests otherwise. In Exeter, for instance, women also made up twenty-two per cent of the subscribers. Of these, about a third (twenty) were related to male subscribers or had some connection with the local Exeter committee. By far the greatest number, however, appear to have taken the decision to subscribe independently of male relatives. Some, like Mary Bennett, a milliner, and Mary Haton, a grocer, were shopkeepers; one, Mrs Pinkstan, ran a boarding school in St Sidwell's. Furthermore, nearly half of the subscribers (twenty-seven in all) were single women. Again, we have very few details, but a significant number were clearly teenage girls or young women. Among those subscribing in 1788 were Mary and Martha Manning, the Miss Sheppards, the Miss Williamses, the Miss Bodleys, and Eliza, Susannah and Sara Godfrey. Together, these sixty women contributed over £40 to the local committee, equivalent to twelve per cent of its total income.[68]

Meanwhile, in Plymouth fourteen per cent of the subscribers were women, as were fourteen per cent in York.[69] But there is little doubt that female support for abolition did vary. Only fifteen women appear in the Nottingham list of 1788 (about eight per cent), while at Bristol, Leeds, Sheffield, and Birmingham the numbers were smaller still. Leicester, it appears, produced no female subscribers.[70] Midgley is surely right in suggesting that religion, radical politics, and socio-economic factors all played a part here. Exeter, like Manchester, had a large dissenting community, and, as we have seen, the town was no stranger to political radicalism. But manufacturing interests did not dominate the Exeter committee in quite the same way as they did in Manchester. Neither were the two areas alike in terms of their developing regional economies. Industrialisation, in other words, only explains so much.[71] Just as important were considerations of status and respectability and the lead taken by prominent local families, whether their wealth derived from manufacturing, banking or the professions.

Subscriptions helped to confirm the status of women as an important part of the public sphere. But at the same time they were excluded from local committees and certainly in 1788 there was never any question that they might be invited to sign petitions. In 1792, however, Norwich radicals suggested sending a separate women's petition to Parliament. 'The idea is certainly a proper one', echoed the *Derby Mercury*, 'for, as *Female Misery* is included in the wretched Allotment of the African, an Appeal on their Behalf from the same Sex must carry great Weight with it'.[72] While the proposed petition never materialised, the debate seems to have prompted some women to join forces with their male counterparts. Among the 433 people who signed the local petition at Belford in Northumberland in 1792 were a number of 'Ladies, who were anxiously desirous to show their abhorrence of this abominable trade'.[73] Meanwhile, William Dickson noted that at Dundee 'some boys and 3 women have been allowed to sign'. Dickson put this down to 'mistaken zeal' and his frank admission that he did not 'know how to act' in such circumstances was a measure of just how unexpected (and undesirable) female participation at this level was.[74] Indeed, it was not until 1830 that women would sign petitions in any significant numbers.

Discouraged from signing petitions, women might nevertheless have a hand in the petitioning process itself. Petition meetings, for instance, did not obviously exclude women and in 1792 the Barnsley petition was left open for signature with a Mrs Roper at the 'White Bear Inn'.[75] During both campaigns women also found a voice in the capital's various debating societies. In March 1788 the abolition of the slave trade was discussed 'by Ladies only' at La Belle Assemblée in Brewer Street, Golden Square, and later that month a woman addressed a mixed audience on the same subject at the School of Eloquence in Panton Street, Haymarket. Women were also present in 1792 at the Coach-makers' Hall Society for Free Debate in Foster Lane, Cheapside, when a motion calling for a boycott of West Indian sugar and rum was carried by 'an almost unanimous vote of near six hundred persons'.[76] Exceptional though they were, these examples illustrate how powerfully abolition spoke to middle-class women, impelling them to take actions that were by their very nature public rather than private.

Another obvious way in which women could make their presence felt was through the boycott of West Indian sugar. Whether apocryphal or not, the story of the man who after a short absence returns home to find that his wife and daughters have 'entirely left off the use of Sugar, and banished it from the tea table', hinted at an important reality.[77] Here, within the domestic sphere, was an opportunity for women to seize the initiative and influence those around them. As Clare Midgley has shown, the campaign was quite often framed in these very terms. 'They [women] are universally considered as the MODELS of every just and virtuous *sentiment*', wrote William Allen in 1792, 'and we naturally look up to them as PATERNS [*sic*] in all the *softer virtues*. Their EXAMPLE, therefore, in ABSTAINING FROM THE USE OF WEST INDIA PRODUCE—must silence every murmer [*sic*]—must refute every objection—and render the *performance* of the Duty as UNIVERSAL as their INFLUENCE'.[78] Women were also appealed to as consumers and arbiters of taste and fashion. The author of *An Address to Her Royal Highness the Duchess of York* (1792) clearly hoped in this way to give the campaign its own status meaning and thereby induce others, including the King and Queen Charlotte, to follow her example.

At its peak the abstention campaign of 1791–92 affected perhaps as many as 300,000 people. The inhabitants of Leicester were said to be 'nearly unanimous in rejecting the use of sugar and rum'.[79] Clarkson later wrote that on his tour of the north of England in 1791 he encountered widespread support for the boycott:

> In smaller towns there were from ten to fifty by estimation, and in the larger from two to five hundred, who had made this sacrifice to virtue. These were of all ranks and parties. Rich and poor, churchmen and dissenters, had adopted the measure. Even grocers had left off trading in the article, in some places. In gentlemen's families, where the master had set the example, the servants had often voluntarily followed it; and even children, who were capable of understanding the history of the sufferings of the Africans, excluded, with the most virtuous resolution, the sweets, to which they had been accustomed, from their lips.[80]

In London 25,000 were said to have joined the boycott on the publication of Fox's *Address*, while newspapers reported that at Norwich 'sugar is now positively banished from the most polite and fashionable tea-tables'.[81]

A great deal of the support for the boycott undoubtedly came from women. As early as 1788, Hannah More had urged a personal friend 'to taboo the use of West Indian sugar in their tea'.[82] Anna Laetitia Barbauld followed her example, as did Katherine Plymley, the Wedgwood family, and Mary Birkett, an

Irish Quaker who wrote a poem on the subject in 1792.[83] Birkett's public stance was unusual, however. More often than not the real impact was felt in the home. By doing away with tea-drinking in the afternoon and substituting ale or cider for punch, women were able to influence patterns of consumption and so make their feelings known without necessarily offending male sensibilities (itself an important consideration).[84] Abstinence, in other words, gave women an opportunity not only to act, but to take the lead. James Gillray plays with these ideas in his cartoon, *Anti-Saccharrites,—Or—John Bull and his Family leaving off the Use of Sugar'*, which visualises the royal couple gathered around the breakfast table being harangued by Queen Charlotte.[85]

Clearly, women played a vital role in the abolition of the slave trade—as authors, subscribers, boycotters, and even, on occasion, as signers of petitions. Nevertheless, activity of this kind could (and did) offend those who sought to keep women in a subordinate position. Many women were themselves deeply conscious of the need to conform to male expectations. The *Lady's Magazine*, for instance, took a close interest in the early abolitionist movement. Yet the editors actively discouraged any *discussion* of the subject; indeed, in April 1792 a correspondent was told that her (or his?) question on the slave trade was of 'too political a nature to accord with our plan'.[86] In short, politics was something that concerned only men. Many women appear to have taken heed of the magazine's advice. Katherine Plymley is a case in point. Plymley's diaries offer a fascinating insight into her brother, Joseph's, activities, but nowhere does she record that she herself took any action to organise or influence her female friends. Plymley's protests, it seems, were confined to the home.

The French Revolution was also a significant factor in determining how women perceived their role in the abolitionist movement. If some like Mary Wollstonecraft and Helen Maria Williams applauded the actions of the revolutionaries and felt inspired by their example, others looked on with increasing concern.[87] Hannah More, for instance, was fervently opposed to the revolution and sought to counteract its levelling principles through her contributions to the Cheap Repository Tracts. Significantly, the first volume of these tracts, published in 1795, contained three stories addressed to slavery and the slave trade. In one, Babay, 'a good Negro woman', rescues an orphaned white child and nurses him back to health, risking her own life in the process. 'The Sorrows of Yamba' tells the story of a young mother separated from her children and sold into slavery. Yamba is a victim, but she finds salvation in the shape of a missionary who tells her that it is 'the Christian lot, / Much to suffer here below'. Converted, she becomes a new creature—sensitive, docile, affectionate. Babay, it transpires, has also been converted to Christianity. The same theme is continued in the third tale, 'A True Account of a Pious Negro', which takes the form of a dialogue between an 'English Gentleman' and a Christian slave whose master is so kind that the slave does not desire his freedom.[88]

What are we to make of these stories? More's obvious intention was to distance herself from any talk of human rights, of freedom and justice, whether it was for colonial slaves or the British working classes. In this sense, her *Tracts* were part of a much more general attempt after 1791 to preach the virtues of social and domestic obedience. More spells this out in a postscript to 'A True Account of a Pious Negro'. 'This story', she tells her readers, 'shows us that religion, and that only, will make a man content and comfortable in the lowest situations'.[89] The answer, More seems to be saying, is not resistance (or perhaps even abolition?), but spiritual rebirth. More was not alone in being caught off balance by the course of events in France. The linkage between anti-slavery, revolution, and the spectre of the mob undoubtedly frightened many women, just as it frightened many men.[90] It also put greater pressure on women to distance themselves from actions that might in any way seem threatening or a challenge to the natural order of things. Viewed in this light, Plymley's reticence becomes all the more comprehensible. But no less striking is the courage of those women who refused to conform and insisted, instead, on making themselves heard.

Just as abolitionists sought to reach and influence women, so, too, did they try and influence children. As J. H. Plumb argues, after 1700 children 'became luxury objects upon which their mothers and fathers were willing to spend larger and larger sums of money, not only for their education, but also for their entertainment and amusement'.[91] Children, in effect, became consumers. The trade in toys, the spectacular growth in children's literature, and the increasing number of private schools and academies were all evidence of 'a remarkable change in the lives of middle- and lower-middle-class children'.[92] There is no doubting either the size or the scale of this 'quiet revolution'. Eighteenth-century children, especially those living in towns, did, indeed, live in a 'new world'—a world that was more open, more exciting, and more stimulating than anything their parents or their grandparents would have known.

What did this mean for the abolition of the slave trade? Children's literature provides one clue. The man usually credited with making children's literature an important branch of the publishing trade is John Newbery, a London printer and bookseller whose publications included such favourites as *The Lilliputian Magazine* (1751–52), *Giles Gingerbread* (1761), and *Goody Two Shoes* (1763).[93] Newbery and his successors made their name through the skilful marketing of cheap books intended both to instruct and to entertain. But the Newbery family did not have the field to themselves for very long. By the end of the century equally resourceful competitors had sprung up in the shape of John Marshall, Vernor and Hood, John Stockdale, and Darton and Harvey.[94] Together, these men transformed children's literature in Britain. The Newberys alone published some 250 juvenile titles before 1800 and John Marshall was more prolific still.[95] When it is remembered that a first printing was usually 1,500 to 2,000 copies, and that many of these works went into three or four impressions, the full extent of this enterprising assault on consumer choice becomes readily apparent. The nineteenth century witnessed further expansion, the Peter Parley series selling over seven million copies in thirty years.[96]

Abolitionists were quick to exploit the potential of children's literature. A case in point is William Darton, a Quaker, who founded the firm of Darton and Harvey in 1787. In one of his earliest books, *Little Truths*, Darton devoted two pages to the inhumanity of the slave trade. 'Great are the hardships these poor people endure on board many of the ships', he explained,

I have read that six hundred and eighty men, women, and children, were stowed in one ship! which was also loaded with elephants' teeth. 'It was a pitiful sight', says the writer, 'to behold how these people were stowed. The men were standing in the hold, fastened one to another with stakes, for fear they should rise and kill the whites; the women were between decks, and the children were in the steerage, pressed together like herrings in a barrel, which caused an intolerable heat and stench'. In this situation the poor creatures frequently die; others attempt to break confinement, try to swim back again, and are often drowned.[97]

By no means as popular as *Tom Telescope* or Thomas Percival's *A Father's Instructions to his Children*, which both went through ten impressions before 1800, *Little Truths* nevertheless demonstrated the speed with which the growing literature on the slave trade, much of it collected and published by the London Committee and enthusiasts like Thomas Clarkson, reached juvenile readers.

The same information made possible a further development, namely, the introduction of black characters in children's literature. An early example of this device is to be found in Thomas Day's immensely popular *The History of Sandford and Merton* (1783–89), in which a black beggar miraculously rescues Harry Sandford from a raging bull. The story is remarkable both for its highly romanticised view of African tribal life, which Day seems to suggest is superior to Western civilisation, and its representation of blacks as helpless innocents dragged away from their 'happy homes' by fraud and violence. Significantly, Day has very little to say about the institution of slavery itself, but the reader is left in no doubt as to its inhumanity and cruelty, or the irrationality of English racial attitudes. 'In some parts of the world I have seen men of yellow hue, in others of a copper colour', the faithful black tells Tommy Merton,

> and all have the foolish vanity to despise their fellow creatures as infinitely inferior to themselves. There, indeed, they entertain these conceits from ignorance, but in this country, where the natives pretend to superior reason, I have often wondered they could be influenced by such a prejudice.[98]

As writers and publishers were quick to realise, black characters brought immediacy and authenticity to the anti-slavery struggle, and the device was widely imitated. Black servants appear in minor roles in *Rambles Further* (1796) and the revised edition of *Little Truths* (1802), a black beggar appears in *The Budget* (1799), and a slave figures prominently in *Excursions in North America*

(1806).[99] Of course, most of these characters had a story to tell, and their introduction proved the ideal way of confronting juvenile readers with the appalling misery of the Atlantic slave trade. Here again, Day's influence was evident. A recurring theme in these books, and one calculated to stir the imaginations of young and impressionable minds, was the way in which slavery disrupted the tranquillity of domestic life in Africa. As the black beggar in *The Budget* laments,

> I was born on the coast of Guinea, far from any white man, and made one among a principal tribe, headed by a valorous chief. United to one of our females, my days rolled on in happiness, and, for a time, the gentle gales of peace wafted to us success and pleasure. For three years we enjoyed the society of each other with mutual delight, till that accursed ambition which pervades the breast of white men drove their fatal barks of merchandise against our happy shores.[100]

Almost without exception, the blacks portrayed in these stories were faithful, honest, and resourceful. The black servant in *Little Truths*, we are told, is a 'tolerable scholar' and a considerable businessman:

> He was master of one of our fishing boats! he understood his business thoroughly. He knew the art of catching fish and selling them to advantage. The people in the market had a very high opinion of his honesty and skill, and he bore the character of being a very fair dealer.[101]

The seeming normality of these men was further enhanced by their eloquence. Few writers before 1800 tried to reproduce West Indian or African dialect, and, except for the obligatory 'massah', let their characters speak in the manner of educated Englishmen. These figures, in short, were recognisable as human beings and not as inhuman objects that could be bought, sold or mutilated.

The same point was made in a rather different way by Priscilla Wakefield in her *Excursions in North America*. One of the first children's books to deal with the issue of American slavery, *Excursions in North America* made no secret of its abolitionist sympathies. In the course of the story the protagonists, two English travellers on a tour of the eastern seaboard, buy a black slave at an auction in Charleston and immediately set him free.

Sancho, as he is called, subsequently becomes their servant and in short time reveals himself to be 'a good marksman', an excellent guide, an authority on local flora and fauna, and splendidly resourceful:

> At night, Sancho, with our assistance, erected a few posts, and formed a shelter from the night dews with pieces of bark, that he found scattered on the ground. In order to furnish our chamber completely, he spread the skin of a buffalo, which he had brought with us, over a heap of dried leaves that he had collected from under the trees, and, I assure you, formed a couch by no means uncomfortable.[102]

Sancho, of course, is an exotic, a composite picture of the black as a child of nature. But there was no denying his humanity or the fact that he was the real hero of Wakefield's book.

By these various means writers and publishers sought to influence how young readers—typically five- to fourteen-year-olds—thought about the slave trade. They sought to inculcate ideas that in time would become social attitudes. The obvious outlet for this literature was the nation's bookshops. London, as usual, led the way with a Juvenile Library at 157 New Bond Street, popularised by Eliza Fenwick in her book of the same name.[103] But the provinces were not far behind. Most booksellers carried a selection of children's books and some, like John Allen of Hereford, boasted stocks in excess of 100 volumes.[104] Those parents who were either unable or unwilling to buy books for their children could always borrow them. Circulating libraries often kept holdings of children's books. One operating in Sheffield in 1806 even had a special juvenile section or 'Children's Library'.[105] And children evidently did read these books, either alone or with their parents. Anna Larpent, wife of John Larpent, the inspector of plays, read *Sandford and Merton* with her son, George, over a period of seven months in 1792–93, diligently recording each session in her diary.[106]

Children's literature may also have been available in the increasing number of private (boarding) schools and academies that sprang up during the eighteenth century. We have no reliable estimate of the total number of these schools, but it was certainly large. Plumb notes that ninety-one schools advertised in the *Ipswich Journal* between 1783 and 1787. In Hampshire well over

100 schools are mentioned in local newspapers after 1740, although not all of them were operating at the same time. As more and more details emerge, it is quite clear that educational facilities for the middle classes exploded during the eighteenth century. Even small towns and villages had their own schools; indeed, a rural location was often considered particularly beneficial for the moral and intellectual training of young minds.[107] With these schools came new influences and new ideas. Many teachers, we know, supported the abolition of the slave trade and it is very likely that these same sympathies were passed on to their pupils, either directly, or, indirectly, through books and pamphlets.[108] How many of Mrs Pinkstan's charges, one wonders, were the same young women who subscribed to the local Exeter committee in 1788?

Through such experiences increasing numbers of children were brought into contact with anti-slavery sentiment. Many more besides were influenced by the example of their parents. Amelia Opie recalled how her parents reacted to her terrible fear of Aboar, a neighbour's black footman:

> . . . missey was forced to shake hands with the black the next time he approached her, and thenceforward we were very good friends. Nor did they fail to make me acquainted with negro history; as soon as I was able to understand, I was shown on the map where their native country was situated; I was told the sad tale of negro wrongs and negro slavery; and I believe that my early and ever-increasing zeal in the cause of emancipation was founded and fostered by the kindly emotions which I was encouraged to feel for my friend Aboar and all his race.[109]

The receptivity of children to abolition was a common theme in anti-slavery literature. Katherine Plymley, for instance, noted with evident satisfaction that her nephew, Panton, had given orders that his shoes 'shou'd not be black'd because he understood Sugar was used in the composition'. Her niece, meanwhile, 'wou'd not use any [sugar] till it came from Sierra Leone'. Plymley appears to have been fascinated by the 'virtue of little children', observing that 'among those who are informed on the subject I have heard of more readiness to give up the use of Sugar than among grown people'.[110] It is also evident that children did, on occasion, sign petitions. At Dundee 'some boys' signed the local petition in 1792, as did three women.[111] We can only guess at the motives of children who came forward in this manner. (Perhaps it was mischief?) Some were no doubt influenced by their parents; others, however, may have been influenced by relatives, schoolteachers or perhaps even their classmates.

The 'new world' of children provided the perfect vehicle for disseminating ideas about the inhumanity of slavery and the slave trade. To some extent, of course, this was an investment for the future. Clarkson made the same point when he told Katherine Plymley's nephew that if he wanted to be of use 'the best thing he cou'd do was to read on the subject [of the slave trade] that he may grow up with a just detestation of it'.[112] But there is enough evidence to suggest that the efforts of parents, writers, publishers, and teachers had a more immediate impact. Further research may yet shed more light on the role of children in the early abolitionist movement. It is even conceivable that in some cases they took the initiative, setting an example for their parents to follow and not vice versa. One thing is certain, however. Children were not simply a 'sales target'—they were also historical actors in their own right.

Abolition, it is clear, spoke to the provincial middle classes in a particularly vivid and forceful manner. Compassion, sensitivity, and considerations of pride and national honour all played a part here, but so, too, did fashion, status, and respectability. The composition of country committees, the details contained in subscription lists, the attitude of local clergy: all of these things were important social indicators that gave the movement its own status meaning. Perhaps there was also something unique about the slave trade, something shocking and yet at the same time comfortably remote, that enabled abolition to unite so many people across the lines of gender, religion, and politics. Whatever the reason, anti-slavery emerged as a potent symbol of middle-class concern during the late eighteenth century, forging alliances that gave the movement outside Parliament an urgent moral force.

Notes

1. Fryer, *Staying Power: The History of Black People in Britain*, p. 106.
2. Ibid., pp. 102–13; Walvin, *Black and White: The Negro and English Society, 1555–1945*, pp. 89–95; *Morning Post and Daily Advertiser*, 21 February 1788.
3. Fryer, *Staying Power*, p. 111. For Ottobah Cugoano see Fryer, pp. 98–102; Ottobah Cugoano (John Stuart) to Sir William Dolben, n.d., Northamptonshire Record Office, D(F)39.
4. Ibid., pp. 125–6; Walvin, *Black and White*, pp. 121–9.
5. Fryer, *Staying Power*, p. 108.
6. Clarkson, *History*, II, pp. 268–76.
7. *Lady's Magazine*, XXII, 1791, p. 556; Diary of Katherine Plymley, 1066/1 (20 October 1791). See also Elizabeth Montagu to Matthew Montagu, July 1792, Montagu Papers, MO 2870, Huntington Library.
8. *Diary, or Woodfall's Register*, 23 November, 1 December 1791.
9. Bradley, *Religion, Revolution and English Radicalism*, pp. 73–4.
10. Ibid., pp. 79 (quotation), 83.
11. Colley, *Britons*, p. 19; Bradley, *Religion, Revolution and English Radicalism*, p. 89.
12. Bradley, *Religion, Revolution and English Radicalism*, p. 167.
13. Ibid., esp. pp. 427–30.
14. *List of the Society, Instituted in 1787, for the Purpose of Effecting the Abolition of the Slave Trade*, London, 1788 (unpaginated).
15. *Newcastle Chronicle*, 18 November 1791; *Newcastle Courant*, 11 February 1792.
16. *Commons Journal*, XLIII, 1788, pp. 212 (Quakers), 248 (Protestant Dissenters of Devizes), 297 (Edinburgh), 364 (Aberdeen), 374 (Kircudbright), 377 (Glasgow).
17. *Commons Journal*, XLVII, 1792, p. 552 (Dundee, Inverness, Garioch, and Paisley).
18. For Turner see Chapter Four, n. 27. The point about leadership can be made in a different way. Significantly, fifteen members of Turner's Hanover Square congregation contributed funds to the local Newcastle committee in 1792, among them the bookseller, Edward Humble, junior, his two brothers, Stephen and Francis, and Thomas Milner, a local ironmonger. See *Newcastle Courant*, 14, 21, 28 January, 4, 11, 18, 25 February 1792; 'Register of the Minister and People who regularly assemble in Hanover Square, Newcastle, 1782', Tyne and Wear Archives Service, Newcastle-upon-Tyne, 1787/10/1; *Universal British Directory*, 1798.
19. A. C. Wood, *A History of Nottinghamshire*, Nottingham, 1947, pp. 276–80; Bradley, *Religion, Revolution and English Radicalism*, esp. pp. 154–5, 163–4, 185–7, 188; *Dictionary of National Biography*, XX, pp. 515–16.
20. *Sherborne Mercury*, 24 November 1788; *Exeter Pocket-Journal*, 1791; *Universal British Directory*, 1798; Brockett, *Nonconformity in Exeter, 1650–1875*.
21. *Sherborne Mercury*, 8 December 1788; *Aris's Birmingham Gazette*, 7

January 1788; *Universal British Directory*, 1798. For Priestley see Anne Holt, *A Life of Joseph Priestley*, Westport, Connecticut, 1970; *Dictionary of National Biography*, XVI, pp. 357–76.

22. *Newark Herald*, 28 December 1791. For Wakefield see *Dictionary of National Biography*, XX, pp. 452–5.

23. *List of the Society, Instituted in 1787*. For Hinchcliffe and Watson see, respectively, *Dictionary of National Biography*, IX, pp. 888–9, and XX, pp. 935–8.

24. Peter Marshall, *The Anti-Slave Trade Movement in Bristol*, 1963, pp. 2–3; *Aris's Birmingham Gazette*, 28 January 1788.

25. For Bidlake see his *Slave Trade. A Sermon, preached at Stonehouse Chapel, on Sunday, December 28, 1788*, Plymouth, 1789. For Peckard see *Dictionary of National Biography*, XV, pp. 632–3; Clarkson, *History*, I, pp. 203–5; *Eighteenth Century Short Title Catalogue*, CD-Rom version, 1992.

26. *Commons Journal*, XLIII, 1788, pp. 223 (Protestant Dissenting Ministers), 354 (Anglican Clergy of Leicester), 416 (Diocese of Chester).

27. Ibid., pp. 223 (Colchester), 230 (Cambridge, Leek, and Staffordshire), 253 (Grantham), 265 (Blackburn), 332 (Exeter).

28. Ford K. Brown, *Fathers of the Victorians: The Age of Wilberforce*, Cambridge, 1961, pp. 72–8, 87, 88; Kenneth Hylson-Smith, *Evangelicals in the Church of England, 1734–1984*, Edinburgh, 1988, esp. pp. 79–93.

29. For Porteus see Brown, *Fathers of the Victorians*, pp. 85–6, 121, 123–4; *Dictionary of National Biography*, XVI, pp. 195–7.

30. Brown, *Fathers of the Victorians*, p. 9. For Gisborne see *Dictionary of National Biography*, VII, pp. 1280–1.

31. The list can be found in the *Sherborne Mercury*, 24 November 1788. Subscribers were checked against *The Exeter Pocket-Journal*, 1791, *The Universal British Directory*, 1798, and indexes in the West Country Studies Library, Exeter Central Library, and the Devon Record Office. I was able to identify 124 names in this way, or approximately half the list of subscribers.

32. Bradley, *Religion, Revolution and English Radicalism*, p. 427.

33. For Nottingham see Everitt, 'Country, County and Town: Patterns of Regional Evolution in England', pp. 96–9.

34. *Nottingham Journal*, 1 March 1788; *Universal British Directory*, 1798.

35. Ibid. The other local doctors and surgeons were: John Davison, Henry Keyworth, John Storer, Snowden White, and Thomas Wright. George Bott, a local dentist, sat on the local Nottingham committee in 1791–92. See *Newark Herald*, 28 December 1791.

36. *Sherborne Mercury*, 8 December 1788; *Nottingham Journal*, 16 February 1788; *Newark Herald*, 28 December 1791; *Universal British Directory*, 1798. In Plymouth the two attorneys were John Prideaux and John Saunders.

37. Porter, 'Science, Provincial Culture and Public Opinion in Enlightenment England', pp. 243–67; Jonathan Barry, 'The Cultural Life of Bristol, 1640–1775', D.Phil. thesis, Oxford, 1985, pp. 94–5, 99, 206.

38. Porter, 'Science, Provincial Culture and Public Opinion in Enlightenment England', pp. 249, 257–8, 250 (n. 64), 260 (n. 67), 263; *Dictionary of National Biography*, XX, pp. 515–16.

39. Wood, *A History of Nottinghamshire*, p. 280.

40. Diary of Katherine Plymley, 1066/2 (21–2 October 1791).

41. *Sherborne Mercury*, 24 November 1788; *Nottingham Journal*, 1 March 1788.

42. *Newcastle Courant*, 14, 21 January 1792. Humble's father, also Edward, had supported conciliation with the American colonies in 1775. See Bradley, *Religion, Revolution and English Radicalism*, p. 379.

43. *Sherborne Mercury*, 24 November 1788; Brockett, *Nonconformity in Exeter, 1650–1875*, pp. 136, 167.

44. Josiah Wedgwood to Thomas Clarkson, 18 January 1792, Wedgwood Papers, microfilm edition, E. 18990.26.

45. *Eighteenth Century Short Title Catalogue*, CD-Rom version, 1992.

46. *Sherborne Mercury*, 16 February 1789; Drescher, *Capitalism and Antislavery*, pp. 218–19 (nn. 56, 58).

47. As one newspaper put it in 1788: 'That the spirit of humanity which now pervades the people at large, on the behalf of the natives of Africa, does not owe its celerity and zeal solely to dissenters, is clear from the active benignity which the University of Cambridge has evinced, and the many Roman Catholics who have subscribed towards the emancipation of their fellow-creatures'. See *Morning Post and Daily Advertiser*, 22 February 1788.

48. Corfield, *The Impact of English Towns, 1700–1800*, pp. 63–4. Corfield estimates that in 1801 women made up fifty-four per cent of the population of Margate, fifty-five per cent of the population of Brighton, fifty-nine per cent of the population of Scarborough, and sixty-one per cent of the population of Bath.

49. J. R. Oldfield, 'Private Schools and Academies in Eighteenth-Century Hampshire', *Proceedings of the Hampshire Field Club and Archaeological Society*, XLV, 1989, pp. 147–56.

50. Colley, *Britons*, p. 281.

51. See Chapter Six.

52. Clarkson, *History*, II, p. 190.

53. Roger Lonsdale, ed., *Eighteenth-Century Women Poets*, Oxford, 1989, p. xxxv.

54. J. Jamieson, *The Sorrows of Slavery, A Poem. Containing a faithful Statement of Facts respecting the African Slave Trade*, London, 1789, pp. 10–11.

55. Ibid., pp. 17–25; further references in text.

56. Of course, Jamieson was not the only male writer who turned his attention to the slave trade, or who chose (deliberately?) to treat the subject in verse. See, for instance, *Aura; or, The Slave. A Poem, in Two Cantos. Dedicated to John Carr, LL.D., Master of the Grammar School, Hertford*, London, 1788; J. N. Puddicombe, *A Poem to the Rev. Messrs. Ramsay and Clarkson, Granville Sharp, Esq., Captain Smith, and the respectable Society of Quakers, on their Benevolent Exertions for the Suppression of the Slave Trade*, London, 1788; Hugh Mulligan, *Poems chiefly on Slavery and Oppression, with Notes and Illustrations*, London, 1788.

57. For an exhaustive and penetrating survey of this literature see Moira Ferguson, *Subject to Others: British Women Writers and Colonial Slavery*,

1670–1834, London and New York, 1992. Ferguson has a wide agenda, namely, the impact of colonial slavery on the development of 'modern' feminism. My own focus is rather more limited. I have drawn on the works of women writers principally to illustrate their involvement in the early abolitionist movement as historical actors in their own right. For a very similar approach see Clare Midgley, *Women Against Slavery: The British Campaigns, 1780–1870*, London and New York, esp. pp. 29–35.

58. Ferguson, *Subject to Others*, p. 171.

59. *Poems on Slavery: by Maria Falconar, aged 17, and Harriet Falconar, aged 14*, London, 1788, p. 14.

60. Quoted in Ferguson, *Subject to Others*, p. 160.

61. *Epistle to William Wilberforce, Esq. On the Rejection of the Bill for Abolishing the Slave Trade. By Anna Laetitia Barbauld*, London, 1791, p. 14.

62. Yearsley had been 'discovered' by Hannah More in 1784. The two women later fell out, however, and by 1786 Yearsley had a new patron in the shape of Frederick Augustus Hervey, Bishop of Derry and Earl of Bristol. See Lonsdale, ed., *Eighteenth-Century Women Poets*, pp. 392–4.

63. *A Poem on the Inhumanity of the Slave-Trade. Humbly Inscribed to the Right Honourable and Right Reverend Frederick, Earl of Bristol, Bishop of Derry, etc. By Ann Yearsley*, London, 1788, pp. 19–20.

64. Quoted in Ferguson, *Subject to Others*, p. 172. See also *European Magazine and London Review*, XII, 1788, p. 424.

65. The words are Hannah More's, quoted in Lonsdale, ed., *Eighteenth-Century Women Poets*, p. xxxiv.

66. Midgley, *Women Against Slavery*, pp. 17–23; *List of the Society, Instituted in 1787*.

67. Midgley, *Women Against Slavery*, pp. 18–19; *Manchester Mercury*, 3 December 1787.

68. *Sherborne Mercury*, 24 November 1788; *Exeter Pocket-Journal*, 1791; *Universal British Directory*, 1798.

69. *List of the Society, Instituted in 1787; Sherborne Mercury*, 8, 22 December 1788, 5, 19 January, 16 February 1789, 1 February 1790.

70. *List of the Society, Instituted in 1787; Nottingham Journal*, 1 March 1788; Midgley, *Women Against Slavery*, pp. 18–19.

71. Midgley, *Women Against Slavery*, pp. 18–19.

72. Quoted in Midgley, *Women Against Slavery*, p. 24.

73. *Newcastle Courant*, 3 March 1792.

74. Dickson, 'Diary of a Visit to Scotland' (entry for 25 February 1792).

75. *Leeds Intelligencer*, 5 March 1792. See also *Manchester Mercury*, 8 January 1788.

76. Midgley, *Women Against Slavery*, pp. 24–5; Drescher, *Capitalism and Antislavery*, pp. 78, 215 (n. 44), 216 (n. 46); *Diary, or Woodfall's Register*, 5, 12, 18 January 1788.

77. *Newcastle Courant*, 7 January 1792.

78. Quoted in Midgley, *Women Against Slavery*, p. 38.

79. *Hampshire Chronicle*, 30 January 1792.

80. Clarkson, *History*, II, pp. 349–50.

81. Diary of Katherine Plymley, 1066/1 (20 October 1791); *Aris's Birmingham Gazette*, 7 November 1791.

82. Quoted in Ferguson, *Subject to Others*, pp. 179–80.

83. Mary Birkett, *A Poem on the African Slave Trade. Addressed to Her Own Sex*, Dublin, 1792. See also Drescher, *Capitalism and Antislavery*, p. 216 (n. 46).

84. *Aris's Birmingham Gazette*, 7 November 1791.

85. Hill, ed., *The Satirical Etchings of James Gillray*, pp. 102–3 (plate 25).

86. *Lady's Magazine*, XXIII, 1792, p. 215.

87. Ferguson, *Subject to Others*, pp. 186–98.

88. *Cheap Repository Tracts, published during the Year 1795*, London, 1795, p. 8 (quotation).

89. Ibid., p. 11.

90. See, for example, Elizabeth Montagu to Elizabeth Carter, 11 July 1792, Montagu Papers, MO 3701, Huntington Library. 'There has been a riot at Edinburgh', she writes, 'occasion'd by the peoples being angry at Mr Dundas' delay of the abolition of the Slave Trade. They endeavoured to pull down his House. The disposition to Insurrection in every part of G. Britain is very alarming'. Later, Montagu told Carter that 'no one in any rank of life in this our land have reason to be discontented' (Montagu Papers, MO 3714). Montagu, it should be said, supported abolition and her nephew, Matthew Montagu, MP for Bossiney (1786), Tregony (1790), and St Germans (1806, 1807), was a close friend of William Wilberforce. See *Dictionary of National Biography*, XIII, p. 690.

91. Plumb, 'The New World of Children in Eighteenth-Century England', p. 310. For the history of childhood see Philipe Aries, *Centuries of Childhood: A Social History of Family Life*, London, 1962; John C. Sommerville, 'Towards a History of Childhood and Youth', *Journal of Interdisciplinary History*, III, 1972, pp. 438–47; Linda Pollock, *Forgotten Children: Parent-Child Relations from 1500 to 1900*, Cambridge, 1983.

92. Plumb, 'The New World of Eighteenth-Century Children', p. 311.

93. For Newbery and his family see S. Roscoe, *John Newbery and his Successors, 1740–1814: a Bibliography*, Wormley, Hertfordshire, 1973; William Noblett, 'John Newbery, Publisher Extraordinary', *History Today*, XXII, 1972, pp. 265–71.

94. Darton, *Children's Books in England*, pp. 137–8.

95. This figure is abstracted from Roscoe, *John Newbery and his Successors*.

96. Darton, *Children's Books in England*, pp. 226–7.

97. William Darton, *Little Truths better than great Fables*, pp. 69–70.

98. Thomas Day, *The History of Sandford and Merton*, 1783–89, new edn., Edinburgh, 1867, p. 514.

99. Charlotte Smith, *Rambles Further: a Continuation of Rural Walks; in Dialogues. Intended for the Use of Young Persons*, 2nd ed., London, 1800; *Little Truths, for the Instruction of Children [A Revised edition of 'Little Truths better than great Fables', by William Darton]*, London, 1802; *The Budget: or, Moral and Entertaining Fragments. Representing the Punishment of Vices and the Rewards of Virtue*, London, 1799; Priscilla Wakefield,

Excursions in North America, described in Letters from a Gentleman and his Young Companion, to their Friends in England, London, 1806.

100. *The Budget*, p. 103.

101. Quoted in Leonard de Vries, *Flowers of Delight: An Agreeable Garland of Prose and Poetry*, London, 1965, pp. 151–2.

102. Wakefield, *Excursions in North America*, p. 89.

103. Eliza Fenwick, *Visits to the Juvenile Library; or, Knowledge Proved to be the Source of Happiness*, London, 1805.

104. *A Catalogue of Allen's Extensive and Increasing Circulating Library; Consisting of a Great Variety of the best Authors on History, Antiquities, Voyages, etc.*, 1790, Hereford Public Library.

105. Plumb, 'The New World of Eighteenth-Century Children', p. 305 (n. 85).

106. Diary of Anna Margaretta (Porter) Larpent, I (1790–95), Huntington Library, HM 3120, entries for 8, 22, 30 October, 17, 22 December 1792, 1, 2, 14, 25 January, 26 March, 4 April 1793.

107. Plumb, 'The New World of Eighteenth-Century Children', pp. 292–300; Oldfield, 'Private Schools and Academies in Eighteenth-Century Hampshire', pp. 147–56.

108. Many clergymen who supported abolition were also schoolmasters, among them John Bidlake, William Turner, and George Walker. Two subscribers to the local Exeter committee in 1788, the Revs. William and John Stabback (both Anglicans), later opened a private school at their home in St. David's Hill. The same list also contains a reference to L. H. Hallaren, who was a master at the Academy in Alphington. See *Sherborne Mercury*, 24 November, 1788, 13 December 1790; *Exeter Pocket-Journal*, 1791; *Universal British Directory*, 1798.

109. Celia Lucy Brightwell, *Memorials of the Life of Amelia Opie*, Norwich, 1854, p. 13.

110. Diary of Katherine Plymley, 1066/9 (9–16 April 1792). For an adverse reaction to this sort of activity among children see *European Magazine and London Review*, XXI, 1792, pp. 185–6.

111. Dickson, 'Diary of a Visit to Scotland' (entry for 25 February 1792).

112. Diary of Katherine Plymley, 1066/2 (21–2 October 1791).

Chapter Six

ABOLITION, VISUAL CULTURE, AND POPULAR POLITICS

THE consumer revolution of the eighteenth century not only affected the household economy, moulding tastes and preferences within the private sphere, but created a market in politics, the public sphere. The size and potential of this market was realised by John Wilkes and his supporters. Wilkite paraphernalia—medallions, badges, prints, ceramics, pewter pots, flagons, and tankards—commercialised politics during the 1760s. As J. H. Plumb observes, 'every trick of modern promotion [was] used to extend his influence and to convince the literate public of his stand for liberty against the tyranny of George III'.[1] Twenty years later the same 'tricks' or strategies were adopted by entrepreneurs and tradesmen (including the members of the London Committee) trying to exploit the market for abolition. As a result, the movement began to acquire its own visual culture, a culture that was at once dynamic, immediate, and malleable.

No one perhaps understood the commercial value of abolition better than Josiah Wedgwood. Wedgwood was no stranger to charitable or philanthropic causes, having set up a sick club at Etruria and lent his support to the establishment of schools in the area. It was his business dealings with James Phillips, however, that brought him into contact with the group of twelve abolitionists who in May 1787 organised the Committee for the Abolition of the Slave Trade.[2] Wedgwood was one of the Committee's earliest supporters—his name appears on the first subscription list—and in August 1787 he went a stage further and agreed to become one of its members.[3] It is easy to dismiss Wedgwood's interest in abolition as commercial exploitation, but his attendance at meetings and his evident enthusiasm suggests otherwise.[4] Never entirely selfish in his motives, Wedgwood's achievement was to make abolition fashionable at a period when social emulation and emulative spending already had a powerful hold over the lives of many middle-class men and women.

Wedgwood's knowledge and influence are discernible, above all, in the design of the London Committee's seal, adopted in October 1787, depicting a kneeling slave together with the motto 'Am I not a Man and a Brother?' The Committee decided on the idea of an official seal at a meeting in July 1787 and entrusted three of its members—Joseph Woods, Philip Sansom and Joseph Hooper—to come up with an appropriate design. But none of these men was qualified or proficient in the visual arts and it seems only natural that they should have turned to Wedgwood for advice.[5] Indeed, Wedgwood's earliest biographer, Eliza Meteyard, notes that it was one of Wedgwood's employees, William Hackwood, who 'modelled the design of a seal for the society, which was laid before the Committee on October 16, 1787'.[6] Whatever its precise origins, the whole concept was brilliantly conceived, drawing on existing images of kneeling black figures as well as religious and secular belief in the equality of mankind. As Hugh Honour points out: it 'neatly encapsulated ideas already widely accepted while giving them a more specific meaning'.[7]

If Wedgwood was responsible for the design of the seal, then it helps to explain the following entry in the Oven Books at Etruria for 7 December 1787:

7 doz. black pyramid seals of a wax blackamoor large
6 doz. do. do. figures do. do.[8]

This black basalt seal, described in *Old Wedgwood* for 1938, was in all likelihood intended for limited circulation among the Committee's corresponding members.[9] Wedgwood, however, had other ideas and took it upon himself to produce a black and white jasper medallion incorporating the same design. The first of these cameos appeared early in 1788—a small consignment was sent to Benjamin Franklin in Philadelphia on 29 February—and thereafter they were produced in their thousands.[10] Many of them were distributed to Wedgwood's friends and sympathisers with the abolitionist cause. But others were marketed in the usual way, that is, through Wedgwood's trade catalogues, his various showrooms, and his small team of travelling salesmen.

Cameos, it needs to be said, were already fashionable consumer goods. Wedgwood's catalogue of 1779 advertised a range of

Wedgwood medallion, 'Am I not a Man and Brother?', 1787

designs 'fit for rings, buttons, lockets and bracelets; and especially for inlaying in fine Cabinets, Writing Tables, Bookcases, etc.' The idea of mounting cameos in this fashion seems to have originated with Wedgwood and his partner, Thomas Bentley, in 1771, and was quickly taken up by Boulton and Fothergill and other Birmingham toy-makers, who bought cameos for setting in cut steel.[11] By 1788, therefore, cameos were highly collectable and it comes as no surprise to learn from Clarkson that some gentlemen had Wedgwood's slave medallion 'inlaid in gold on the lid of their snuff-boxes', or that 'of the Ladies, several wore them in bracelets, and others had them fitted up in an ornamental manner as pins for their hair'.[12] Later, in the nineteenth century, items like these were mutilated and the cameos mounted in frames for enthusiastic Victorian collectors, but happily some examples still survive. One of the finest, now in the British Museum, is a gold pendant with a toothed border. Another, formerly in the Harry M. Buten Wedgwood Collection, has a cameo set in gold on a glass patch box. And a third, in the Manchester City Art Gallery, features a medallion mounted in a very simple metal frame, presumably intended for display.[13]

Such pieces are evidence of a bold and enterprising assault on eighteenth-century consumer choice. Clarkson went so far as to claim that the taste for wearing cameos became 'general'. Clarkson undoubtedly exaggerated, but he did speak with some authority. No stranger himself to new marketing devices, Clarkson used Wedgwood's cameos on his tour of southern England in the summer of 1788, as did William Dickson, who toured Scotland on behalf of the London Committee in 1792. While he was in Paisley Dickson dined with 'the Rev. Mr Alice'. 'His grandson 10 yrs old won't touch sugar since he read Fox's tract', Dickson noted in his diary on 24 January. 'Gave him a cameo for himself and another for any lady he chose to give it to'.[14] The reference here to women and, by implication, women of a certain social standing, is revealing, not least because it points to their role as the arbiters of taste and fashion. More likely than men to possess decorative goods, women were an obvious target of marketing influence, as entrepreneurs like Wedgwood understood only too well.[15]

Wedgwood medallion mounted in a gold pendant, c. 1790

For the moment at least, Wedgwood's cameo, and the message it conveyed, was fresh, engaging and, above all, novel. Not wishing to be outdone, some of Wedgwood's competitors also began producing slave medallions. A good example, possibly manufactured by T. and J. Hollins of Hanley, can be found in the Wedgwood Museum at Barlaston, Stoke-on-Trent. Mounted in a solid wooden frame, the cameo in this instance is slightly larger than Wedgwood's and, if anything, more crudely modelled, but in all other respects bears a striking resemblance to the original.[16] Such imitations were a further indication of just how fashionable abolition had become. Not all producers of consumer goods were innovators like Wedgwood. Most of them survived by keeping abreast of prevailing London high fashion, and what they chose to copy is therefore highly significant.[17]

We cannot be sure how many slave medallions were produced during the late eighteenth century. But we do know that fresh batches were fired at Etruria in March and April of 1792, to coincide with the petition campaign of that year, and again in January and April of 1807, to coincide with the debates on the Foreign Slave Bill.[18] In short, they became an instantly recognisable feature of abolitionist activity during this period. Moreover, the same design was incorporated in a number of other artefacts, among them trade tokens. Eighteenth-century society suffered from an acute shortage of all kinds of specie, and of small change (pennies and halfpennies) in particular. By the late 1780s this shortage had grown to such proportions that a flood of new token coins was produced to ease the problem. The first of these, an issue of token pennies, was minted by the Powys Mining Company of Anglesey in 1787, and thereafter they became increasingly common. Most eighteenth-century tokens were genuine coins; that is to say, they bore the issuer's name and address, usually with a promise 'to pay the current value on demand'. But others, notably those with fictitious names of towns and issuers, were made for sale to collectors, while quite a number had no identifying marks and were sold in bulk to anyone who would purchase them.[19]

Tokens, especially those without any locality or issuer's name, proved a perfect vehicle for political propaganda. Thomas Spence of Holborn, for instance, was responsible for several hundred tokens, many of them made to advance his own ideas on reform of the land laws. Other efforts included a 1792 farthing depicting on the obverse a figure of a kneeling slave together with the motto 'Am I not a Man and a Brother?', and on the reverse Adam and Eve in the Garden of Eden with the words 'Man over Man He made not Lord'.[20] Spence may also have been responsible for a series of anti-slavery pennies and halfpennies. Here again, the obverse of both coins bore the now familiar figure of a kneeling slave. The reverse of the penny, however, was inscribed with the words 'Whatsoever ye would that men should do unto you, do ye even unto them', while the reverse of the halfpenny displayed a pair of clasped hands, together with the motto 'May slavery and oppression cease throughout the world'.[21]

None of these tokens were genuine coins, although they undoubtedly passed as such. The pennies, especially those struck in white metal, were probably intended as medals or medallets. A penny in mint condition in the British Museum even has the figure of the kneeling slave painted over in black enamel, a sure indication that it was a collector's item.[22] Surviving examples of the halfpennies are more common, some of them quite pitted and worn, but most have false edges and bear no issuer's name. In effect, these were advertising tokens circulated at the expense of enthusiasts like Spence or possibly even at the urging of the London Committee. If these objects suggested how formalised (and ubiquitous) the image of the kneeling slave had become, they also made clear the linkage between anti-slavery, commercialisation and radical politics. Significantly, the reverse of a slave token (farthing) dating from 1795 bears the inscription 'Advocates for the Rights of Man: Thos. Spence, Sir Thos. More, Thos. Paine'.[23] Such sentiments caused many abolitionists deep embarrassment, but radicals like Spence were obviously less circumspect about exploiting abolition's political message.

If Wedgwood's cameo gave abolition status meaning, a meaning that was inseparable from its novelty value, then Spence's tokens helped to make it cheap and accessible. Dalton in his *Provincial Token Coinage of the Eighteenth Century* (1910) lists no fewer than fifteen different versions of the pennies and nineteen of the halfpennies, noting small but significant variations in spelling, punctuation, spacing, and edges. Of course, none of this would have been possible had it not been for the dictates of fashion and the emergence of a rapidly expanding consumer society. Abolition, like any other new idea, was open to commercial development and exploitation. Viewed in this light, anti-slavery artefacts not only provide an insight into the beliefs of those who made, commissioned, purchased or used them. They also reveal how eighteenth-century consumers were influenced and exploited. Entrepreneurs like Wedgwood had an intimate knowledge of the workings of the market, and through their ingenuity they ensured that abolition became a commodity to be purchased and possessed.

Abolitionists fully appreciated the importance of artefacts in arousing public feeling against the slave trade. In July 1794, at a time when the movement was languishing, James Phillips approached Matthew Boulton of Birmingham about producing 'an Abolition Halfpenny'. 'I think thy operator might design some good allusion to the subject', Phillips told Boulton, 'and I wish to know the terms upon which thou exercisest this part of the prerogative, i.e. the price per cwt or m and the quantity to be taken payable at London, Bristol and York'.[24] Perhaps more revealing are Clarkson's thoughts on the subject. Alluding to 'a little Engraving' sent to him by Joseph Taylor early in 1807, Clarkson admitted that 'as far as our Cause is concerned, this is not the most desirable Time for its Circulation'. 'As to myself', he went on, 'I should like some thing more substantial–such as Cameos—or Medals—I should also like to have the Profile of

[a]

[b]

T. Webb, Wilberforce commemorative medal, 1807,
(a) obverse, (b) reverse

Wilberforce on one Side and a Device on the other'.[25] Clarkson's preference for cameos and medals, which were highly collectable and could be passed easily from hand to hand, was not simply a matter of personal taste. It also reflected assumptions about fashion, status and, above all, consumer choice.

Clarkson wrote at a time when the outcome of the debate on the Foreign Slave Bill remained very much in the balance. Victory brought with it a series of commemorative medals and medallets. Many of these items were really quite simple, bearing no design and very little by way of ornamentation. One, struck in white metal with milled edges, has on the obverse only 'Wilberforce for ever' and on the reverse 'Humanity is the cause of the people'. Far more elaborate, however, was a larger portrait medal by T. Webb which bears the profile of Wilberforce, while on the reverse the figure of Victory hovers above that of Britannia seated upon a dais inscribed with the words 'I have heard their cry'. Another medal from the same period carries the motto 'We are all brethren', together with a design depicting an 'Englishman' proffering a hand to a native African, while in the background five (black) figures dance jubilantly around a tree. Underneath is the legend 'Slave trade abolished by Great Britain 1807'.[26]

Some of these medals were clearly made with the intention of being worn. Among the examples in the British Museum, several have small holes, indicating perhaps that a loop or clasp was originally attached to the rim, or perhaps that they were suspended by a piece of ribbon or braid. Others were more likely to have been collectors' items and kept in purpose-built metallic boxes or display cabinets. Not only did these medals commemorate the abolition of the slave trade; they were also a form of self-advertisement. They were a means of identifying, individually and collectively, with a noble, humanitarian cause. This comes across very clearly in another of the medals struck in 1807. Here the obverse bears the motto 'William Wilberforce Esq. Returned to the British Parliament the Sixth Time for the County of York June 1807', while the reverse carries the message 'Africa Rejoice!! Yorkshire-Men have acted independently. The Hero of Freedom, the Pride of his Country and the Ornament of Human Nature'.[27]

In short, the early abolitionist movement produced a range of artefacts—cameos, tokens, medals and medallets. The nineteenth century would witness further initiatives, not least in the area of ceramics. Anti-slavery jugs, plates and even dinner services were all familiar sights during the 1820s and 1830s.[28] Nevertheless, the central image, that of the kneeling slave, remained easily the most popular and identifiable abolitionist motif. Remodelled and reworked, it reappears time and time again in the nineteenth century, sometimes as a transfer print on a piece of china, sometimes in the form of a sulphide set in a piece of glass.[29] All of which brings us back to Josiah Wedgwood. Not only did Wedgwood make abolition fashionable, he also helped to fix in the public's mind an image that would be forever associated with the abolition of slavery and the slave trade.

Next to artefacts, prints and printed images were perhaps the most important means of giving abolition visual identity. The market for prints grew enormously during the eighteenth century, thanks largely to William Hogarth, whose dramatic social commentaries captured the imagination of an increasingly leisured middle class. Hogarth's success spawned a host of imitators. Satirical prints were especially popular, but so too were engravings of old masters and pictures by English artists like Reynolds and Gainsborough. Prints, according to one authority, rapidly became 'the favourite decoration of middle-class staircases and dining rooms'.[30] Robert Sayer, a fashionable London print seller, advertised his 'sets of fine prints' as

> proper to collect in the cabinets of the curious, and also make furniture elegant and genteel when framed and glazed, or may be fitted up in a cheaper manner, to ornament rooms, staircases etc. with curious borders representing frames, a fashion much in use, and produces a very agreeable effect.[31]

Here, in other words, was a market ripe for exploitation. The problem for abolitionists, however, was to find an appropriate image. This they did in the form of the plan and sections of a slave ship. As noted earlier, this simple design originated with William Elford and the members of the Plymouth committee in December 1788.[32] Fashioned after the *Brooks* of Liverpool, the print depicted the lower deck of a slave ship, as if viewed from above, 'with Slaves stowed on it, in the proportion of not quite one to a ton'. The plan was accompanied by a crude representation of

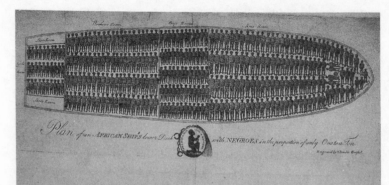

Plan of an AFRICAN SHIP's lower Deck, with NEGROES in the proportion of only One to a Ton.

THE above Plate represents the lower deck of an African Ship of 297 tons burthen, with the Slaves stowed on it, in the proportion of not quite one to a ton.

In the Men's apartment, the space allowed to each is six feet in length, by fixteen inches in breadth.—The Boys are each allowed five feet by fourteen inches.—The Women, five feet ten inches, by sixteen inches; and the Girls, four feet by one foot each.—The perpendicular height between the Decks, is five feet eight inches.

The Men are fastened together two and two, by hand-cuffs on their wrists, and by irons riveted on their legs.—They are brought up on the main deck every day, about eight o'clock, and as each pair ascend, a strong chain, fastened by ring-bolts to the deck, is passed through their Shackles; a precaution absolutely necessary to prevent insurrections.—In this state, if the weather is favourable, they are permitted to remain about one-third part of the twenty four hours, and during this interval they are fed, and their apartment below is cleaned; but when the weather is bad, even these indulgences cannot be granted them, and they are only permitted to come up in small companies, of about ten at a time, to be fed, where after remaining a quarter of an hour, each mess is obliged to give place to the next in rotation.

It may perhaps be conceived, from the crouded state in which the Slaves appear in the Plate, that an unufual and exaggerated inftance has been produced; this, however, is fo far from being the cafe, that no Ship, if her intended cargo can be procured, ever carries a lefs number than one to a ton, and the ufual practice has been to carry nearly double that number: The Bill which was paffed during the laft Seffion of Parliament, only reftricts the carriage, to five Slaves for three tons; and the Brooks, of Liverpool, a capital ship, from which the above fketch was proportioned, did, in one voyage, actually carry 609 Slaves, which is more than double the number that appear in the plate.—The mode of ftowing them was as follows:—Platforms, or wide fhelves were erected, between the decks, extending fo far from the fides towards the middle of the veffel, as to be capable of containing four additional rows of Slaves, by which means the perpendicular height between each tier, after allowing for the beams and platforms, was reduced to two feet fix inches; fo that they could not even fit in an erect pofture; befides which, in the Men's apartment, inftead of four rows, five were ftowed, by placing the heads of one between the thighs of another.—All the horrors of this fituation are ftill multiplied in the fmaller veffels.— The Kitty, of 137 tons, had only one foot ten inches, and the Venue, of 146 tons, only one foot nine inches perpendicular height above each layer.

The above mode of carrying the Slaves, however, is only one, among a thoufand other miferies, which thofe unhappy and devoted creatures fuffer from this difgraceful Traffick of the Human Species; which in every part of its progrefs, exhibits fcenes that ftrike us with horror and indignation.—If we regard the firft ftage of it on the Continent of Africa, we find that a hundred thoufand Slaves are annually produced there for exportation, the greateft part of whom confifts of innocent perfons, torn from their deareft friends and connections, fometimes by force, and fometimes by treachery. Of thefe, experience has fhewn, that five and forty thoufand perifh, either in the dreadful mode of conveyance before defcribed, or within two years after their arrival at the plantations, before they are feafoned to the climate.—Thofe who unhappy furvive their hardfhips, are deftined like beafts of burthen, to exhauft their lives in the unremitting labours of a Slavery, without recompence, and without hope.

The Inhumanity of this Trade, indeed, is fo notorious, and fo univerfally admitted, that even the advocates for the continuance of it, have refted all their arguments on the political inexpediency of its abolition; and in order to ftrengthen a weak caufe, have either malicioufly or ignorantly confounded together the emancipation of the negroes already in Slavery, with the abolition of the Trade; and thus many well-meaning people have become enemies to the caufe, by the apprehenfions that private property will be materially injured by the fuccefs of it.—To fuch, it becomes a neceffary information, that liberating the Slaves forms no part of the prefent fyftem; and fo far will the prohibition of a future trade be from injuring private property, that the value of every Slave will be very confiderably increafed, from the moment that event takes place, and a more kind and tender treatment will immediately be infured to them by their Mafters, from the neceffity every Planter will then be under to keep up his ftock, by natural means; a practice which fome humane inhabitants of the Iflands have purfued with the greateft fuccefs, and upon whofe eftates no new Negroes have been purchafed for a number of years, the death vacancies having been fupplied by young ones, born and bred in their own Plantations.— Thus then the value of private property will not only fuffer no diminution, but will be very confiderably inhanced by the abolition of the Trade.—It now only remains to fee how the Public and the Slave Merchants will be affected by it.

It is faid by the well-wifhers to this Trade, that the fuppreffion of it will deftroy a great nurfery for feamen, and annihilate a very confiderable fource of commercial profit.—In anfwer to thofe objections, Mr. Clarkfon, in his admirable treatife on the impolicy of the Trade, lays down two pofitions, which he has proved from the moft inconteftible authority.—Firft, that fo far from being a Nurfery, it has been conftantly and regularly a Grave for our feamen; for that in this Traffick only, more Men perifh in ONE Year, than in all the other Trades of Great-Britain, in TWO Years: And, fecondly, that the balance of the trade, from its extreme precarioufnefs and uncertainty, is fo notoriously againft the Merchants, that if all the veffels, employed in it were the property of one Man, he would infallibly, at the end of their voyages, find himfelf a lofer.

As then the Cruelty and Inhumanity of this Trade muft be univerfally admitted and lamented, and as the policy or impolicy of its abolition is a queftion which the wifdom of the Legiflature muft ultimately decide upon, and which it can only be enabled to form a juft eftimate of, by the moft thorough inveftigation of all its relations and dependencies; it becomes the indifpenfible duty of every friend to humanity, however his fpeculations may have led him to conclude on the political tendency of the meafure, to ftand forward, and to affift the Committee, either by producing fuch facts as he may himfelf be acquainted with, or by fubfcribing, to enable them to procure and tranfmit to the Legiflature, fuch evidence as will tend to throw the neceffary lights on the fubject.—And people would do well to confider that it does not often fall to the lot of individuals, to have an opportunity of performing fo important a moral and religious duty, as that of endeavouring to put an end to a practice, which may, without exaggeration, be filled one of the greateft evils at this day exifting upon the earth.

By the Plymouth Committee,

W. Elford, Chairman.

Plan of an African Ship's lower Deck, 1788

the London Committee's seal, together with the motto "Am I not a Man and a Brother?' Underneath, in its 'remarks', the Plymouth committee set out the dimensions of the *Brooks*, taking this opportunity to launch an attack on the cruelty and inhumanity of the slave trade, before closing with an appeal for individuals to come forward with information that might be used as evidence before the bar of the House of Commons.[33] As propaganda the print was shocking, yet neither sentimental nor unduly graphic. Here, in diagrammatic form, were human beings reduced to the level of inhuman objects, treated as so much merchandise and stowed on board ship in the most appalling conditions.

In all, some 1,500 copies of this print were circulated locally in Plymouth during the early part of 1789. Copies were also sent to the Committee in London, which in April produced a similar engraving, again based on the *Brooks* of Liverpool.[34] Now, instead of just a view of the lower deck, there was a similar plan of the quarter deck, as well as longitudinal and cross sections of the entire vessel. The seal was this time omitted—indeed, there was nothing to suggest that the engraving had anything at all to do with the London Committee—but parts of the original text were retained, supplemented by more information about the dimensions of the *Brooks* and a lengthy quotation from Alexander Falconbridge's *Account of the Slave Trade on the Coast of Africa* (1788).[35] While distinctly an improvement, therefore, it is clear that the London print owed a great deal to the Plymouth committee, both in conception and in design.

The plan and sections of a slave ship were to prove among the most arresting of all anti-slavery images. In Edinburgh, as we have seen, the engraving was posted up in the streets. In Glasgow, it was printed in a slightly modified form, without the text, so as to fold easily into a small pamphlet (the way it appears, in fact, in Clarkson's *History*).[36] Some had the engraving framed and displayed in their homes. Clarkson relates how it was one of only two or three prints he ever encountered among his Quaker friends, the others being a 'plan of the building of Ackworth School' and a 'representation of the conclusion of the treaty between William Penn and the Indians of America'. Clarkson put this down not to pride or a sense of their own achievements, but to a genuine desire to draw the 'attention of those, who should come into their homes, to the case of the injured Africans, and of procuring sympathy in their favour'. The significant thing for our purposes, however, is that 'all the prints, that have been mentioned, were hung up in frames'.[37]

While the London Committee financed the printing of the plan and sections of a slave ship and distributed them in large quantities (over 8,000 were produced in 1788–89 alone), it was understandably reticent about identifying itself too closely with anti-slavery publications.[38] This explains, I think, the Committee's reluctance to exploit the obvious potential of the figure of the kneeling slave. An impression of the seal appeared for the first time in the *Gentleman's Magazine* for March 1788.[39] Thereafter, it was used selectively in a range of abolitionist literature, including Peter Peckard's *Am I not a Man and a Brother?* (1788), James Stanfield's *Observations on a Guinea Voyage in a Series of Letters Addressed to the Rev. Thomas Clarkson* (1788), and *Slavery: An Essay in Verse* (1792) by Captain J. Marjoribanks. But the total number of these books and pamphlets is surprisingly small. Significantly, the London Committee did not use the seal (or any other device) on its own publications, preferring to publish anonymously through James Phillips. Local societies, too, seem to have used the image only sparingly. Indeed, Marjoribanks's *Slavery*, which was published at the urging of the Edinburgh committee, is one of the very few examples of the seal being used in this way as a mark of identification.

Wedgwood, needless to say, had other ideas. In January 1792 he wrote to Clarkson about an 'addition' to Fox's address on the consumption of West Indian sugar and rum. 'I would propose', he suggested,

> to have a wooden cut of the negro kneeling with the motto 'Am I not a man and a brother' in the place of the advertisement in the title page. The bookseller's name and edition may be underneath. This pathetic figure will then be immediately under Mr Cowper's verses and he may be considered as uttering the ejaculation, Why did all creating nature etc. I would leave out 'Cowper's negroes complaint' which is written under the verses. If you approve of this addition I will gladly pay for the wooden print and I wish you would speak to the printer to know if it would make any addition to the price he having the print given him and 2,000 being ordered by me.[40]

Wedgwood spoke as a businessman who understood the value of such innovations, both to himself and to the movement. The Committee, however, was unwilling to lend its name to the abstention campaign, at least in its official capacity, and so the idea was dropped.

Nevertheless, the device did appear in a somewhat modified form on the title page of the *Abstract of the Evidence Delivered before a Select Committee of the House of Commons*, published by the Newcastle committee in 1791.[41] Here the artist was the engraver Thomas Bewick, who, with his partner, Ralph Beilby, was an enthusiastic supporter of abolition. Bewick's interpretation of the London Committee's seal gave fresh life to what was by now a familiar image. Characteristically, he set the figure of the kneeling slave against an appropriate background, in this case a plantation scene, the whole within a border bearing chains and the motto 'Am I not a Man and a Brother?'. Several versions of this engraving appeared after 1791, each one of them more elaborate than the last. Figures were added, among them a master or overseer who is shown striking another slave, again in a kneeling posture. The background, meanwhile, becomes fuller and deeper.[42] In short, Wedgwood's image, really a profile, had become a picture, complete with its own frame or border.

Of course, the kneeling slave, like the plan and sections of a slave ship, was an 'official' image devised and sponsored by abolitionists. At the same time, abolition attracted the attention of artists working outside the movement, chief among them being George Morland. Morland was one of the more colourful characters of the eighteenth century. Generous and good-natured but thoroughly dissolute, he lived recklessly and seemingly without regard for either his health or his reputation. His boon companions, it is said, were 'ostlers, potboys, horse jockeys, moneylenders, pawnbrokers, punks and pugilists'. Pursued by dealers and creditors, he was at last imprisoned for debt in 1799 and some time after died in a sponging house in Eyre Street, Cold Bath Fields.[43] Though he was frequently drunk for days on end, Morland's output was prodigious, running not into hundreds but into thousands of paintings. Appropriately, perhaps, his name became synonymous with scenes of lowly life, the inside of cottages, stables and inn yards. These he tended to portray in an affected, sentimental manner. Yet, as John Barrell suggests,

Morland was also capable of providing insights into the 'dark side of the landscape', the pain, the suffering, the hunger.[44]

Between 1788 and 1792 Morland was at the height of his powers. Many of his paintings from this period have a moralising tone, reflected in such titles as *The Miseries of Idleness* and *The Comforts of Industry*. Morland's art, however, was more subtle than this might suggest. He had a keen eye for the foibles of genteel society. In *A Visit to the Boarding School* (c. 1789) a young girl, perhaps no more than fourteen years of age, is being brought in to see her fashionably dressed mother. Two friends, meanwhile, hover in the doorway, obviously deeply affected by the scene they are witnessing. The schoolroom is relatively bare and uninviting, save for a few books strewn along a mantelpiece, some prints and a hat left on the floor by the young girl's brother in his excitement to see his sister again. It is a scene of disorder but not just in a formal, decorative sense. Morland was also making a comment on contemporary family values. Compare this picture with *The Comforts of Industry* (1790). Here a young family, obviously farm labourers, are captured together inside their cottage. The parents and children are well dressed, their home clean and neatly arranged. But more obviously they are a family, sharing in each other's comfort and happiness.[45]

A year earlier, in 1789, Morland had produced *The First Fruits of Early Industry and Economy*. The title was intended to be ironic or at least ambiguous. At the left a merchant is seated at a table discussing business with a clerk. Outside, through a window, are warehouses and river boats. To the right, with her back to her husband, is the merchant's wife, who is offering one of her children a bunch of grapes. The child stands on an expensive leather chair, while her hat, a recurring motif in Morland's paintings from this period, lies abandoned on the floor. As witness to this scene, with his hands balancing a basket of fruit, is a black servant who looks on with boredom or disgust, it is difficult to say which. Above them hangs a picture of a country house.[46] The painting, in effect, was a commentary on middle-class aspirations. Here again, the contrast with *The Comforts of Industry* is striking. The interior, the liveried servant, the country house—all of this suggested not contentment or even harmony but luxury, ostentation and display. These, it seems, were the 'fruits' of the merchant's industry.

Given these preoccupations, and Morland's evident sympathy with outsiders (the lowly, the degraded), it is perhaps not surprising that he should have turned his attention to the subject of the slave trade. The painting in question, *Execrable Human Traffic*, was exhibited at the Royal Academy in 1788. Based on a poem by his friend, William Collins, it dealt in visual terms with a familiar theme in abolitionist literature, namely, the enforced separation of black families. In the centre of the picture an African chief is being restrained by two slave traders, while his wife Ulkna and their child are dragged away to an awaiting boat. She looks back in fear and horror as one of the traders brandishes a 'bludgeon' over her husband's head. Meanwhile, another slave sits in the boat head in hands, clearly in a state of shock.[47] The scene is brutal, graphic, frightening. Far more impassioned than anything produced by the London Committee, *Execrable Human Traffic* confronted the public with the inhumanity and injustice of the slave trade,

John Raphael Smith, *The Slave Trade*, 1791, engraving after George Morland, *Execrable Human Traffic*, 1788

demanding a response even at the risk of alienating them altogether.

The following year Morland produced a companion piece to *Execrable Human Traffic*, again based on Collins's poem. 'Suppose', asked Collins, 'by tempest's rage, on Afric's shore',

> Your ship is driv'n, with all her pallid crew,
> What help from Blacks!—dare you their aid implore?
> Will they forget their foes, and save them too?

> Unspotted Truth, triumphant, answers yes!
> The sympathetic spark of heavenly fire
> Pervades a Negro's breast, he feels that bliss
> Which human kindness ever must inspire.

> Dauntless they plunge amidst the vengeful waves,
> And snatch from death the lovely sinking fair;

John Raphael Smith, *African Hospitality*, 1791, engraving after the painting by George Morland

> Their friendly efforts, lo! each Briton saves!
> Perhaps their future tyrants now they spare.[48]

African Hospitality visualises this scene. Amid a fearsome storm a group of blacks nurse and comfort the (white) survivors they have just dragged ashore from a shipwreck off the coast of Africa. Dominating the canvas, bathed in moonlight, sits a young family (man, woman and child) supported by a complementary black family, their rescuers.[49] So while *Execrable Human Traffic* was about separation and the sundering of families, *African Hospitality* celebrated unity; not just family unity, and, in this case, a family restored, but unity among races. As Collins put it,

> Hence vain distinctions, prejudice of sight!
> The social union knows no diff'rent hue,
> And Nature's pencil paints him purest white,
> Who feels for others, and must good will do.
>
> (p. 13)

Taken together, these paintings not only attacked the slave trade, and those who were engaged in it, but portrayed blacks as men and women capable of noble, generous actions. This idea of the 'essential goodness' of Africans was becoming increasingly popular in the late eighteenth century. (As Hugh Honour points out, when first exhibited *Execrable Human Traffic* was subtitled *The Affectionate Slaves*.[50]) If at times such ideas threatened to create stereotypical black images, they nevertheless helped to undermine the justification for a trade that denied the basic humanity of black people. Morland, for his part, in portraying blacks as 'fellow creatures', as historical actors in their own right, extended the range of anti-slavery images still further.

Such was Morland's popularity that hundreds of his paintings were quickly engraved and published as prints, some of them by his brother-in-law, William Ward, others by John Raphael Smith, whom Morland had first met in 1780. Morland's slave trade paintings were no exception. On the contrary, with the outcome of the Parliamentary contest still uncertain, they were an obvious subject for exploitation of this kind. Ward, it seems, did an engraving of *Execrable Human Traffic*, possibly as early as 1788 or 1789. Another version, under the title *The Slave Trade*, was published by John Raphael Smith in February 1791, along with an engraving of *African Hospitality*, while copies of both prints were published in France in 1794 to mark the abolition of the slave trade by the National Convention.[51] It is conceivable, therefore, that the final figure may have run into the thousands. In this way, Morland's startling images came to enjoy wide circulation on both sides of the English Channel, finding their way into the homes of the middle classes, many of whom undoubtedly had the prints framed and glazed or fitted up with 'curious borders' in the manner suggested by Robert Sayer.

Smith's intervention could not have been more timely. His prints of Morland's two paintings were part of an onslaught on public taste and sensibility—books, pamphlets, cameos, tokens, the plan and sections of a slave ship—that was at its peak during 1791–92. Morland's appeal, as we have seen, was to the emotions, to his viewers' finer feelings. This is perhaps best summed up in the figure of the brutal slave trader in *Execrable Human Traffic*. Thomas Bewick used the same image in the various woodcuts of the kneeling slave that he produced after 1791. And it appears again in *Abolition of the Slave Trade, or the Man the Master*, an anti-abolitionist print published in 1789. Here an elegantly dressed black master is depicted wielding a bludgeon over the head of a kneeling white slave.[52] The other details of the print are unimportant here. Its message and its meaning derived from the deliberate inversion of two abolitionist emblems, further evidence of the role played by visual images in helping to frame the discourse on slavery and race in the late eighteenth century.

During the 1780s and 1790s the marketing and distribution of prints became increasingly specialised. Alongside old-established printsellers like Carrington Bowles and Robert Sayer, with their humorous mezzotints and 'Drolls', there sprang up newer businesses keen to exploit the huge potential market for personal and political satires. Chief among these were the caricature shops of Samuel Fores, William Holland and Hannah Humphrey, all of which opened in London during the 1780s. Political prints were already popular; they had been a marked feature of the Wilkite agitation, for instance. But enterprising printsellers, new techniques (etching, stipple engraving, aquatints) and artists like Thomas Rowlandson, Isaac Cruikshank and James Gillray, whose association with Humphrey dates from 1791, raised the genre to higher levels of visual expression. Quick and easy to produce, satirical prints provided a biting and seemingly uninhibited commentary on eighteenth-century politics and society.[53]

From Hogarth to Rowlandson, English satirists helped to popularise an image of blacks as servants, sailors, rioters, and beggars; in short, as part of plebeian culture.[54] Worse, they were often the butt of jokes or introduced only to make a wider political point. During the Westminster election of 1784, for instance, Rowlandson portrayed the Duchess of Devonshire in the act of buying the vote of a disreputable-looking black publican. Another engraving from this period, again by Rowlandson, depicts Mrs Hobart rounding up more potential voters, in this case 'an old and decrepit Chelsea pensioner and a negro supported on stumps and crutches'. Blacks, in other words, were being used here to discredit the electioneering tactics of Fox's supporters. In a similar manner, references to black rioters during the Westminster by-election of 1788, although based on fact, were clearly intended to tell 'readers' something about the origins of the mob, its character and its complexion.[55]

Some of these prints also had obvious sexual overtones. Rumours that the Duke of Clarence had kept a black mistress on board the *Pegasus* during his return from Jamaica in 1787 were seized upon with great delight by satirists. An engraving by Gillray, published in January 1788, depicts the Duke tenderly embracing his mistress in a hammock below deck. Another of April 1788, at about the time of Pitt's motion against the slave trade in the House of Commons, shows the 'royal couple' in their cabin. Even as late as 1791 satirists were still referring to the Duke's supposed infatuation with his 'lovely Wowski'.[56] The same prurient interest in black–white sexual relations is evident in Rowlandson's *The Disaster* (n.d.), which depicts a black servant fondling a white maid in partial view of their master, who has been incapacitated by a bad case of gout. And it is implicit again in *The Girl in Stile* (1787), where a black footboy waits on a fashionable white prostitute.[57]

At best, therefore, satirists were ambivalent in their attitude towards black Britons, something that undoubtedly affected the way in which they responded to the abolition of the slave trade. Almost without exception, early references to the subject treat it as a metaphor or device to rehearse old themes and arguments. In

The Slave Trade, published in April 1788, the target was ministerial corruption. George III is pictured surrounded by obsequious ministers. Their heads are shaded to indicate a black complexion and Lloyd Kenyon, Master of the Rolls, kneels before the King with clasped hands, that is, in the manner of a kneeling slave. In other cases the target or point of the engraving was more personal. *English Slavery; or, A Picture of the Times*, again published in 1788, was actually a commentary on the foibles of fashionable society: the Queen's miserliness; the Duke of York's weakness for gambling; Lord Derby's infatuation with Miss Farren, an actress. All of these men and women were 'slaves' of one description or another. Later in the series Mrs Fitzherbert is shown leading the Prince of Wales by a chain attached to his wrists.[58]

Significantly, none of these prints addressed the slave trade as a subject worthy of comment in its own right. The Commons debate of 1791, however, and the ensuing petition campaign, elicited a quite different response. The shift is evident in Gillray's *Barbarities in the West Indias*, published in April 1791. A swarthy overseer is depicted stirring a huge vat of steaming sugar juice. He

James Gillray, *Barbarities in the West Indias*, 23 April 1791

stands on a ladder, while in his right hand he holds a whip or rattan. Above him, to the right, are nailed up on the wall a fox, a bird, some rats, two black ears and a black arm. To the left, meanwhile, the flailing arms and legs of a black slave protrude from the stone vat. As he stirs, the overseer exclaims, 'B———t your black Eyes! what you can't work because you're not well?— but I'll give you a warm bath to cure your Ague, and a Curry-combing afterwards to put Spunk into you'. Outside, through a doorway, are palm trees and the outline of a building, possibly the plantation house.[59]

Barbarities in the West Indias was based on an incident reported by Sir Philip Francis in the Commons debate of 18 April 1791.[60] As such, the print could be read as a piece of abolitionist propaganda. But its meaning was more ambiguous than this might suggest. Like any good satirist, Gillray sought to embellish Francis's evidence before the House of Commons, improvising at will. In doing so, however, he cast doubt on the authenticity of the story and the reliability of its source. For those unaware of the sig-nificance of the vermin pinned on the wall of the sugar refinery, Gillray etched under the title a caption directing readers to 'Mr Frances [sic] speech, corroborated by Mr Fox, Mr Wilberforce etc. etc.'. Thus *Barbarities in the West Indias* could just as easily be interpreted as an anti-abolitionist print, a confusion of images that in part reflected popular feeling on the subject of the slave trade.

The same ambiguity is evident in Isaac Cruikshank's *The Abolition of the Slave Trade*, published a year later, in April 1792. Here again, the engraving was based on an alleged incident, in this case Captain John Kimber's part in the murder of a young black woman for refusing to dance naked for him on deck.[61] The print shows Kimber at left, whip under his arm and a lascivious smile on his face. To the right, the slave girl swings by a leg from a pulley-rope. She is caught in half profile, clutching her head in her hands, and is naked except for a crude loincloth which has ridden half way up her back. Even those looking on appear to find the spectacle distasteful. Two sailors are depicted exiting at the far right. 'My Eyes Jack', says one, 'our Girles at Wapping are never flogged for their modesty'. 'By G———d that's too bad', replies the other. 'If he had taken her to bed it would be well enough. Split me I'm allmost [sic] sick of this Black Business'.[62]

The ABOLITION of the SLAVE TRADE.
Or the Inhumanity of Dealers in human flesh exemplified in the Cruel treatment of a young Negro Girl of 15 for her Virgin Modesty

Isaac Cruikshank, *The Abolition of the Slave Trade*, 10 April 1792

But there was a light-hearted banter about these exchanges (no one had ever accused the girls at Wapping of being modest), while the central image itself bordered on 'the shady frontier of pornography'.[63] Put a different way, was Cruikshank trying to instruct or titillate or both?

It is interesting to compare *The Abolition of the Slave Trade* with *Practical Christianity* by Richard Newton, also published in April 1792. The scene is a plantation somewhere in the West Indies. At the right a female slave is tied by her wrists to a palm tree. She is naked from the waist up and is being whipped by an overseer or slave driver. A white woman, possibly the mistress, looks on. She appears to smile, directing her left hand at the slave as if to encourage the overseer in his work. Again, there is something almost pornographic about this image. At the left, however, a male slave is also being whipped. He is suspended naked from a palm tree, his deeply scourged back turned towards the spectator, his arms outstretched and his head tilted to one side in a Christ-like posture.[64] Thus *Practical Christianity* begins to take on a very different significance. Is the white mistress, after all, trying to stop the whippings? And what about the bags of sand attached to the slave's feet to prevent him from offering any kind of resistance? Were details like these evidence of a more deliberate moral purpose?

Taken together, *The Abolition of the Slave Trade* and *Practical Christianity* reveal how easily images of this kind could be misinterpreted or misconstrued. Often only an exaggerated gesture, an ironic title or a carefully worded caption offered the viewer a clue as to the artist's moral and political viewpoint. Just as often the same image could be read in a number of different ways, which was obviously the intention. Moreover, by focusing on barbarities in the West Indies, on sensational incidents reported in the House of Commons, artists like Gillray and Cruikshank frequently tended to blur the distinction between slavery and the slave trade, thus making the task of abolitionists that much more difficult.

Another subject that caught the attention of satirists during the spring of 1792 was the boycott of West Indian sugar and rum. Gillray and Cruikshank both produced prints on the campaign, in each case using it as a vehicle to poke fun at the miserliness of the King and Queen Charlotte. Gillray's *Anti-Saccharites,—Or—John Bull and his Family leaving off the Use of Sugar* (March 1792) visualises the royal family around the tea table. The King holds a cup of unsweetened tea to his lips, exclaiming as he does so, 'O delicious! delicious!' To the right the royal princesses look on with a mixture of horror and dismay. Each has a cup of tea in her hands, one idly stirs the uninviting brew, but none of them dares to drink it. The Queen, meanwhile, implores her children to but taste the tea. 'You can't think how nice it is without Sugar', she tells them, 'and then consider how much Work you'll save the poor Blackamoor by leaving off the use of it!—and above all remember how much expence [sic] it will save your poor Papa!—O it's charming cooling Drink'.[65]

Within weeks, Cruikshank produced a similar satire, entitled *The Gradual Abolition of the Slave Trade. Or leaving of Sugar by Degrees*. This time the royal couple are pictured around a circular breakfast table. The Queen, again seen as the chief protagonist in this affair, takes tiny pieces of sugar from a basin to weigh them in a small pair of scales. As she does so she grins at Mrs Schwellenberg, Keeper of the Robes. 'Now my Dears only an ickle Bit', she says, 'do but tink on de Negro girl dat Captain

Isaac Cruikshank, *The Gradual Abolition of the Slave Trade, or leaving
of Sugar by Degrees*, 15 April 1792.

Kimber treated so *cruelly* ha, Madame Swelly and Rum too'. At
the Queen's side George III holds a brimming saucer in one hand
and a cup of tea in the other. 'Poo Poo', he tells Princess Elizabeth,
'leave it off at once, you know I have never Drank any since I was
married Lizzie'. Lizzie, however, is hesitant. 'I can't leave of [*sic*] a
good thing so soon', she blurts out. 'I must have a bit now and
then'. Her sister, on the extreme left, turns away in disgust,
protesting that 'for my Part I'd rather Want altogether than
have a small Piece'.[66]

The abstention campaign provided satirists with a fresh
perspective on the slave trade. Individual examples of violence
and brutality soon lost their novelty value and Wilberforce and
the other leading proponents of abolition seem to have offered
little by way of comic potential. Indeed, personal attacks on
Wilberforce were extremely rare. One of the very few, by Gillray,
following the defeat of the Foreign Slave Bill in 1794, shows him
relaxing with the Bishop of Rochester in a black brothel. Rochester
sits to the right kissing a black prostitute who balances herself
precariously on his knees. Wilberforce crouches on a sofa to the
left smoking a crude-looking pipe. His black companion, as large
and shapely as he is thin and scrawny, also smokes. She stares into

178

the distance, her breasts exposed and a large straw hat perched on top of a patterned turban. Entitled *Philanthropic Consolations*, the print is chiefly remarkable for its rather belated attempt to link abolition with the collapsing of racial and sexual categories.[67]

By their very nature satirical prints offered a jaundiced view of eighteenth-century politics and society. Those dealing with slavery and the slave trade were no exception. Ambiguous, irreverent, and mocking, they sought to highlight (and exaggerate) the bizarre, the novel, and the sensational. Nevertheless, it would be wrong to dismiss the significance of these prints for the early abolitionist movement. Unwittingly, perhaps, they helped to popularise abolition and give it a political voice. They helped to familiarise the public with scenes of the most appalling cruelty. And, finally, they helped to make people think about the slave trade, its meaning, its relevance, and its significance, even as they smiled or laughed nervously out loud.

Anti-slavery cameos, tokens, medals and prints were all part of the growing commercialisation of politics during the eighteenth century. Relatively inexpensive to produce, they made abolition immediate and accessible. They made it fashionable. Here again, the initial impetus came from abolitionists and the London Committee, in particular. But just as abolitionists borrowed ideas from the world of business, so entrepreneurs like Wedgwood, Spence, and John Raphael Smith were quick to seize on abolition and exploit its value as a marketable commodity. For the most part, the results were beneficial for all parties concerned. Only satirical prints offered any serious threat to the ability of abolitionists to control anti-slavery images, and even then the threat was perhaps more apparent than real. By 1807 abolition had acquired its own visual culture. At the heart of that culture was the figure of the kneeling slave. It appears again in Robert Smirke's illustrations for James Montgomery's *The West Indies, a Poem in Four Parts* (1809) and Richard Westmacott's funerary monument for Charles James Fox (1812–22).[68] Instantly recognisable, this simple device became a form of abolitionist shorthand, a visual cue that made explicit the relationship between abolition, consumption and popular politics.

Notes

1. *The American Experience: The Collected Essays of J. H. Plumb*, p. 151. See also Brewer, 'Commercialization and Politics', pp. 238–9.
2. Josiah Wedgwood to James Phillips, 1785, and James Phillips to Thomas Byerly, 26 October 1787, Wedgwood Papers, 24260–61.124. See also James Phillips to Josiah Wedgwood, 17 March and 9 December 1788, Wedgwood Papers, 24262.124 and 24264.124.
3. Wedgwood Papers, 21074.111 (circular letter dated 22 May 1787); London Committee Minutes, 27 August 1787. Wedgwood attended his first meeting of the Committee on 11 March 1788.
4. See, for instance, McKendrick, 'Josiah Wedgwood and the Commercialization of the Potteries', pp. 122–3. Wedgwood attended seven meetings of the London Committee in 1788, one in 1789, six in 1790, four in 1791, four in 1792 and one in 1793. His son, Josiah Wedgwood, junior, was elected a member of the Committee in 1791.
5. London Committee Minutes, 5 July, 27 August, 16 October 1787.
6. Eliza Meteyard, *The Life of Josiah Wedgwood from his Private Correspondence and Family Papers*, London, 1865–66, II, p. 565.
7. Hugh Honour, *The Image of the Black in Western Art*, IV, i, pp. 63–4.
8. Oven Book (17 February 1786 to 28 December 1787), Etruria 53 (30016), entry for 7 December 1787, Wedgwood Museum, Barlaston, Stoke-on-Trent.
9. *Old Wedgwood*, V, 1938, pp. 57–8.
10. Josiah Wedgwood to Benjamin Franklin, 29 February 1788, Wedgwood Papers, microfilm edition, E.19085.26.
11. Eric Robinson, 'Matthew Boulton and Josiah Wedgwood, Apostles of Fashion', *Business History*, XXVIII, 1986, pp. 105–6.
12. Clarkson, *History*, II, pp. 191–2. Announcing the arrival of Wedgwood's cameo on 3 April 1788, the *Morning Post and Daily Advertiser* noted that '*fashion* has extended her influence to the *cause of humanity*, and figures, similar to what we have described, are making in *cameo* as bracelets for the ladies'.
13. British Museum, Reg. No. 1909, 12–1, 261; Harry M. Buten, *Wedgwood and Artists*, Merion, Pennsylvania, 1960, p. 59 (plate 31); Manchester City Art Gallery, Reg. No. 1906.146. The Birmingham Museum of Art, Birmingham, Alabama, has photographs of a medallion set in a nineteenth-century glass patch box, which was later taken out (dismounted) for display purposes. Personal communication from E. Bryding Adams, Curator of Decorative Arts, Birmingham Museum of Art, 16 September 1991. Other examples sometimes come up for sale at auctions or antique fairs.
14. Thomas Clarkson to Mr Wedgwood's agent, 27 August 1788, Wedgwood Papers, 21982.115; Dickson, 'Diary of a Visit to Scotland' (entry for 24 January 1792).
15. Lorna Weatherill, 'A Possession of One's Own: Women and Consumer Behavior in England, 1660–1740', *Journal of British Studies*, XXV, 1986, pp. 150–1.
16. Josiah Wedgwood, '*The Arts and Sciences United*': *An Exhibition of Josiah*

Visual culture and popular politics

Wedgwood's Correspondence, Experiment Books and the Ceramic Products He Developed and Manufactured. Held at the Science Museum, London, 21 March to 24 September 1978, Barlaston, 1978, p. 67 (No. 193).

17. See John Styles, 'Manufacturing, Consumption and Design in Eighteenth-Century England', in Brewer and Porter, eds., *Consumption and the World of Goods*, pp. 543–7.

18. Oven Book (3 and 10 December 1790 to 26 August and 2 September 1802), Etruria 53 (30017), I, p. 78 (entry for 30 March and 6 April 1792), Wedgwood Museum; Ornamental Ware Order Book (1801–12), pp. 78 (entry for 31 January 1807), 143 (entry for 27 April 1807), Wedgwood Museum. I am most grateful to Lynn Miller for supplying me with this information.

19. For token coinage see Arthur W. Waters, *Notes on Eighteenth-Century Tokens (being Supplementary and Explanatory Notes on the 'Provincial Token Coinage of the Eighteenth Century')*, London, 1954, pp. vii–viii; Brewer, 'Commercialization and Politics', pp. 207–8; Peter Seaby, *The Story of British Coinage*, London, 1985, pp. 138–42.

20. British Museum, Department of Coins and Medals, Cabinet No. 1013, Tray G8 (DH 1089).

21. R. Dalton, *Provincial Token Coinage of the Eighteenth Century*, London, 1910, pp. 119, 195, 541–2.

22. British Museum, Department of Coins and Medals, Cabinet No. 4034, Tray 236 (1787).

23. Ibid., Cabinet No. 1013, Tray G9 (DH 1118).

24. James Phillips to Matthew Boulton, 23 June 1793, Matthew Boulton Papers, Birmingham Public Library, 252/1/117. This piece of evidence suggests that the London Committee may, indeed, have been behind the tokens produced by Spence, although there is no reference to coins in the Committee's minute books.

25. Thomas Clarkson to Joseph Taylor, January 1807, Clarkson Papers, St. John's College, Cambridge.

26. British Museum, Department of Coins and Medals, Cabinet No. 4035, M5283, M5292, M5319.

27. Ibid., Cabinet No. 4035, M5291.

28. John and Jennifer May, *Commemorative Pottery, 1780–1900: A Guide for Collectors*, London, 1972, pp. 131–4.

29. In February 1990 Christie's of London sold an Apsley Pellatt scent bottle and stopper, c. 1830, inlaid with a sulphide of a kneeling slave. Personal communication from Rachel Russell, Christie's, London, 11 October 1991.

30. J. H. Plumb, 'The Public, Literature and the Arts in the Eighteenth Century', in Paul Fritz and David Williams, eds., *The Triumph of Culture: Eighteenth-Century Perspectives*, Toronto, 1972, p. 38.

31. Quoted in Charles Saumarez Smith, *Eighteenth-Century Decoration: Design and the Domestic Interior in England*, New York, 1993, p. 303.

32. *Sherborne Mercury*, 5 January 1789. See Chapter Four for the activities of the local Plymouth committee and its chairman, William Elford.

33. 'Plan of an African Ship's lower Deck with Negroes in the proportion of

only One to a Ton', Bristol Record Office, 17562/1. The plan was engraved by T. Deeble of Bristol, but it is not at all clear who was responsible for the original design. The *Sherborne Mercury* simply records that at a meeting held on 29 December 1788 it was agreed that '1500 plates, representing the mode of stowing slaves on board the African traders, *with remarks on it*, be struck off and distributed gratis'. My italics. There appear to be no other references to the print in local records.

34. London Committee Minutes, 17 March, 21, 28 April 1788. Clarkson hints that the London Committee improved on the original design by giving it the form of an actual ship, that is, the *Brooks* of Liverpool. Clearly, this was an exaggeration. See Clarkson, *History*, II, pp. 28–9, 111–15.

35. Honour, *The Image of the Black in Western Art*, IV, i, p. 65 (plate 24).

36. See Chapter Four.

37. Clarkson, *A Portraiture of Quakerism*, I, pp. 208–10.

38. London Committee Minutes, 28 July 1789. A further 1,000 copies of the plan and sections of a slave ship were printed and distributed early in 1791. See London Committee Minutes, 1 February 1791.

39. *Gentleman's Magazine*, LVIII, 1788, pp. 161, 208–9.

40. Josiah Wedgwood to Thomas Clarkson, 18 January 1792, Wedgwood Papers, microfilm edition, E.18990.26.

41. *An Abstract of the Evidence Delivered before a Select Committee of the House of Commons in the Years 1790 and 1791*, Newcastle, 1791, Tyne and Wear Archives Service, DX 112/1; Thomas Hugo, *A Bewick Collector: A Descriptive Catalogue of the Works of Thomas and John Bewick; Including Cuts, in Various States, for Books and Pamphlets, etc.*, 1866, rpt., Detroit, 1968, pp. 460–1 (Nos. 3441–50), 512–13 (No. 3768).

42. Blanche Cirker, ed., *1800 Woodcuts by Thomas Bewick and his School*, New York, 1962, plate 218 (No. 5); Robert Robinson, *Thomas Bewick: His Life and Times*, London, 1887, p. 76.

43. For Morland see William Collins, *Memoirs of that Celebrated, Original and Eccentric Genius, the Late George Morland, an Eminent Painter*, London, 1806; George Dawe, *The Life of George Morland*, London, 1904; *Dictionary of National Biography*, XIII, pp. 961–4.

44. John Barrell, *The Dark Side of the Landscape: The Rural Poor in English Painting, 1730–1840*, Cambridge, 1979, pp. 89–129. Barrell notes that many of Morland's darker images were softened by engravers like James Ward. This sort of retouching is in some cases quite striking. See, for example, Ward's treatment of Morland's *The Door of a Village Inn* (pp. 120–1).

45. Smith, *Eighteenth-Century Decoration*, pp. 341 (plate 337), 343 (plate 341).

46. Ibid., p. 342 (plate 340).

47. Honour, *The Image of the Black in Western Art*, IV, i, pp. 67–8 (plates 25, 26). Honour also notes that several painted copies of *Execrable Human Traffic* were made 'within a decade or so of the original' (pp. 74, 316 n. 162). One of these, in the Menil Foundation Collection, Houston, Texas, is dated 1789.

48. *The Slave Trade; A Poem. Written in the Year 1788*, London, 1793, pp. 12–13. The timing of this publication is itself significant. Collins was obviously

hoping to capitalise on the interest generated in Morland's paintings by the engraver, John Raphael Smith.

49. Honour, *The Image of the Black in Western Art*, IV, i, pp. 68–72 (plates 27, 28).

50. Ibid., p. 71.

51. See Julia Frankan, *John Raphael Smith, 1752–1812, Catalogue Raisonné*, 1902, rpt., Amsterdam, 1975, pp. 20, 215; Ralph Richardson, *George Morland, Painter*, London, 1895, pp. 90, 142, 148, 160; Honour, *The Image of the Black in Western Art*, IV, i, p. 74. According to Richardson, both prints were also published again in 1814.

52. Honour, *The Image of the Black in Western Art*, IV, i, pp. 73–4 (plate 29).

53. M. Dorothy George, *Catalogue of Political and Personal Satires Preserved in the Department of Prints and Drawings in the British Museum*, London, 1978, VI, pp. xxxiii–xxxiv; Smith, *Eighteenth-Century Decoration*, pp. 303–5.

54. For Hogarth see David Dabydeen, *Hogarth's Blacks: Images of Blacks in Eighteenth-Century English Art*, Manchester, 1987.

55. George, *Catalogue of Political and Personal Satires*, pp. 112, 120 (No. 6566), 520 (No. 7367), 521–2 (No. 7369). For black rioters see *London Chronicle*, 24–6 July 1788.

56. George, *Catalogue of Political and Personal Satires*, pp. 455 (No. 7260), 473 (No. 7296), 829 (No. 7926).

57. *The Watercolor Drawings of Thomas Rowlandson, From the Albert H. Wiggin Collection in the Boston Public Library. With a Commentary by Arthur W. Heintzelman*, New York, 1947, pp. 20–1; George, *Catalogue of Political and Personal Satires*, p. 433 (No. 7226).

58. George, *Catalogue of Political and Personal Satires*, pp. 475 (No. 7301), 477 (No. 7303).

59. Ibid., pp. 781–2 (No. 7848).

60. Clarkson merely records that Francis 'instanced an overseer, who, having thrown a Negro into a copper of boiling cane-juice for a trifling offence, was punished merely by the loss of his place, and by being obliged to pay the value of the slave'. See Clarkson, *History*, II, p. 269. Francis (1740–1818), a keen Whig and one of the founders of the Society of the Friends of the People (1793), was MP for Bletchingley.

61. Wilberforce made this charge in his Commons speech of 2 April 1792, basing it on the evidence of the ship's surgeon, William Dowling. As a result, Kimber was arrested and tried at the Admiralty on 7 June. Although Wilberforce believed Kimber 'substantially guilty', the court acquitted him, whereupon Kimber pressed Wilberforce for 'a public apology, £5000 in money, and such a place as will make me comfortable'. See *Life of Wilberforce*, I, pp. 356–9; Furneaux, *William Wilberforce*, pp. 113–14; Wilson, *Thomas Clarkson*, p. 85.

62. George, *Catalogue of Political and Personal Satires*, pp. 899–900 (No. 8079).

63. Honour, *The Image of the Black in Western Art*, IV, i, p. 74.

64. Eduard Fuchs, *Die Karikatur der europäischen Völker, vom Altertum bis zur Neuzeit*, Berlin, 1901, p. 247 (fig. 249).

65. George, *Catalogue of Political and Personal Satires*, p. 806 (No. 8074). See also Hill, ed., *The Satirical Etchings of James Gillray*, pp. 102–3 (plate 25).

66. George, *Catalogue of Political and Personal Satires*, p. 900 (No. 8081). Note here the Queen's West Indian dialect and the reference to Captain Kimber. Both were clearly intended to be ironic and are all of a piece with Cruikshank's ambivalent, even hostile, attitude towards abolition.
67. Furneaux, *William Wilberforce*, pp. 94–5 (plate 7a).
68. Honour, *The Image of the Black in Western Art*, IV, i, pp. 97–9 (plates 48–50).

EPILOGUE

IN 1792 a massive petition campaign, involving some 400,000 people, was instrumental in forcing a Commons vote to abolish the slave trade, albeit gradually, shifting the burden of responsibility to the House of Lords. As we know, it was to prove a hollow victory. The Lords refused to follow the Commons' lead and voted, instead, to hear evidence at their own bar. Desperately, Wilberforce tried a fresh approach, a proposed Bill to prohibit the carrying of slaves in British ships to foreign territories, but by 1794 that, too, was stalled in the upper chamber.[1] The abolitionists' moment had passed. It seems likely that neither of these measures would have made it through both Houses, whatever the circumstances. There was, after all, a strong West India lobby and many members were understandably reticent about voting for a measure that might result in an increase in trade for Britain's maritime competitors. It was the French Revolution, however, that effectively killed abolition in Parliament, sapping the energies of its supporters and forcing the movement out of the political spotlight.

Outside Westminster, too, the Revolution took its toll. Hannah More's natural distaste for 'insurrections', reflected in her contributions to the Cheap Repository Tracts, was symptomatic of a broader social and intellectual shift that drove a wedge between Evangelical Anglicans, on the one hand, and radical dissenters, on the other.[2] Thomas Clarkson noticed the change in the public mood, admitting to Josiah Wedgwood in 1794 that his 'Notions of Liberty' were unpopular; indeed, that many people considered him a 'political apostate'.[3] Under this sort of pressure the movement outside Parliament began to show signs of disintegration and decay. The London Committee met only twice in 1796, before ceasing operations altogether, while the local committee in Manchester collapsed after 1794 following the arrest of Thomas Walker for treason.[4] A similar fate befell Daniel Holt, editor of the *Newark Herald*. In 1793 Holt was found guilty of publishing two reform pamphlets and imprisoned for four years, a sentence that, if anything, reinforced the linkage between abolition, revolution, and the spectre of the mob.[5]

Wilberforce went on presenting his annual abolition motion in the Commons, even winning a partial victory in 1804, but all to no avail. Finally, he tried a different tack. In 1806 the Ministry of All the Talents brought in a Bill for the 'Guiana Order', prohibiting the slave trade to conquered Dutch Guinea. Inspired by James Stephen, Wilberforce now began quietly to attach the provisions of his own Foreign Slave Bill to the proposed legislation. Abolitionists, in other words, were trying to turn the Napoleonic war to their own advantage. And the tactic worked. The Foreign Slave Bill passed into law in 1806, paving the way for the Abolition Act of 1807.[6] As these few details suggest, the final struggle took place in Parliament. Success, when it came, depended not on appeals to the public or popular protests, but on the ability of Wilberforce and his supporters to outwit their opponents in the House of Commons. If anything, Wilberforce deliberately avoided the sort of tactics employed by abolitionists between 1787 and 1792, using the London Committee, for instance, as a vehicle only for information-gathering.

Yet there is little doubt that public opinion was behind abolition. Touring England in the summer of 1805, Thomas Clarkson found that 'the ardour of all the former friends of the abolition with whom he had conversed [remained] unabated and that wherever he had been all ranks of people were warm in the cause and desirous of lending their aid'.[7] Clarkson was particularly impressed by the enthusiasm of the younger generation.

> When . . . I conversed with these, as I travelled along, I discovered a profound attention to what I said; an earnest desire to know more of the subject; and a generous warmth in favour of the injured Africans . . . Hence I perceived that the cause furnished us with endless sources of rallying; and that the ardour, which we had seen with so much admiration in former years, could be easily revived.[8]

The organisation of the African Institution within three weeks of the passing of the Abolition Bill was just one indication of the continuing interest in the welfare of black people. So, too, were the

800 petitions condemning slavery presented to Parliament in 1814.[9]

Seen in this light, the campaigns of 1788 and 1792 succeeded in sensitising the British public to abolition. Through books, pamphlets, prints, and cameos the London Committee and its supporters set Britain on a course that would lead, ultimately, to the abolition of colonial slavery in 1833. Some of the continuities are, indeed, striking. At the local level, for instance, many of those involved in the early abolitionist movement were at the forefront again in the petition campaigns of 1814 and 1829. William Elford is a case in point. Chairman of the local Plymouth committee between 1788 and 1792, Elford was still active in the 1820s, drawing up the petition sent to the Prince Regent in 1828.[10] Clarkson is another important figure who went on to devote himself to the abolition of slavery, not only in the Caribbean but in the United States as well. We could multiply these examples. The important point is that the fervour of the nineteenth century did not spring into existence overnight. It had its origins in the early abolitionist movement and the activities of the London Committee, in particular.

There were also important continuities in terms of techniques and strategies: the committee system, petitioning, the use of anti-slavery prints and artefacts. Indeed, some of the most successful opinion-building techniques of the nineteenth century were first devised during the 1780s and 1790s. One thinks, for instance, of the recurring image of the kneeling slave, which originated with Josiah Wedgwood. Such innovations transformed abolition into a potent political force, shifting attention away from the confines of Parliament to the wider world outside Westminster. Abolitionism, in other words, helped to redefine the shape of British politics. Like the Wilkite agitation of the 1760s, the petition campaigns of 1788 and 1792 were a demonstration of strength and independence. They were harbingers of change, further evidence of the growing assertiveness of the middle classes in the public sphere.

Notes

1. Pollock, *Wilberforce*, pp. 124–5; Clarkson, *History*, II, pp. 461–3.
2. Midgley, *Women Against Slavery*, pp. 27–9; Ferguson, *Subject to Others*, pp. 214–20.
3. Thomas Clarkson to Josiah Wedgwood, 18 April 1794, Wedgwood Papers, 24743.32.
4. Frida Knight, *The Strange Case of Thomas Walker: Ten Years in the Life of a Manchester Radical*, London, 1957; *The Whole Proceedings of the Trial of an Indictment against Thomas Walker, etc. . . . for a Conspiracy to Overthrow the Constitution and Government, and to Aid and Assist the French*, Manchester and London, 1794.
5. Wood, *A History of Nottinghamshire*, p. 280.
6. Pollock, *Wilberforce*, pp. 187–9, 199–200, 213–14; Anstey, *The Atlantic Slave Trade and British Abolition*, pp. 343–90.
7. Abolition Committee Minutes, 9 July 1805.
8. Clarkson, *History*, II, pp. 502–3.
9. Griggs, *Thomas Clarkson*, pp. 94–5; Colley, *Britons*, pp. 354–8.
10. 'Papers relating to Meetings against the Slave Trade and Negro Slavery and for the Mitigation of Slavery in the Colonies, 1826–28', Plymouth Record Office, W669.

INDEX

Index

Brighton, 133
Brissot de Warville, Jacques Pierre, 55, 80
Bristol, 10, 21, 43, 46, 79, 85, 96, 103, 129, 138, 161
British Museum, 157, 160, 162
Brough, 60
Brougham, Henry, 79
Brown, Moses, 53
Buckinghamshire, 3, 107
Burbage, George, 132
Burgh, William, 108
business techniques, 9
    application to reform sphere, 44–5
Butcher, William, 130
Buten, Harry M., 157

Cambridge, 70, 105, 125, 129
cameos, 81, 133, 156–9, 163, 187;
    see also Wedgwood, Josiah
Cardigan, 106
Caribbean, see West Indies
Carlisle, 109, 116
Cartwright, John, 33, 131
Charlotte, Queen Consort to George III, 57, 140, 141, 177–8
Charnley, William, 132
Chesham, 3, 107
Chester, 7, 46, 75, 81, 129
children, 3, 5, 132, 142–8
    role in abolitionist movement, 147–8
children's literature, 3, 16–20, 22–3, 125, 143–7
Churchill, Samuel, 130
civic pride, 13, 104
Clapham Sect, 86, 88, 129–30
Clarke, Richard Hall, 98
Clarkson, Catherine, 73, 85, 90
Clarkson, John, 86
Clarkson, Thomas, 2, 42, 45, 49, 50, 52, 59–60, 61, 63, 70–91, 100, 131, 132, 133, 140, 144, 148, 157, 161–2, 165–6, 186, 187

books and pamphlets:
    Abstract, 58–9, 76, 77, 101–2, 103, 167
    Essay on the Comparative Efficiency of Regulation or Abolition of the Slave Trade, 56, 76, 77
    Essay on the Impolicy of the Slave Trade, 55, 56, 76, 77
    Essay on the Inhumanity of the Slave Trade, 43, 54, 72, 76, 77
    History, 47, 72, 83, 85, 86–7, 88, 165
    Letters on the Slave Trade, 76
    Potraiture of Quakerism, 85
    Strictures on the Life of William Wilberforce, 87–8
    Summary View of the Slave Trade, 44, 76, 77
    health, 84
    Lake Years, 84–5
    personality, 77–84
    political views, 80–1, 185
    relationship with Wilberforce, 87, 90–1
    tours, 46, 47, 58, 74–6, 97, 98, 99, 101, 103, 126, 140, 158
    views on abstention campaign, 58
    visit to France, 42, 55–6, 74, 80, 86; see also London Committee; Wilberforce, William
clubs and societies
    debating, 13, 133, 139
    literary and philosophical, 12–13, 19, 54, 131
    political, 20, 118
Coddrington, William, 111
Colchester, 129
Coleridge, Samuel Taylor, 77, 82–3, 85
Colley, Linda, 33, 118
Collins, William, 169, 170–1
Committee for the Abolition of the

Index

Index

Index

Index

Index

98, 101, 102, 128, 131, 137,
165–6
London Meeting for Sufferings,
41
Society to Effect the Enforcement
of His Majesty's
Proclamation against Vice
and Immorality, 129–30
Somersett, James, 126
South Carolina, 52
Southampton, 12
Southerne, Thomas, 23–4, 27, 31
Oroonoko, 23–4
Southey, Robert, 85, 88
Southwell, 110
Spadafora, David, 118
Spain, 51, 54
Sparkes, Thomas, 98
Spence, Thomas, 159–60, 179
Stanfield, James, 166
*Observations on a Guinea
Voyage*, 166
Stafford, 116
Staffordshire, 105, 106, 129
Stanley, Henry, 106
Stephen, James (1758–1832), 63,
85–6
Stephen, James (1789–1859), 86, 88
Stirling, 106
Stockton, 125
sugar
abstention campaign, 57–8, 62,
76, 81, 89, 100, 139–41, 147,
177–8; *see also* West Indies
Surrey, 50
Sussex, 21, 50

Tarleton, Banastre, 61, 113
Taunton, 9–10, 20
Taylor, Joseph, 161
Teston, 72
Tewkesbury, 111
Thompson, Edward, 32–3
Thornton, Henry, 129
Tingcombe, John, 99
Tiverton, 75–6, 108, 127
Tokson, Elliot, 23

Topsham, 116
trade tokens, 159–61
transport, 9–10
Tregony, 3, 114
Trewman, Robert, 132
Turner, Thomas, 19
Turner, William, 101, 128, 131
Tuxford, 110

United States
anti-slavery movement in, 45,
51–4, 90
Congress, 53, 56
Philadelphia Convention, 52–3
universities, 70, 105, 129
urban renaissance, 7–8, 13, 133

Vickery, Amanda, 15
Virginia, 53

Wadström, Carl, 44
Observations on the Slave Trade,
44
Wakefield, Gilbert, 128, 131
Wakefield, Priscilla, 145–6
Excursions in North America,
145–6
Wales, 7, 79, 113, 114
Walker, George, 102, 128–9, 131
Walker, Thomas, 2, 43, 47–8, 54,
96, 185
Walvin, James, 1, 22, 126
Warwickshire, 128
Washington, George, 81
Washington, D. C., 53
Watson, Richard, 129
Watts, Joseph, 12
Waymouth, John, 130
Wedgwood, Josiah, 1–2, 3, 9, 11,
12, 32, 42, 43, 45, 57, 77, 81,
132, 133, 140, 155–9, 163,
166–7, 179, 185, 187; *see
also* cameos
Wedgwood Museum, 159
Weatherill, Lorna, 8
Wenlock, 108, 111
West Indies, 4, 56, 63, 75, 187

STUDIES IN SLAVE AND POST-SLAVE SOCIETIES AND CULTURES

Series Editors: Gad Heuman and James Walvin
ISSN 1462–1770

Other Titles in the Series

Unfree Labour in the Development of the Atlantic World
edited by Paul E. Lovejoy and Nicholas Rogers

Small Islands, Large Questions
Society, Culture and Resistance in the Post-Emancipation Caribbean
edited by Karen Fog Olwig

Reconstructing the Black Past
Blacks in Britain 1780–1830
by Norma Myers

Against the Odds
Free Blacks in the Slave Societies of the Americas
edited by Jane G. Landers

Routes to Slavery
Direction, Ethnicity and Mortality in the Atlantic Slave Trade
edited by David Eltis and David Richardson

Slavery and Colonial Rule in Africa
edited by Suzanne Miers and Martin Klein

Classical Slavery
by M.I. Finley